GYPSIES IN THE CITY

SISTER EVA
Gifted Reader & Advisor

Come see why you are so unhappy, why everything seems to go wrong. If sick, worried, troubled, you can be helped and everything made clear by consulting this gifted reader. She asks no questions but tells you what you want to know giving dates & facts of business, love, health, family affairs. Tells if the one you love is true & what to do to be successful.

Don't let time or distance stand in the way of your happiness

MRS. EVE

READER, ADVISOR
GUARANTEED RESULTS
IN 3 DAYS
A visit to her will be
of immense value to you

Are you facing difficult problem? Poor health? Money or job trouble? Are you unhappy in your married life? Do you have drinking, love or family problems? Are you lonely, heart broken or depressed? Do you want to know yourself or others? Does bad luck follow you? Do you want to know how you can have success and good fortune in life? She will help you she has helped many. There is no pity for those who need help and do not come for it.

A visit to her will be of immense value to you.

SHE GIVES SOUND AND

important advice on all affairs of life. There is no problem so big that she can't solve. If you are in trouble, sick or in love; if you can't win the one you cherish, see this Gifted Lady who. can and will help you on all your problems.

Dont Classified her with Gipsy or other Readers

GYPSIES IN THE CITY
Culture Patterns and Survival

by

Rena C. Gropper
Associate Professor
Hunter College of the City University of New York

THE DARWIN PRESS
Princeton, New Jersey

Library of Congress Cataloging in Publication Data
Gropper, Rena C
    Gypsies in the city.
    Includes bibliographical references.
    1. Gipsies—United States. I. Title.
DX201.G76   1975   301.45'19'1497073   70-161055
ISBN 0-87850-008-1

Printed in the United States of America

If I knew where I was going to fall, there would I place my bedding.

Nomad Gypsy proverb

To my teachers, Ruth Fulton Benedict and Alfred Louis Kroeber, who gave me the tools of my trade and demonstrated by their example that the good fieldworker should be a warm and sensitive human being—

To my informants, the Nomad Gypsies, who became my friends and adopted kinsmen, and taught me how to survive and mature, come what may—

To my students, matriculated and non-matriculated, of the School of General Studies of Hunter College of the City University of New York, who put the joyous excitement into teaching and make it all worthwhile—

This book is lovingly dedicated.

CONTENTS

PREFACE

To write a book is not easy, especially if the topic to be covered has been a fascination for more than a quarter of a century. There is the material the author wants to share with those of kindred spirit; there is the data that must be passed on for the sake of those who will continue the scientific inquiry. There are also promises made to Gypsy informants, long since become friends, of things to be explained to the outside world—and also of things to be kept secret. But there is also a belated realization that so much of the total experience has become part of the author's own being that writing it all down almost constitutes an invasion of privacy. What I have put into this book is a distillation of years of study by many people, for my own contacts with the Gypsies have been supplemented by reading all I could find on these people and by discussions and correspondence with some—most notably Mr. Jan Yoors—who have also lived with and studied the Nomads.

Cultures keep changing and human beings are highly varied. There is no way to promise you that you will find the same situations if you undertake fieldwork beginning tomorrow. However, a good researcher should be able to utilize anecdotal accounts as a partial fieldwork experience and to study the illustrations in much of the literature as an additional data source. To encourage such new research and to make it easier for you than it was for me when I began, I append an annotated bibliography.

The chapter headings of this book would seem to promise a standard anthropological/analytic approach to the data, and this is somewhat misleading. The major focus is the Gypsy culture itself, and this has in large measure determined the organization of the material. Thus, the connective links between the various topics come from their close association within the Gypsy culture, not from the expectations of outsiders. Consequently, I have also tried to frame the material so that each chapter can stand alone; in this way, perhaps, I shall have the best of both possible worlds: I shall not wreak undue havoc with the organizing principles of Gypsy culture, and yet I shall not excessively inconvenience my patient readers. Of course, this has led to some repetition, but I have been a teacher long enough not to feel apologetic about that.

Some of you may take offense at a few of the terms I use in this book, and I readily apologize in advance. However, the Gypsies learned about non-Gypsies from a European standpoint and to them "voyages of discovery to the New World" is a sensible phrasing; so is "American Indian," for, compared to the Gypsies, almost all outsiders seem by contrast to be "Native Americans," and, unlike indigenous Europeans of long standing, the Gypsies are not at all impressed by details of nativity.

If my fellow anthropologists take offense at some of the passages in this book, they owe me an apology; for their objectivity will be in doubt if their egos are involved in pet theoretical positions that cannot be demonstrated in the only genuine testing ground we have—that of the real world of live human beings who have the sense to exist and survive without having read the polemics of our professions.

I take full credit for whatever is wrong with this book. To all those people who have educated me must be attributed whatever merits this book may have. My teachers at Hunter College were persistent and encouraging; some of the grey hairs on the heads of Elsie Viault Steedman, Dorothy Cross Jensen, Dorothy Keur, Ethel Aginsky, and Alice Galligan James were doubtless mementoes of their attempts to make me an anthropologist. Professor George Herzog left Columbia University a year after I arrived; perhaps my problems were too much for that gentle human being. Professor Joseph H. Greenberg started his teaching service by being one of my advisors; he passed this acid test with flying colors as we all know. The Nomad Gypsies have stubbornly remained in New York City despite my frequent visits; they probably realize there is no escape from me, no matter where they were to go. But the man who deserves the most sympathy from my readers is Mr. Albert McGrigor, who demonstrated supreme lack of judgment by functioning as my editor for four weary years (so he tells me). He knows when to cajole and when to scold; more important, he knows when to leave an author alone. He returns copy to you with all kinds of corrections and revisions, and then puts balm on your bruised ego by announcing that he likes the chapter very much. I wholeheartedly recommend his services to all my academic colleagues. If anybody can get us to produce a worthwhile piece of writing, my editor can.

GYPSIES IN THE CITY

1
INTRODUCTION

They have been called "Heathen," "Bohemian," "Tartar," "Tinker," "Egyptian," *"Tzigane,"* *"Zigeuner,"* and "Gypsy," the mysterious, little known people who are the subject of this book. For five hundred years they have succeeded in being themselves against all odds, fiercely maintaining their identity in spite of persecution, prejudice, hatred, and cultural forces compelling them to change. We may have something to learn from them on how to survive in a drastically changing world. Who are they?

Evidence for the Origin of the Gypsies

In 1763, Stefan Valyi, a Protestant student of theology at Leyden University, discovered quite by accident that there was a similarity between the Gypsy language of the Kormorn district of Hungary and the languages of the Indian subcontinent. With the aid of three Indian students from Malabar, he compiled a vocabulary list of one thousand words; these words were then read off to a group of Gypsies, who recognized almost all of them. Thus began a long series of philological investigations by such linguists as Pott (1844), Miklosisch (1872-1880), Paspati (1870), von Wlislocki (1890), and Turner (1926, 1927) that led to the conclusion that *Romany* is akin to modern Hindi.

When the ancient Aryan speakers entered India, they spoke a proto-Sanskritic language. In the course of time, the resultant Classical Sanskrit became the language of literature and of religion (like Latin during the medieval period in Europe) whereas the masses spoke a Prakrit vernacular as the everyday language (like the Romance languages that sprang from Latin). By the tenth century A.D. these vernaculars had assumed roughly the form of the modern Indo-Aryan languages; it was in this period that Romany apparently differentiated as a separate language in its own right. Today this fact is accepted by all linguists. The only linguistic problem remaining to be solved revolves around the fact that the Prakritic parent-forms seem to have been of three basic types, and presently we are unsure to which subgroup Romany properly belongs.

The linguistic evidence of an Indian origin is paralleled by the evidence of physical types. Although blond Gypsies do occur, they are comparatively rare except in those groups known to have intermarried with Europeans and those in which an extensive first-generation intermarriage between two formerly widely separated Gypsy groups (i.e., different breeding isolates) has been followed by intensive inbreeding in the succeeding filial generations. Most Gypsies tend to fall within the darker ranges of Caucasoid skin color; hair shades ordinarily are very dark, and hair form varies from slightly wavy to curly. Light-colored eyes are rare, and there is no evidence of an epicanthic fold. The large aquiline nose characteristic of parts of the Indian subcontinent is present in many Gypsies. But the most convincing evidence comes from the study of blood-type frequencies. A comparison was made of the relative frequencies of the ABO(H) blood groups of Gypsies in Hungary with other Hungarian populations on the one hand and with Asiatic Indians on the other; results showed a closer approximation of Gypsy blood phenotypes with those of the Indians than with neighboring Hungarians.[1]

The evidence from cultural comparisons is the least clear. To understand the reasons behind the apparent conflicts, it is necessary to make a small digression into Indian prehistory and early history. Archaeology and linguistics have shown that the subcontinent of India has been peopled by a number of different groups, each quite distinctive from the others. Each wave of immigrants tended to push some of the already-settled inhabitants further south. In some cases, however, there was a coexistence of the older and the newer groups, with the result that

[1]Buettner-Janusch 1973: 361-62 provides critical discussion of this issue.

cultural (and physical) exchanges occurred. The incoming groups borrowed some cultural items from the settlers, and the older groups, in turn, borrowed from the newcomers; furthermore, a dominant group usually imposed its language over the conquered peoples.

Apparently the stock from which the Gypsies arose was akin to groups that today are most numerous in the southern part of India and speak Dravidian languages. With the Aryan invasion of *ca*. 1500 b.c. the speakers of Indo-European languages arrived in India, and some members of the proto-Gypsy groups moved southward while others remained in the midst of the Aryan speakers and eventually began speaking Indo-Aryan languages themselves while retaining close bonds of culture with their southerly kin.[2] Such a hypothesis seems necessary to explain the situation of the groups referred to as the "Criminal and Wandering Tribes" today. These groups have representative bands throughout India and Sri Lanka (Ceylon). The similarities among these groups are of sufficient magnitude to warrant the assumption that they share a common history; nevertheless, some of the Criminal and Wandering Tribes speak Dravidian languages and others speak Indo-Aryan languages. Furthermore, some of these groups have tribal status (i.e., they do not participate in the caste system and hence do not partake of the dominant Indian civilization) whereas other groups are integrated into the total Indian caste hierarchy.[3]

The Gypsies probably stem from the northern branches of these Criminal and Wandering Tribes. Whether the Gypsies left India as a single tribal group or as a collection of several tribes is not known. For that matter, we do not know when the emigration took place or whether it took place as a single mass exodus or in the form of small bands leaving over a relatively long period of time.

My personal feelings, based on the combined evidences of the earliest historical records of the Gypsies in the Near East and Europe and the great cultural discrepancy that exists today

[2]Woolner 1928: 108 thinks they originated in southeastern India and migrated to the northwest, leaving by way of Peshawar.

[3]Surveys on these groups may be found in Crooke 1888: 68-75, 1910: 35-40; Williams 1912-1913: 34-58, 110-35. Up to date ethnographies by Indian anthropologists are Bhargava (1949), Biswas 1960, Sher Singh 'Sher' 1967, 1965.

between the nomad and sedentary groups, are that some proto-Gypsy bands left India from time to time throughout their existence. This is a sensible hypothesis since they are and were Criminal and *Wandering* Tribes. Some of the groups may have elected (or been forced) to leave and remain away from India, thus becoming one of those problematic groups that have been wandering in Near Eastern areas for a number of centuries.

The exodus leading to the dispersion of the Gypsies throughout all of Europe must have been stimulated by a highly unusual set of circumstances. Nomads do not usually depart from annual migration routes without strong justification. Since the Gypsies first appeared in western Europe in the first quarter of the fifteenth century, it would appear logical to link their appearance there with the prior entrance of Timur the Great (Tamerlane) into India (Grellman 1807: 205-07; Pittard 1902: 130). The Mongol scourge accomplished this feat at the end of the fourteenth century. This theory, however, requires an ability to predict the future (a typically Gypsy occupation, of course!) because it must have taken considerably more than twenty-five years to make the migration route from India to Europe. The proto-Gypsies, according to this view, decided to leave India because of the *expected* Mongol invasions.

But why was it necessary for the Romanies to make such a long leap in space? As these Gypsies passed through the Near East and into southeastern Europe, they probably came into contact with related groups already established in these areas. These distant kinsmen not only possessed prior territorial claims but also a different set of cultural practices. The lack of cultural rapport, one might say, precluded intermarriage and alliance with the resident groups. Furthermore, most of them were attached to monasteries or estates as slaves. If the Gypsies were fleeing from possible slavery under Timur, they certainly were not knowingly going to put on shackles elsewhere. The newcomers pushed on, westward and northward.

It has also been suggested that contact with Europeans in the Near East during the Crusades provided the impetus for a migration. (I am indebted to my husband, Mr. Murray Gropper, for this suggestion.) This hypothesis has the merit of integrating two disparate data: (1) the fact that we have historical evidence of Gypsy-like groups in the Near East at an early date; and (2) the fact that, when the Gypsies arrived in Europe, they had intimate knowledge of European ways. It does not share with the other non-Timur hypotheses the disadvantage that we would have the Gypsies coming out of India before the postulated emergence of their language.

Early History in the Near East

The Persian poet Firdusi (*ca.* 940- *ca.* 1020 A.D.) in his famous epic poem, the *Shâh Nâmah* (Book of Kings), makes reference to a fifth century A.D. king by the name of Behram Gour, who received "12,000 Luri musicians" as a gift from an Indian potentate. To this day, Iranians refer to Gypsies as Luri. Furthermore, Hamzod of Isfahan, some fifty years before Firdusi, mentions the same story and calls the musicians Zott, which is the Arab term for Gypsies (Grierson 1888: 73).

During the Persian-Arab wars of the seventh century, Zotts were inducted into the Persian Army; they defected to the Arabs when the Shah suffered reverses. Around 670, the Caliph Mouwia brought Zott followers and their families from Basra to Antioch and other Syrian towns. By the third century of the Moslem era, there were separate Zott quarters in the city of Antioch.

At the beginning of the ninth century, Zotts were living in the lower Tigris valley, and in 834 some were captured, apparently as slaves, and were transported to an area about 100 miles northeast of Baghdad and northern Syria. In 855, they are mentioned in reference to the Byzantine Empire (de Goeje 1886: 14-58; Grierson 1888: 74; MacRitchie 1886: 77-90). By the eleventh century, it would seem, Gypsies or Gypsy-like groups were scattered throughout the Near East.

Today there are a number of groups in the area (as well as in North Africa) that are a source of aggravation to natives and to visiting anthropologists alike. The Arabs haughtily insist they are not Arabs; the Iranians and Turks disclaim them. Many of them cannot speak Romany while others are bilingual, speaking dialects of Romany not readily understandable by European Gypsies. Again this seems to indicate that some proto-Gypsy groups left India at different times and that migrations into the area continued sporadically, perhaps sometimes in small, scat-

tered groups and sometimes in larger waves. The group of
Zingari in Samarkand mentioned before 1406 must have had
contact with Timur, for Borrow (1907: 35-36) quotes an Arab
source that details a fierce slaughter of rebellious Zingari by
Timur before he swept into India.

Early History in Europe

Table 1.1 indicates the earliest recorded mention of the Gypsies
in different areas of Europe. The span of several hundred years
between southeastern Europe on the one hand and central western Europe on the other bears out the contention of at least two
separate migration waves. However, as Latin chronicles make
reference only to a given number of tents of *Atsigani* assigned to
a monastery, we can only speculate that the name seems to be
cognate with other, later, European names designating the Gypsies and that the sparse details of appearance and customs furnished as incidentals to the accounts do correspond to Gypsy
ways. The reader must judge for himself.

While it is true that a Georgian monk of Mt. Athos mentions
some magicians and sorcerers by the name of *Atsincani* or
Athingani in 1100, these were probably not Gypsies. However,
there are indications that Gypsies were in the Balkans before the
fourteenth century. A Minonite friar by the name of Symour
Simeonis recorded in the *Itinerarium* his pilgrimage from Ire-
land to Palestine. He documents his meeting in 1322 with a
group of people outside the city of Candia, Crete, who claimed
to be of the race of Ham but who followed the Greek rites of
Christianity. They lived in caves or low, oblong black tents, and
they were reported never to stay longer than thirty days at any
one place. Later that year in Egypt, the friar encountered some
Danubian captives who were very dark-skinned and who impressed him by their resemblance to Asiatic Indians. These
prisoners were adherents of Islam, and they practiced the art of
tattooing. A plausible hypothesis is that the Gypsies entered the
Balkans with the Arab and Turk invaders, having followed the
normal Romany procedure of ostensibly embracing the dominant religion of the area (Block 1939: 55; Clébert 1963: 27;
Groome 1899: xix).

The Empress Catherine de Courtenay-Valois (1301-1346) au-

TABLE 1.1

EARLIEST APPEARANCE OF THE GYPSIES IN EUROPE

Southeastern Europe
Corfu—before 1346
Crete—before 1322
Greece—before 1346
Hungary—before 1383
Rumania—before 1350
Serbia—before 1340

Northeastern Europe
Poland—1501
Russia—1501
Sweden—1512

Western Europe

Belgium—
  1421 Tournais
  1427 Tournais
England—ca. 1506
Flanders—1420
France—
  1419 Macon
  1419 Sisteron
  1419 Provence
  1422 Alsace
  1427 Paris
  1427 Amiens
  1427-1434 Metz and environs
Germany—
  (?1407 Hildesheim?)
  (?1414 Hessen?)
  (?1416 Meissen?)
  1417 Bavaria, Hanseatic League, etc.
    Greifswald
    Hamburg
    Lübeck
    Lüneburg
    Rostock
    Stralsund
    Wismar
  1418 Augsburg
  1418 Frankfurt am Main
  1418 Leipzig
  1424 Ratisbon (Regensburg)
  1426 Ratisbon

Italy—
  1422 Bologna
  1422 Rome
  1422 Forli
Netherlands—
  1420 Deventer
  1427-1434 Arnheim
  1427-1434 Utrecht
Scotland—ca. 1430
Spain—1447
Switzerland—
  (?1414 Basel?)
  (?1417 Lindau?)
  1418 Basel
  1418 Bern
  1418 Solaure
  1418 Zurich
  1422 Basel

thorized the Corfu suzerains to treat wandering people from the Greek mainland as vassals, and by the end of the fourteenth century Gypsy groups were established under a Baron Gianuli de Abitabulo in a fief known as the "feudum Acingarnorum." This group of some hundred adults followed such typically Gypsy occupations as smith, tinker, animal-dealer, and mechanic. Our sources indicate that they were subject to a semi-annual tax and paid for their marriage dues in hens (Groome 1899: xix-xx).

Other Atsigani are mentioned around 1340, when a Serbian prince gave some families as slaves to the Tismana monastery at the foot of the Carpathian Mountains. Thirty years later, a document from Rumania chronicles a similar gift of forty families by a Wallachian prince. Thus, it would seem that Gypsies were slaves in Rumania before the mid-fourteenth century. In 1386 and 1387, Vlad II and Wercea I, waywodes of Wallachia, received forty tents of Atsigani from the monastery of St. Antoine; these slaves had been given to that monastery by the waywodes' uncle Vladislas in 1370. Gypsies continued to be slaves of the boyars until the nineteenth century (Block 1939: 55; Bataillard 1889-1890: 187; Clébert 1963: 27).

There is evidence that a certain amount of unrest occurred among Gypsy slaves living in Hungary, for in 1383 Sigismund of Hungary gave a group called the *Sincani* the right to choose their own leaders. Part of this rebellious spirit may have been occasioned by the better living conditions enjoyed by Gypsies in Greece and Cyprus, where the only obvious burden they had to bear was the payment of taxes to the royal treasury. We have the testimony of Florio Bustron to that effect in his *Chronique de Chypre* (1468). Still earlier, around 1398, at Nauplion in the northern Peloponnesus, we have a recorded confirmation of separative privileges (Bataillard 1889-1890: 187; Groome 1899: xx).

Certainly it is sensible to expect the Gypsies to have entered those parts of Europe adjoining the Near East at a comparatively early date. Moreover, all Romany dialects spoken in Europe (and the Americas) contain many Greek and Slavic loan-words; this is probably evidence of a long sojourn in southeastern Europe.

I should think it might be equally sensible to postulate that it was these Gypsies of southeastern Europe who began to move into western Europe in the fifteenth century, were it not for the problem of the Romany language. There are Gypsy groups in southeastern Europe and in Hungary and Rumania that do not speak Romany. We might postulate a gradual and continuous migration from India into the Near East and thence to southeastern Europe. If this were the case, there would be a culturolinguistic bridge between some of the resident Gypsies and any newcomers. I believe it would be the more recent arrivals who collected necessary survival information from their kin and then continued to move on, as I have indicated.

The appearance of Gypsies in the Hanseatic League towns of northern Germany was an event, and the chroniclers accordingly devoted considerable space to the details.[4] Examination of these documents allows us to map the routes taken by the Gypsies and to reckon the size of the traveling parties that split from the main group (see Map 1.1). The Romanies seem to have taken the precaution of sending advance scouts into the area before the main party entered. We have some debatable documentation supporting the hypothesis that small groups went through Germany and Switzerland before the first major influx in 1417. Apparently scouts went to Hildesheim in 1407 and returned with their report. Seven years later, in 1414, a small vanguard appeared in Hessen and Basel, presumably to obtain additional information. In 1416, an advance party may have been in Meissen, perhaps to prepare the way for the entrance of the main group the following year.

The Gypsies appeared near the North Sea in 1417. They referred to themselves as "Lords of Little Egypt" (the English word, "Gypsy," is a corruption of "Egyptian"). All in all, there were some three hundred Gypsies in the traveling party between 1417 and 1427. They were headed by King Zindolo; Dukes Michael, Andreas, and Panuel led smaller groups. Several earls are mentioned as well as Count Johannis and Knight Petrus. These leaders rode magnificent horses; they dressed in European clothing tailored in the fashion of the nobility, their heads covered by hats with flowing plumes and appropriate jewels, and

[4]This section is based on the following sources: Bataillard 1889-1890; Grellman 1807; Groome 1899; Hopf 1870; Vesey-Fitzgerald 1944: 5-29.

MAP 1.1
**DATES AND AREAS OF FIRST APPEARANCES OF THE
GYPSIES IN EUROPE**

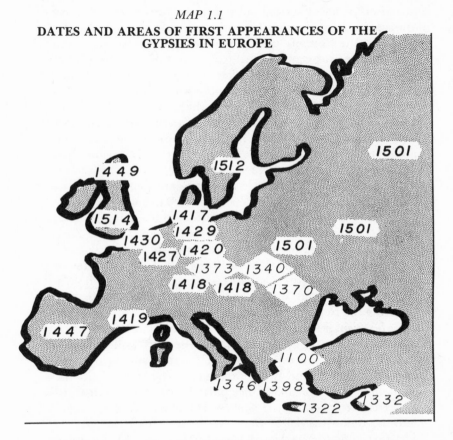

on their wrists they carried hunting falcons. The commoners, clothed in rags, walked at the end of the procession. The women were draped in sari-like garments, wearing pendant earrings and bracelets.

It is possible that an initial stop was made at Lindau on Lake Constance in 1417. We know that the Pope was sojourning there at the time, and the Gypsies carried a letter from His Holiness when they appeared in north Germany later that year. Then they swung back southward to Switzerland in 1418. For the next year or so apparently they split into two smaller bands led by Dukes Andreas and Michael and made rendezvous in Switzerland late in 1419. By 1422, the Gypsies had a new letter of safe-conduct from Emperor Sigismund of Hungary. This would indicate either the arrival of a new group or reentrance of part of the original group after a return to southeastern Europe. In 1422, the Gypsies again broke into two groups while winding their way through Italy, for one hundred Gypsies were reported at Bologna on the eighteenth of July while two hundred were seen at Forli on the seventh of August. They may have rejoined ranks when they arrived at Rome.

Throughout their travels the Romanies exploited the tale that their ancestors had failed to provide sanctuary to the Holy Family on the Flight and as a result God had condemned them to wander for seven years to expiate their sin and atone for their apostacy. Among the worthy men who were impressed by this inspiring Christian tale were the Emperor Sigismund and the Pope himself. Both these pious personages provided letters of safe-conduct for the repentant Gypsies, instructing all Europeans in their domains to shield them from harm and to provide them with food and money to allow them to fulfill their sacred mission.

With the aid of the letters given them, the Gypsies traveled through central and western Europe, making a living as fortunetellers and necromancers. When rumors began to circulate that valuables seemed to disappear with more than magical consistency whenever Gypsies were around, the Gypsies made known the Story of the Fourth Nail. According to this legend, a Gypsy blacksmith had refused to forge the nails required to crucify Christ; instead, he managed to steal the nails from a non-Gypsy smith. The Romans had to nail both of Christ's feet together at the execution, and in gratitude for the attempt to save His Son, God granted permission to all the descendants of that daring Gypsy smith to steal once every seven years.

The second story was not as well received as the first. In fact, the legend backfired in time, and Europeans began to tell a different version wherein the Gypsy smith was the only one willing to forge the nails, thereby automatically excommunicating himself and his descendants from the company of Christians everywhere for eternity.

There is a bewildering hiatus in the chronicles between 1422 and 1427. Did the Gypsies return to southeastern Europe after their fifteen-year trek? Did they go back to organize a systematic invasion by larger groups? All we know with certainty is that from 1427 to 1434 Gypsies expanded their traveling routes westward on the continent.

Between 1434 and 1438, there is another blank period in the history of the Gypsies; soon thereafter, however, we find them all over Europe and the British Isles in great numbers. Sympathy gave way to active dislike of the strangers as they entered country after country and failed to leave after the promised seven years. Their European hosts made systematic plans to eject the unwanted guests. Preventing them from entering towns and cities did not keep them away. The Gypsies definitely were not townspeople. They were nomads by habit and preference, and they merely pitched their tents in the countryside while their womenfolk visited the neighboring farms to tell fortunes, doctor animals, and sell potions.

An attempt was made to force the wanderers to conform to European customs. They were to settle down, stay in one place, renounce their traditions, and become members of the community. Both the carrot and the stick were used with the stubborn Gypsy donkey. Maria Theresa of Austria generously subsidized the resettlement and outfitting of her "neo-Austrian" subjects; she also set a time limit in which to do it, under penalty of death. Other countries chose to banish the Gypsies entirely, or punish them physically. Gypsy children were to be removed forcibly from their parents and brought up as Christians.

Country after country tried to banish them or make them conform, but each new measure proved as ineffectual as the last. It was like outlawing the wind. The Gypsies remained in Europe and multiplied. Before the Nazi decimations and Communist attempts to settle them into collective farms, there were Gypsies in every country of Europe.

Types of Gypsies

Gypsy groups may be divided into two types on the basis of their settlement patterns. There are groups that remain within the confines of one country or even of a single district for generations. Of these, some preserve the Gypsy language while others speak the tongue of their adopted countries. These settled, or Sedentary Gypsies, frequently intermarry with non-Gypsies, contrary to the other groups. In former times, Gypsy musicians, dancers, and other entertainers were often under the patronage and protection of a noble, and a beautiful Gypsy girl was often his mistress or wife.

The Sedentary groups are called *Sinte* by the Nomads, and the term is one of opprobrium. Sinte groups, such as the Spanish Gypsy groups that make a living as dancers and musicians in Granada and the Hungarian cymbalom players, are so well known to the outside world that they are assumed to be typical Gypsies. Actually the divergence between Sinte and Nomads is so great that they will not associate together. Sinte women often act as prostitutes as well as entertainers, whereas chastity and post-marital fidelity is the absolute rule for Nomads. There is a much stronger emphasis by the Sinte on the woman's side of the family, even allowing their women to be the boss of the household.[5]

In the Americas, there are representatives of many of the Sinte groups. The Spanish *Calé* are in the cities of North America as well as throughout Central and South America. There are colonies of Hungarian and Rumanian entertainers settled in many of the larger cities. Relatively large numbers of Russian Sinte live in New York City. English basket-makers still exist in the rural areas of New England.

The Nomad groups of Gypsies are themselves divided into a number of different tribes, sometimes with friendly alliances and sometimes with traditional hostilities. Nevertheless, all Nomads acknowledge the legitimate claim of all other Nomads to the designation *Rom* (literally, "husband" or "man"), true Gypsy, merely specifying *amare Roma* ("our own Gypsies") when reference is made to the same tribe. Intermarriage is permissible among all Nomad tribes, and the different dialects are on the whole mutually intelligible. (This is in marked contrast to the lack of mutual understanding between Nomad and Sinte dialects. I have found myself acting as interpreter between these two groups on several occasions.)

The Nomad tribal divisions in western Europe include the *Lovara* (supposed to be derived from the Gypsy word for money; in other words, "the money people"); the *Ćurara*, "the people of

[5]An excellent ethnography on Spanish Sinte is Quintana and Floyd 1972.

the knife"; the *Mačvaja*, or traders; and the *Kalderaša*, or coppersmiths. A tribe is distinguished by a common Romany dialect and a shared set of cultural patterns. Tribal lines are of little practical importance in daily life, and, although the Gypsy nearly always knows his own tribal affiliation, he often is quite vague about the tribal provenience of other Gypsy groups with whom he interacts.

The Mačvaja are most numerous in the United States, but in most of the Americas the Kalderaša outnumber them. The Lovara are represented only by a very few groups in the United States despite the fact that large numbers of them travel through Spain, the Low Countries, and Italy. The Čurara, who tend to be avoided by the other Nomads because of their familiar ways with weapons and violence, are the least known by outsiders and by Gypsies alike, and consequently it is difficult to make even an educated guess about their numbers. I am sure they do exist in the Americas; they must be the group alluded to under the rubric "Killer Gypsies."

The designation of the bands within tribes are common knowledge since the bands are the true functioning socio-political units. These *vitsas* take their names from the "king" of the *vitsa*; i.e., from the name of the band chief. Thus, the vitsa name may change through time. There are several vitsas whose home territory is the United States and who seem to be acting as small nuclei for the formation of new tribes. For example, the *Arxentina* actually are members of a Kalderaš vitsa whose original home base was Argentina. Its members arrived in the United States through a pattern of extensive intermarriage with a large and very important Kalderaš vitsa already well established here. Initially the Arxentina acknowledged the suzerainty of their in-laws because of the numerous advantages of allying with such powerful kin. However, as the power situation in New York City changed, the affinal kin no longer were able to function as protectors; the Arxentina realigned into a functionally independent unit, and linguistic differentiation was the logical result. The *Meksikaja* are a small group reluctantly conceded to be Mačvaja by the other Mačvaja groups.[6] They are looked at as-

---

[6]Most recently, the Meksikaja have laid successful claim to being part of the Kalderaša network of New York City. Currently, this is more advantageous than belonging to the Mačvaja, for the Kalderaša are in control now.

kance because the grandmother from which they are descended was a non-Gypsy in Mexico and their men do not object to work in order to earn a daily living. Their ingenuity on that score is enviable: they have invented a new insurance racket (at least it is new from the Gypsy vantage point) whereby they throw themselves in front of moving vehicles and collect indemnity for the alleged injuries suffered. Another group, the *Russ*, seem to be composed of some Kalderaša that had formerly claimed Russia as home territory and some Russian Sedentaries. The so-called "French" are actually Lovara, and in the East at least they have begun to intermarry with some of the vitsas of mixed Russ and Kalderaša.

As an interesting aside, perhaps I should add that this confusion of tribal designations and affiliations is characteristic of Gypsies.[7] It probably constitutes a significant mechanism for the maintenance of Gypsy solidarity, for it acts as a counterbalance to a splintering tendency encouraged by all tribal and band groups. Furthermore, I would suspect that equal confusion exists for many tribal groups in large parts of Asia; surely not all the apparent chaos in tribal groupings and affiliations can be attributed to inept ethnographic methods.

Relevance of Contact Situations for the Study of Culture

An intensive study of Nomad Gypsies is of particular interest to anthropologists concerned with cultural changes arising from the meeting of members of different cultures and societies. This is because the Nomads have had contacts with a number of different cultures in turn—Persian, Arabic, Greek, Serbian, German, Russian, and American. Some seem to have influenced Gypsy culture more strongly than others. However, most important of all is the fact that after half a millenium of living in the midst of alien cultures, often under great pressure to assimilate, Gypsies have managed to maintain their identity, preserve their language, and retain their culture. This record is extraordinary in view of the overwhelming numbers of cultures reported to disappear under exposure to the forceful persuasion of Euro-

[7]Discussions of the problem may be found in Brown 1929; Clébert 1963: 23-25; Cohn 1973: 17-26; Cotten 1955: 20-28.

American technology. Because of the large numbers of peoples who have lost their separate cultural identities within a relatively short time period, the majority of anthropologists believe that capitulation is inevitable for all non-Western cultures. Thus the ability of the Gypsies to resist acculturation (or at least that extreme form called assimilation) warrants close analysis, not only for its own sake but also for the lessons that may be learned for all groups determined to preserve their cultural integrity. For example, the new Afro-Asian nations are anxious to participate with their Euro-American brothers in a world community but not at the cost of their newly gained identities. They have many vital questions to ask the social scientists: "May we pick and choose among the cultural items being offered us in the world supermarket? Will the price prove exorbitant? Will we have to buy items we do not truly want through a hidden 'package deal'?"

Perhaps the Gypsies can help provide some of the answers.

2

GYPSIES IN THE UNITED STATES AND IN NEW YORK

During the Age of Exploration and Colonization, Spain, Portugal, France, and Great Britain attempted to get rid of the Gypsies by resettling them in the New World. Thus, Gypsies arrived in the Americas along with the European settlers. Thereafter, each wave of European immigration usually brought along a group of Gypsies.

From the 1880s to about 1914, numerous Gypsy bands arrived in the Americas, many from Serbia and from Russian-dominated areas. Those that made their way into the United States quickly made themselves at home, dividing the country into territories and following seasonal migration routes. They led a nomadic existence during the summer, spending most of the cold winter months in camps pitched in out-of-the-way places. This typically Gypsy way of life was continued until about 1925.

Stages of Culture Change in the United States

For the purposes of this volume, we can recognize four periods in Gypsy contacts with Americans. My original study, done between 1947 and 1950 with the Kalderaš groups, gave promise of more acculturative behavior than actually materialized in the next decade and a half. An inherent danger of ethnological studies on culture-borrowing pursued in a period of crisis is that as more time passes (or perhaps as the investigator becomes more experienced and more mature), the particular crisis under consideration takes on a more realistic perspective. What seemed to be sharp, contrastive angles and jagged lines mellow into more gentle curves and waves, indicative of a much less important pulsation within the inevitable dynamics of cultural processes. The fact is that all cultures exhibit change through time. Contrary to opinions expressed by numerous colleagues at the time of the study, the Romanies have successfully weathered the more recent storm just as they have survived all the past crises.

The first period may be called the Camp Period, named after their major settlement pattern. As far as the Nomads are concerned, it stretches from the time they entered the United States in significant numbers, in the 1880s, until about 1925. This period was a direct continuation of Gypsy life in Europe and Latin America. Families wandered freely thoughout the United States, following Gypsy rules of territoriality. During the winter period, they established relatively large camps in forests, with all or most of the members of a given band living in the same camp; the principal religious and social feasts were all held during the winter. Marriages and religious rites, some of mixed Gypsy and Christian origin, were held at the beginning of winter, coinciding with the Christmas period. In the spring, as the weather warmed up and travel became easier, the Gypsies began their annual migrations, traveling in relatively small groups motivated by the need to make a living (whereas life in winter camps was oriented towards sociopolitical activities) and camping in fields near towns and hamlets. Spring rites were held to celebrate the break-up of communal camps.

The second period, from about 1925 to 1933, I shall call the Transition Period. This period is characterized by a gradual decrease in the frequency with which winter camps were established. A number of factors contributed to this change. One factor was the acceptance and growing popularity of cars as the favored mode of transportation, instead of horses. Horsetrading decreased in importance, affecting Gypsy economy, and with the need for land on which to build roads and highways, unclaimed lands in which to camp decreased. After the Crash of 1929, the Gypsies suffered from the general economic depression; money for luxury items like entertainment and fortunetelling became scarce, and the rural areas experienced a severe loss

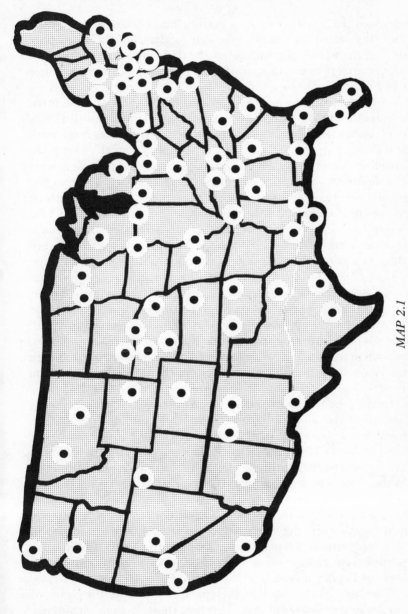

of spare pocket-money. As a result, the Gypsies were pushed into the towns. At first, they began to abandon their camping during the winter months. Then, as their familiarity with town life increased, they gradually began to relinquish their summer camps as well.

In 1933, with the election of Franklin Roosevelt and the institution of various relief and welfare projects (lasting until 1956), the Gypsies began to flóck to the large cities, such as New York and Chicago, to take advantage of the money available there. In order to claim benefits, it was necessary for them to have at least one member of the nuclear family constantly available to the social agencies in charge of relief. Thus the Gypsies were forced to stay in the cities at this time. When the Second World War began, money problems were alleviated through the general economic boom, but the Gypsies were still forced to remain in the cities because of gasoline rationing. Thus the years from 1933 to 1945 I shall call the Crisis Period.

Since the Gypsies were directly dependent upon non-Gypsies for subsistence money, they found themselves under the heel of the *gajo* ("outsider," "non-Gypsy"). The Gypsies had to fulfill non-Gypsy requirements to entitle them to welfare. They had to remain in the cities in order to receive these monies, and living in the city required extensive changes in their social and political structuring.

During the war, New York City, formerly Kalderaš territory, became Mačvaja headquarters. For a while, until the mid-1950s, there was a great voluntary influx of Gypsies into New York, most of these being Mačvaja. Power play among the Mačvaja groups had the unfortunate effect of calling additional attention to the Romanies on the part of city officials.

In 1946, when I started working with the Gypsies, they were still an uncommon element of the population. However, by the mid-1950s, even the newspapers made frequent reference in their columns to Gypsy stores, and many of my students reported Gypsies in their neighborhood. As a result, anti-Gypsy feelings began to be felt.

The New York City Police Department adopted a policy of deliberate harrassment. For instance, there is a city ordinance requiring all storekeepers to affix the name of the proprietor or owner somewhere on the store-front. Gypsies often neglect to adhere to this inconsequential ruling; or, when the men paint a name on the front, they neglect to tell their wives what the name is. The women, being illiterate, cannot read it when the police come by to ask the name of the proprietor. The detectives now made it a practice to utilize this common failing to arrest the Gypsies. In addition, the same type of offense that formerly would have called for a mild fine now brought a jail sentence. All the techniques the Gypsies had learned in coping with the new urban environment failed to meet the changing set of circumstances. The Gypsies had become a logical scapegoat group for New York law enforcers.

By 1960, most of the Gypsies who had moved into the area in the previous decade had left New York City for other parts of the country, leaving only the long established groups in the city. Not only was the city their legitimate domain by Gypsy law, but as they lacked the experience to make a living somewhere else, they would be at a disadvantage elsewhere.

Since the mid-1950s, there has been a general crackdown against Gypsies in parts of the country traditionally hospitable to and cooperative with them. Anti-Gypsy feeling has forced the Gypsies to break up and scatter into smaller, less visible groups. They have reached another Plateau Period in the history of their relations with the gaje.

The history of New York City's Gypsies varies in detail from that of Gypsies in other cities, but the patterning remains the same—periods of population concentration are succeeded by periods of population sparcity, and then a gradual increase ensues. For example, in the late 1960s, certain parts of Washington, D. C. had a Gypsy fortunetelling location every few blocks; by 1972, however, Gypsy stores were becoming scarce in the city proper.

Having explored the history of Gypsies from the vantage-point of a single city (a most un-Gypsylike approach), let us now follow the story of one particular band, beginning the epic in the decade before the turn of the century.

The Bimbulesti

At the time when we pick up the story, the *Bimbulesti vitsa* ("Bimbo's band") was a Kalderaš group based in Russia but spending much time wandering throughout eastern Europe.

Life was fairly comfortable for the band, and peace reigned until Bimbo's son Tinja was about thirteen years old. This youth was regarded as a promising young man destined to succeed his father as group leader. However, Tinja was both ambitious and impatient; he began to plot to wrest leadership from his father. Making secret visits to the heads of families in his father's band, he managed to convince many of them that he would be a better ruler than his father. As a result, Bimbo was informed that he was being deposed. In this way trouble began for the Bimbulesti, one of the oldest, most powerful and proudest groups of Coppersmiths in Europe.

Tinja's usurpation of position was severely condemned by most of the other Kalderaš bands of eastern Europe. Although kings had been deposed before, tribal law prescribed the exact circumstances for such action. Bimbo, however, was still perfectly eligible for leadership, and consequently many Gypsies continued to regard him as the legitimate head of the Bimbulesti. Moreover, tribal custom prescribed that a leader should be an older man with experience, so Tinja was not really eligible. The other Kalderaš chiefs were prepared to capture and discipline the young renegade, but Bimbo prevented harm from coming to his son. To protest such a decision, some of the Bimbulesti families left to ally themselves with kinsmen in other groups. The leaders of the other bands refused to cooperate with Tinja, and the Bimbulesti found themselves in an isolated (and hence vulnerable) position in eastern Europe.

Had Tinja remained in the same general vicinity as the Bimbo sympathizers, he would have had difficulty in maintaining his leadership. Thus he showed considerable astuteness and daring in taking his band across the Atlantic Ocean to South America, where his notoriety would not follow him easily.

In South America, the Bimbulesti joined the caravans of a large band ruled by Adolf Dimitro. Dimitro's group had territorial rights in Argentina and Brazil, and it was wise for a fledgling ruler to become friends with this considerably older, considerably more powerful chief whose sphere of influence extended to some four or five hundred Gypsy families. In accepted Gypsy fashion, Tinja became a supporter of Dimitro, supplying to his mentor youthful strength and craftiness; in return, Dimitro recognized and protected Tinja's rights to headship of the Bimbulesti.

Dimitro was indeed powerful, and the South American Gypsies followed his lead in considering Tinja a legitimate ruler. When a suspected case of theft occurred in one of the groups, Tinja was requested to function as judge of the trial (in itself, one of the ways in which leadership is acknowledged). Tinja's success in handling the trial and enforcing the verdict established his reputation, and soon the original Bimbulesti families were joined by others under Tinja's domination.

Dimitro and Tinja got along very well, and as a gesture of friendship (also as a traditional means of cementing the partnership) a number of marriages were contracted between the two groups. All went well, and the Bimbulesti congratulated themselves upon a wise choice of leader and environment.

Some time later, however, Tinja and Dimitro went into the hills together. Tinja's family claims that they met some other Gypsies who asked Tinja to stay with them for a while to baptize their children. According to one version of the story, this was a group of Killer Gypsies, and they kept Tinja prisoner. The young man was able to escape one night after a drinking party had taken place. Dimitro, however, was unable to protect his own people against a group that refused to recognize his power and that failed to obey the basic laws of Gypsy society. Since the Killer Gypsies had many friends, Tinja and his group decided to leave South America; they made their way up through Central America to Mexico.

This version of the Bimbulesti story has a few odd elements in it, and our suspicions are increased when the story is continued in Mexico. There, we are informed, more Killer Gypsies were now encountered—apparently friends and allies of the first group—and Tinja was forced to flee.

Inquiries among other Gypsy groups reveal quite a different version of the Mexican interlude. According to non-Bimbulesti informants, Tinja's behavior while in Mexico made him many enemies. He utilized strong-arm coercive methods to become the most powerful leader within the territory, and then he extorted money from the Gypsy groups in a gangster-like insurance racket. It is said that he also forced families to give brides to his group without the rightful (and legitimizing) brideprice. Thus it is a non-Bimbulesti contention that Tinja was forced out of Mexico when his deeds began to catch up with him.

If the unofficial version of the story is true, one may assume that Tinja also got into difficulties in South America and fled for the same kind of reasons. I do not believe that Tinja had either the stupidity or temerity to be so irresponsible toward *Dimitrulesti*, because Tinja subsequently returned to Dimitro to ask for Dimitro's favorite granddaughter as a bride for one of his sons. It is quite possible, however, that Tinja's behavior earned him the enmity of other South American Gypsies and consequently he was forced to flee.

The Bimbulesti arrival in the United States in 1910 must have been like a tornado, for the next year Tinja Bimbo was already an established power in Gypsy circles. His group obtained territorial rights to the Midwest area around Chicago and settled in it. As the Depression began to affect the Gypsies, Tinja found it harder to keep his group prosperous and contented. Around 1935, they relocated in New York City, where more welfare money was available than in Chicago.

Soon after arriving in New York City, Tinja "got into trouble." This expression covers a multitude of situations in Gypsy society, the common denominator of which is the fact that some sort of jail sentence is involved. For a Gypsy to get into trouble is a fact of life, with so many non-Gypsies in the world, and the ordinary Gypsy reaction is one of sympathy. But, like Caesar's wife, a Gypsy chief must be above suspicion, for he acts as representative of his group to the outside world. Thus, when a chief gets into trouble, he jeopardizes the welfare of the entire band, and he is punished by removal from leadership. Such a dethroned head may never hope to be reinstated.

The acknowledged leader of the Manhattan Gypsies at that time was Steve Kaslov, and Manhattan was rated in Gypsy eyes as a superior territory to Brooklyn or the Bronx. (At that time, the borough of Queens was largely uninhabited by Nomad Gypsies.) Kaslov was a shrewd and experienced Kalderaš chief, who had consolidated his power through a wily manipuation of non-Gypsy authorities. He had many Gypsy families under his protection, mostly Kalderaš. The Brooklyn boss was Gio, a tough Mačvaja leader, who knew Tinja's reputation in the Midwest and was loath to allow Bimbulesti settlement within his borders. The Bronx was a mixed territory of both Gio-affiliated Mačvaja and also Kalderaš families, and both groups often came to Kaslov for guidance.

The now leaderless Bimbulesti needed desperately to remain in New York City, and so they were forced to ally as subordinates to Kaslov in order to obtain protection and relief money. When World War II broke out, gasoline rationing precluded any hopes for extensive emigration. The Arxentina, continuously increasing in numbers, were growing restive under a double-subordinate position and threatened to break away. Bimbulesti history had reached a new low. As the war continued, however, conditions improved. Kaslov got into trouble with the authorities for draft evasion, having submitted medical certificates that some of his sons were females and that the others (bachelors all) were married with children. After serving the usual year-and-a-day, Kaslov returned to New York; but of course he was no longer eligible for leadership.

In the ensuing struggle for chieftainship, the Bimbos reasserted their independent status, for Tinja's son Steve was old enough to assume leadership. Steve's wife had been the favorite grandchild of Dimitro and had inherited many of his forceful traits. Since she managed to dominate Steve, the Arxentina were content to remain within the Bimbulesti group, confident that through her they would have a stronger voice in the affairs of the vitsa. The Bimbulesti carved out a large part of the old Lower East Side territory formerly bossed by Kaslov and tried to take up a self-respecting life anew.

Steve was not the forceful leader his father had been, and he had difficulty in reconciling the demands of the Bimbo group with the equally vociferous demands of the Arxentina led by his wife. The band was in an uneasy balance, but it counted on two factors to pull it through. Although Tinja was no longer official leader, he still had enough of a reputation left within the group to keep it together, and he was still feared by other groups to the extent that they would not attempt to outmaneuver his Bimbulesti. Needless to say, Tinja still told Steve what to do, and the Bimbos pretended not to notice that Steve was being bossed both by his father and his wife. However, there was hope for a solution since some of Steve's sons were showing good leadership potential; the boys were also blood relatives of the Arxentina, and it was believed one of them would be acknowledged as a legitimate Arxentina leader as well as a Bimbulesti heir. Who could foresee that American baseball would be the Bimbulesti nemesis?

On October 9, 1948, the Boston Braves defeated Cleveland; with it began the final destruction of the Bimbos. Steve had placed a bet with some Brooklyn bookmakers, who refused to pay off. Steve and his wife filed a formal complaint with the Brooklyn District Attorney's office. Since all the Gypsies had been gambling heavily with the bookmakers, this move endangered the entire band when the syndicate threatened revenge. A Gypsy chief is supposed to protect his people from danger; Steve's precipitous action forced them all to run from the gambler's revenge. Finally, in 1951, Steve was arrested; his wife had complained to the authorities that he had stolen her money (two weeks before she had pressed un-Gypsylike charges against her own son and daughter-in-law). Steve lost leadership forever, not only because he had gotten into trouble with the law but also because he showed quite conclusively and most publicly that he could not even control his own wife, a mere woman.

Thus in a most ignominious fashion ends the epic of the famous Bimbulesti.

Other New York City Gypsies

The Bimbulesti had broken the hold of the Kaslov group in New York. No other Kalderaš was strong enough, or able enough, to take over Manhattan leadership. Gio still was the undisputed ruler of Brooklyn; as a Mačvaja, he was not averse to having Manhattan brought over to his own tribe's sphere of influence. He agreed to lend his support to Balano, a young, self-proclaimed Mačvaja chief who operated in Manhattan. I suspect that the wily old veteran of many a power struggle entertained hopes of ruling over the two boroughs himself. Gio probably planned to have the *Balanulesti* do all the rough in-fighting and then to lay claim himself to overlord rights by virtue of seniority. One of the older men from a California-based Mačvaja group also came to New York City at this time. This man (we shall call him Big Toma) was related to both the Gio vitsa and the Balanulesti; his father had been a very influential chief in California. The old man's death left two close contenders for the leadership: Big Toma, one of his sons, and the son of the old chief's brother. When headship finally went to the cousin, Big Toma felt his position in California to be compromised—he had lost prestige. I suspect Gio took advantage of the situation to invite Big Toma to come to the New York area to make a bid for leadership against Balano, knowing that the California man would follow Gypsy law and defer to Gio as an older, more established chieftain.

Big Toma's mistake was to come to New York without sufficient manpower. Within his own extended family he had only three young adult sons, all of whem were adopted. Actually they were the sons of Toma's brother, who gave them to his brother (who had only a daughter and could expect no more children from his wife) upon the death of his first wife. Toma's brother and his present wife had only young children; therefore, only Toma's brother himself could be counted as an ally in that nuclear family. A married (adopted) daughter and her husband also came to New York upon Toma's summons. Since this family was without male issue, one adult male was added to the roster. Another, unrelated extended family traveled with Toma out of friendship; this unit included its leader and three adult sons. Thus the total band strength was only ten adult males. The Manhattan Mačvaja, on the contrary, had well over thirty adult males supporting their contender.

Big Toma's first step was to establish peaceful relations with all the Mačvaja families in and around New York City. He also renewed an old baptismal relationship with old Tinja Bimbo—a wise move whereby he might gain additional strength from the support of the remaining Kalderaš in the area. The Bimbulesti proper threw in with Toma, but the Arxentina dragged their heels, hoping to become leaders themselves.

The second part of the campaign was for Toma to carve a reputation as a just and courageous judge in court trials, a wise and objective adviser and confidant, a generous host, and a stalwart friend and protector. With ample time to look Toma over and to test his abilities, some of the Manhattan Mačvaja, it was hoped, would be won over to Toma's side. In point of fact, Toma did succeed in winning much respect from all the Mačvaja, and the other tribes respected the fact that he acted according to Gypsy traditions.

Toma was becoming a power in New York City, and his adversary Balano had to work quickly to protect his own claims. Toma would have to be discredited in Gypsy eyes. The first strategem was to have the New York Police Department informed that Toma, Gio, and another influential man who supported Toma were traffic-ticket scofflaws. (In fact, like many fellow citizens of New York, most Gypsies were scofflaws, including Balano.) If Toma and Gio went to jail, they would be disqualified from leadership automatically. However, Toma was too clever for this ruse; he managed to convince his cohorts not to panic and run away. He also convinced the gajo judge that there had been no deliberate attempt to circumvent the law. He and his friends were allowed to pay all the fines without serving time, upon promise of cooperation with the police department in explaining the legal requirements to the Gypsies of New York. Since the Romanies knew that Toma also shared part of the expenses of his friends' fines, pawning his valuables for the purpose, they were more impressed than ever.

The next major attempt to shame Toma's name came after one of Balano's followers was convicted of a confidence game. Rumors began to circulate that Toma or one of his people had acted as a stoolpigeon. This was a very serious accusation, rendered more heinous since the woman in question was a distant relative of Toma's wife. Toma was hurt when the Gypsies took the rumors seriously enough to question him about it. But he refused to take notice of the talk in any official way, leaving it to Gio to smooth things over.

Meanwhile New York City had become increasingly inhospitable to Gypsies. The police were more demanding; the various vitsas were suspicious of one another; many Gypsies resorted to gajo means to solve band problems instead of resorting to the traditional Gypsy courts. When old Gio died, Toma's position worsened. Despite many close relationships to the Gio vitsa, Toma did not, or could not, take over leadership. Toma and his immediate supporters returned to California, and many of his sympathizers in New York City went down South, where they had a claim to vitsa and territory membership.

Currently, New York City has representatives of Kalderaš and Mačvaja extraction. The Meksikaja maintain a nominal (and uneasy) affiliation with the Kalderaš bands but are attempting a vigorous affirmation not only of independence but also of importance in the territorial structuring of Manhattan. The Arxentina are based in Manhattan as an independent group. The Borough of Queens is experiencing an influx of Gypsies, and Queens is changing from being regarded as a minor outpost of Gypsydom to becoming a prime territory in its own right.

3

THE ECONOMICS OF BEING A GYPSY

The economic sphere of life is regarded by the Gypsies as the only link between themselves and the gaĵe among whom they live. With few exceptions, no Gypsy group makes its living from other Gypsies. It is for such a reason that the anthropologist A. L. Kroeber referred to the Gypsies as a "half-culture" (Kroeber 1948: 279) and that many non-Gypsies called the Romanies "parasites." These remarks are neither fair nor true; economic interdependence is a form of "symbiosis," not "parasitism." It is an established culture pattern in many parts of Asia; the Gypsies have carried it into Europe and the Americas. For a study of culture borrowing, the enforced contacts required by Gypsy economic practices are significant.

Daily Routine

During the Camp Period, life patterns were influenced by the lack of electricity and central heating. People went to bed a few hours after dark and awoke at sunrise. The women arose early to start the fires and make breakfast (breakfast was normally served to the men in bed). In a Kalderaš camp, the men prepared for a day of metalworking; in a Mačvaja camp, they looked after the horses. The women left for their day's fortunetelling chores. The men and those older women no longer able to walk all day were responsible for supervising the camp and the activities of the children. People in camp were able to take a light meal whenever they desired from a cauldron that simmered over the fire throughout the day. The women returned to camp around four or five in the afternoon, bringing with them whatever supplies they had bought, been given, or had stolen. Then the entire camp had its main meal of the day; this meal was cooked outdoors and served in the tents. Early evening was devoted to visiting; the families sat around the campfires telling stories and sipping tea or coffee or else dancing and singing under the warming influence of alcohol. Then the Gypsies retired for the night, when darkness and cold drove them into their featherbeds. The hours of working and sleeping maintained by the Gypsies during the Camp Period corresponded well with those followed by non-Gypsies.

When the Romanies moved into towns, they found that most of the fortunetelling business came to them later in the day. Whereas formerly the women would go to the farmhouses to find the non-Gypsy women at their chores in kitchen or yard, now the Gypsies had to wait until gaje women had completed their chores at home. Fortunetelling stores rarely do any business until eleven o'clock in the morning, and experience a rush from six or seven in the evening until as late as ten o'clock because most of the modern clientele consists of working women, who are free only after five-thirty or six in the afternoon.

Today a typical Gypsy day does not begin until ten or eleven o'clock in the morning; the women are the first to rise, the youngest daughter-in-law being the first in accordance with tradition. Most of the men continue to take their breakfast in bed. Thereafter the women prepare a major meal for noon-time or one in the afternoon and then leave for the fortunetelling store; the children and men remain behind. The women in the household who happen to remain at home prepare the evening repast for the men and children; the men may also do the cooking. But most fortunetellers eat in a restaurant near their stores. Often the Gypsy men congregate in the homes of some of the more important older men until it is time to pick up the women from their work. The Gypsies then may visit until three or four in the morning; this evening pattern is analogous to the one followed in the Camp Period, except that it starts and ends later and may involve watching television or going out to a nightclub.

A significant alteration in the life of a woman has resulted from changing the site of fortunetelling; formerly, it was the customer's home (necessitating frequent long walks from place to place); now it is a fixed location. Older women who cannot endure such walks may now take taxis or be driven to their place of business by their sons, remain there for a number of hours, and then be driven home. As a result of this change, old women continue to be economically productive.

I have the impression that the modern situation has placed much of the risk-taking involved in Gypsy confidence games on the women past forty. The fact that these older women are away from their families for a part of the day means that they cannot supervise the children as was their custom during the Camp Period nor do they have an immediate and direct knowledge of what the men are doing. However, because they tend to earn more than the younger women, they work shorter hours and put in fewer working days.

Vacations and Sundays as a day of rest are concepts borrowed from the gaje. Nowadays, most Gypsies rest on Sunday and devote Saturday evenings for leisure. Once a year, the women may take a vacation with their families, sometimes spending part of the winter in California, Florida, or Mexico, and traveling through the Southwest and Mexico in the summer. Traditional patterns, however, are preserved; there is a difference in mobility between the winter and summer months, and even now there is greater movement during the warm months.

Some Gypsies are beginning to be exposed to the idea of different daily schedules for children. But many still oppose it because they do not believe that children are qualitatively any different from adults. Children should have the right to participate in all the affairs of the adults; in such manner they can learn the ways of their forefathers.

Masculine Occupations

Coppersmithing was the traditional occupation of the Kalderaš[1] men. Their skills provided them with a livelihood in the New

---

[1]The word *Kalderaš* is supposedly derived from the Rumanian *Calderari*, "coppersmiths."

World during the Camp and Transitional Periods. Many industrial firms utilized their services for the repair and maintenance of equipment, and commercial laundries relied on them almost exclusively for the repair of the large vats essential to their business operations.[2] In addition, the Kalderaš also repaired copper cooking pots; many of their customers waited for their annual return in order to have their utensils fixed. An additional source of revenue was furnished by repairing furnaces.

An older Rom might serve as contractor in a village or industrial location. He made the contacts, discussed the terms of employment with the gaje, and arranged the work allocation and division of profits among the Gypsy men of his group.

Performing the coppersmithing in the seclusion afforded by a Romany encampment served a number of different purposes for the Kalderaš. Kalderaš smithing technique was a secret process jealously guarded from non-Gypsies. Involved in this desire for secrecy were both a pride in craftsmanship and the realization that some work night be lost if the gaje learned the Romany techniques of rivetless metalworking that forced commercial laundries to rely exclusively upon Kalderaš maintenance of their basic equipment.[3]

Another advantage of Kalderaš working conditions was that of apprentice-training. The adult men were assisted by the young boys of the band in their work. This afforded an opportunity for the boys to observe their mentors at all stages of the processing and learn the secret techniques. As the boys grew older, they were encouraged to try their skills; thus under close but casual supervision the youths were incorporated into the men's work group. As a result, many hands were available to help with the work, and the work took place in a congenial atmosphere.

Working conditions were in their own hands and thus they could determine their own schedules, working days, rate of

[2]Lee 1972: 6-9, 11-14, 54-55 presents detailed case histories showing expenses and profits. Mitchell 1945: 57, Weybright 1938: 142 and 1945: 3 list some of the large commissions obtained in the past.

[3]Detailed technological descriptions of Canadian coppersmithing may be found in Lee 1972: 7-8, 11-12, 54-56, 121-22 and Moriarty 1929: 177. Starkie 1933: 294 and Tillhagen 1947: 92 provide a few details for Transylvania and Sweden respectively.

speed, etc. This meant, of course, that the Gypsies could celebrate holidays, take time off for emergencies, and fulfill their total obligations to Gypsy culture without having to sacrifice financial profit. They were their own bosses and did not have to accommodate to non-Gypsy working conditions.

Working with the elders also enabled the boys to learn the Gypsy way of life. The men talked about current affairs, mostly about such tribal news as trials and feasts, sang, and told tales. The young were there to hear and learn.

Working in isolation also kept down to a minimum any contacts with non-Gypsies. Their link with the outside world was the Rom who acted as group contractor. He was always an older man, a family head interested in preserving the status quo because of his influential position therein.[4] Thus, we have a buffer-zone that effectively kept out acculturative influences.

With the introduction of stainless steel in the manufacture of laundry and factory equipment, demand for coppersmithing decreased appreciably.[5] Moreover, mass-production made cooking pots so inexpensive that it was cheaper and easier to replace a broken pot with a new one than to wait for the Gypsies to repair the old one. Thus it was no longer profitable to tour the countryside in search of commissions, and the Kalderaš were forced to make a living out of repairing furnaces, and, later, fenders.[6]

This economic loss was accompanied by a loss of morale, for the Kalderaš had enjoyed great pride in their coppersmithing craftsmanship. In addition to coppersmithing (which included decorative copper objects), they also worked in gold and silver, making jewelry for themselves and other Gypsies and sometimes even selling pieces of Kalderaš design and execution to outsiders. This work gave them aesthetic satisfaction and a genuine feeling of achievement in a job that required artistic skills. Most blacksmithing and tinsmithing had been done half-heartedly. When the transition to fender-repairing was effected, the goal

---

[4]A detailed analysis may be found in Cotten 1951.

[5]Beginning in the thirties in the United States but affecting the Canadian Kalderaš only in the sixties, Lee 1972: 103.

[6]These economic reversals are covered in detail in Mitchell 1945: 43, 56-57; Parry 1941: 21; Weybright 1938: 142, 1945: 3.

became that of making money with a minimum of energy. Eventually the quality of the work degenerated. Instead of a legitimate repair job, the men merely rough-hammered a few of the larger dents and then covered the rest of the faults with a judiciously thick application of shoe polish. The Kalderaš viewed their change to fender- and furnace-repairing as a capitulation to the non-Gypsy world. Metalworking as a masculine occupation was downgraded from a highly satisfying way of life to a despised confidence game without honor within the group or toward the gaǰe.

There is no true art to be learned in the new type of work, and nowadays the youths are no longer needed to assist the men in their work. Consequently, the young males have begun to take on their own set of occupations, and metalwork is a dying trade. The younger boys often become bootblacks; as they grow older, they may become delivery boys, packers in supermarkets, and the like. On occasion they also resort to pickpocketing and stealing.[7] All this work is on a part-time basis. I suspect that this represents a carry-over of work habits which were functional and necessary in the days of coppersmithing.

In the Camp Period, the old days of metallurgical glory, work was discontinuous. Travel time between contracts was an integral aspect of the life of Gypsies; they moved to their work instead of their customers coming to them. They could not run a forge and work metal in a moving wagon. Futhermore, smithery required the use of corrosive acids that literally ate away the flesh.[8] After a series of commissions the men were physically incapacitated; their hands had to heal and this took time. This periodic enforced idleness was part of their life pattern; it became firmly engrained into the habitual patterns of Kalderaš men to the extent that it has remained even when circumstances no longer required it.

The men of the Mačvaja tribe knew little about metalworking; the traditional masculine occupation was animal trading. In Europe, the Mačvaja men traded in horses, donkeys, mules, and

---

[7]Both boys and girls sometimes beg; this is a hold-over from the traditional way of life.

[8]Lee 1972: 8, 19 indicates that the more recent use of the blowtorch has aggravated the occupational hazards by harming the eyes as well.

cattle, depending upon their particular country; in the United States, they traded mostly in horses. They bred, traded, and doctored them. Like the Kalderaš, the Mačvaja followed seasonal routes through the country, but their migrations followed the circuit of animal fairs. At these fairs, the Romanies not only exhibited their horses but also raced them, often gambling on their own animals. From time to time, other types of trades were accepted, and, at the end of the fair season, the men might follow other trading endeavors.

Trading, of necessity, was seasonal work, but the animals must be cared for at all seasons of the year. Thus, the work of the Mačvaja, although less demanding than that of the Kalderaš in some ways, took more of their time. The men did their chores all by themselves, because women were neither expected nor allowed to assist in the care of the animals. The origin of this custom dates back to an ancient prohibition against females touching the horse, a sacred animal, because of the possible contaminating influence of womanhood upon this holy animal. It is interesting to note that women similarly were kept away from automobiles until very recently. Part of the lack of female auto drivers, of course, may be due to illiteracy; women cannot read road signs. (But the reading ability of men and boys is often not much better.)

The economic operations of the Mačvaja men differed significantly from those of the Kalderaš. Trading relationships were on a face-to-face basis, and so each individual Mačvaja man had contacts with the gaje. Shrewd trading demanded a good knowledge of the current economic situation, of gajo needs and desires in different parts of the country and of the latest items available. They had to keep up with the gajo world for the sake of their own economic pursuits; hence, their men got to know much about the outside world.

The greater male/female cooperation of the Mačvaja has carried over into modern days. Their women are ever ready to complain that the men are not paying enough attention to "business." The men are very active in obtaining fortunetelling stores for their women. Wherever they go in the city, they spend much of their time seeking favorable spots in which to open a store, exploring a neighborhood to observe the number and types of people who pass and the times of day when the flow of traffic is heavy. They check out local stores to get some idea of the prosperity of the customers and of their psychological preparedness to spend money. They may chat with the proprietors in an effort to find out the local situation in respect to the police and resident criminal operators (procurers, bookmakers, policy-runners, etc.). In short, they perform a thorough analysis of the neighborhood.

The Mačvaja also devote time and energy to the task of devising new ways to cover the illegalities of fortunetelling. They seize upon any business scheme that will provide a safe cover for fortunetelling without imposing upon the seers undue demands. For example, any sale of an object with an accompanying "free" demonstration satisfies the gajo legal requirements. Thus, Gypsies may display used books on dreams, numerology, and palmistry in their store window, ostensibly for sale to customers, and assert they will give a free demonstration with each purchase.

The New York City Mačvaja were responsible for the widespread establishment of licensed Gypsy tearooms in the fifties. Their men had somehow discovered the relative simplicity of obtaining such licenses,[9] and the women already knew how to boil water and dump tea leaves into cups. The customer paid for the cup of tea and received a free reading of the leaves. Previously, they had pioneered the use of automatic picture-taking machines as a cover for fortunetelling (a sort of combined photograph of one's physique plus a picture of one's life). Their association with traveling carnivals probably made them familiar with such machines, and inquiry revealed that they were not expensive to buy and only needed periodic refilling of paper and chemicals, for the actual exposure and processing was done by the machine itself. The men learned how to change the rolls of photographic paper and mix the chemical solutions and then taught the necessary skills to their women and girls. When coin-operated photo-machines were placed in most five-and-dime stores, the resultant competition brought to an end their exploitation by the Gypsies.

[9]Rom understood the general concept of licensing from their sojourns down South, where palmistry locations were legal if a license were purchased, and the technique of bribing inspectors was a mere extrapolation from the need to bribe other city officials.

Masculine occupations vary according to tribal provenience, historic time-period, and geographic location. For example, the European Lovara are said to specialize in bank robbery and jewel thefts. In former times, the Anglo-Romanies, both in Great Britain and in New England, made and sold baskets, brooms, clothespins, lace, and artificial flowers.[10] Some of the Polish Gypsies were cobblers; some Hungarian Gypsies were hangmen; both were despised occupations rejected by the gaje. There have been Gypsy prizefighters in Europe and the United States and Gypsy bullfighters in Spain and Latin America.

The following may be taken as a general principle: Gypsies, like their Asiatic cousins, the Indian Criminal and Wandering Tribes, tend to follow occupations that do not put them into direct economic competition with non-Gypsies. Gypsy economic activity either exploits a void in the economic structure of a country or else follows occupational lines in which the outsiders have convinced themselves that Romanies excel, such as folk-doctoring, musical entertainment, and other show-business pursuits. In these ways, the Gypsies manage to keep some anti-Gypsy feelings under control: they do not take jobs away from non-Gypsies while supplying needed products and services that the gaje are either unable to do or are loath to do for themselves.[11] At best, Gypsies thereby become an integral part of the overall society; at worst they are a necessary evil.

The Female Breadwinner

In all Gypsy societies, the woman functions as the family treasurer, and the Romany definition of the role differs considerably from ours. In Gypsy terms, part of the treasurer's responsibility is to ensure that there is always something in that treasury. It is the woman who is expected to bring in the daily money for routine expenses. It is true that often the men earn more in one fell swoop than the women do in their daily occupations, but the woman's contribution to the family funds is usually steady whereas that of the men is periodic and relatively uncertain.

[10]This activity continues today, but to a lesser extent. In fact, in New York City, young Kalderaš have been hawking artificial flowers for the last several years.

[11]This point is discussed at length in Cotten 1954 (July-Oct.): 112-16.

Therefore, the woman is the one required to furnish daily food provisions and even pocketmoney for the men whenever they need it.

In the past, surplus family funds were usually converted into jewelry to be worn by the treasurer in the form of gold and precious stones. In this manner, the family's reserves were easily portable and under surveillance constantly. (Oddly enough, non-Gypsies rarely realize that Gypsy women are wearing a considerable fortune about their persons.)[12] Furthermore, a family's funds are available for emergency use, either directly (to be used for bribes or barter) or indirectly (to be pawned and thereby converted into cash).

In the form of jewelry, funds can be transported across borders without having to be converted into different currencies. This is a decided advantage at times when the Gypsies are forced to move on in the middle of the night on short notice. Then, too, gold and diamonds, unlike paper currency, are not subject to sudden depreciation in value; inflation is thus curbed, for the equivalent monetary value of the jewelry rises in proportion to the inflationary upswing.

At least some of the treasury funds, however, were always carried in the form of necklaces of *galbe* (gold coins). The coins were fitted into holders, not punctured, so that their value was not affected. These coins were worth the value of the gold contained therein regardless of the fluctuations of a country's currency. Since the galbe were heirlooms, in any necklace before the 1930s, one could find coins from several different countries with mint dates going back to the 1790s or earlier. When the United States went off the gold standard in 1933, the Gypsies, like the rest of the country, were forced to surrender the American gold coins; this in turn altered their savings habits. Until the present day, the Romanies patronize old coin dealers to buy gold coins, despite the premium prices involved. From the 1940s to the 1950s, Gypsies were reluctant to use banks, but they have learned, the Mačvaja particularly, to use banks in connection with their ownership of real estate. Now there is extensive knowledge of banks and banking practices and confidence in their

---

[12]New York Gypsies have stopped wearing their jewelry in the city because of fear of being mugged.

reliability. A bank account is somewhat limited, however, because withdrawals from out-of-town or in the middle of the night cannot be made. Unless a complicated series of aliases is used, the Gypsies run the risk of having their monies impounded in the event of criminal proceedings against them.

When the Kalderaš men established a work camp, their women searched the countryside to find customers for fortunetelling. In the course of their daily work, the women and older girls covered many miles. Usually several went together for companionship and safety. The Gypsies entered a farm and talked the women into getting their fortunes told; on occasion some of the men would also want to consult the Romanies, usually about illness among their livestock. Readings were usually held in the farmhouse kitchen, but on occasion the women had a chance to inspect other parts of the building as well, and in the process also had an opportunity to observe housekeeping routines and child-care patterns. The readings themselves concerned matters of interest to the non-Gypsies; the most intimate psychological details were revealed to the seers. Thus, in contrast to the men, the Gypsy women got to know a large amount about non-Gypsy life.

Complaints about the disappearance of valuables and livestock when there were Gypsies in the vicinity were often heard. It is true that there was ample opportunity for the women to steal when they were in the houses. If they were given a bad reception by the gaje, many would avail themselves of the chance to obtain revenge by stealing. Often, too, in traveling through the countryside the women dropped their voluminous skirts over a choice chicken or two and walked away with dinner. The men frequently took advantage of a farmer's pastureland and put their horses to graze at night. However, where the Gypsies were well treated, they were careful to take nothing that did not belong to them and to pay for all their needs. The daily winter routine followed by women in the days of permanent winter headquarters differed little from that of summer.

The transition to an ofisa in a town took place during the period when the Gypsies began spending winters in towns.[13]

[13]Exactly when this happened is impossible to determine for lack of references covering the period involved. The Rom themselves are not a reliable source of information on the subject because of their vague sense of historical time and the gradualness of the transition.

The entire pattern of fortunetelling altered. The women established stores for fortunetelling, and their customers came to them. The women usually sat near the large display windows or outside and coaxed prospective customers inside for a reading. At first, the front of the store was used as an ofisa, while the rear, carefully separated from the place of business, functioned as the living quarters of the family. With increasing frequency in the forties and fifties, the women of the Mačvaja tribe began to rent separate stores for the sole purpose of fortunetelling, sometimes maintaining two or three simultaneously in different neighborhoods.

As more time was being spent in the cities, a reversal of winter/summer alternation occurred whereby the women bought concessions in traveling shows or in Coney Island-like amusement parks.

In some parts of the country, especially such southern states as Mississippi, Tennessee, Missouri, and in parts of Florida (and in California and the province of Quebec in Canada), it was possible to purchase a legal license for fortunetelling until a decade or so ago. (The situation is beginning to change even as I write.) Where this occupation was legal, the fortunetellers might build up a steady and remunerative clientele, often advertising in the newspapers, on billboards, and even by spot announcements over local radio stations. In New York City, today, handbills are distributed in the streets and on subway stations.

In many of the larger towns and cities of the United States, however, fortunetelling is usually illegal. For example, in New York City there is an ordinance making it illegal for anyone except a minister or teacher to make predictions about the future. As soon as a Gypsy departs from reading the past and present and begins to look into the future, she is breaking the law and subjects herself to a fine, jail sentence, or both. Since the women can easily run afoul of the law, fortunetelling is not a desirable occupation, the amount of income accruing therefrom not warranting the high risks involved.

Another, much more remunerative, source of income for the women is the so-called Big Lie (*xoxano baro*), a confidence game. The marks, or victims, are found through regular fortunetelling contacts. A likely mark is asked to return at another time, and the problems bothering the gaĵe are then attributed either to a curse or to pollution affecting the money the victim has saved. The gullibility of the victim often is increased through a demonstration of the curse (Mačvaja women are particularly adept at this practice). The egg of a black hen is broken open in full view of the victim, and, as the contents of the egg fall into a bowl, a small devil's-head is seen to drop in as well. This, of course, is a sleight of hand, the little plastic head having been palmed in advance. The Gypsy woman promises to remove the curse by prayers, the lighting of special candles (to be purchased by the victim), and incantations. At the victim's next visit, the Gypsy seer may claim to have received a revelation that the curse's full impact cannot be broken or else that good luck may be ensured by blessing the victim's money. The Gypsy is to have the money brought in a package (of such and such dimensions and wrapping), and, after the blessing, the parcel is to be buried or hidden, unopened, for a set number of days. Needless to say, a rapid substitution of parcels is effected during the blessing, and the Gypsy woman moves away with alacrity, her treasury greatly improved by the contact.

Another variation of the Big Lie, and the one favored by the Mačvaja, is to convince the victim that the money is tainted permanently, and that the only salvation lies in its destruction. In this variant, the Gypsy "tears up" the money in view of the victim and either burns it or flushes it down a toilet. She then pronounces a total cure for the sufferer. Actually, the Romany palms the money and substitutes worthless paper in the final destruction.

The readiness with which the victims enter into these confidence games has never failed to amaze me. Usually the Gypsy practitioner is exceedingly careful to assure herself of the victim's gullibility. The New York Police Department and the press appear to believe that the success of Gypsy confidence games is due to the embarrassment of the victims and their reticence in admitting that they have been taken; according to them, the victims suffer in silence, not wanting to make fools of themselves in public. I am not sure that they are correct in this interpretation, for I have watched the games played any number of times. The victims often continue to believe sincerely in the efficacy of the Gypsy's magic. The relationship may continue for many months, until the Gypsy decides to stop seeing the customer. It would be more accurate to say that the Big Lie results in as many satisfied customers as any other service-type business enterprise. In fact, as a matter of policy, the Gypsy will return the money, should her customer return to express dissatisfaction. The Gypsies themselves are always surprised at the foolish be-havior of their customers.

Gypsies cannot understand why the gaje take bogus readings so seriously; they assume that it is because non-Gypsies are stupid. What the Gypsies fail to take into account is that it is mostly the less intelligent or maladjusted who come to them for readings. Occasionally, the Gypsies are approached by younger people or a courting couple who want their palms read merely for a lark. (The Gypsies recognize that this type of one-time contact is different, but its innocent, frivolous nature tends to be forgotten when the Rom begin to generalize about all gaje from their experiences with their own customers.)

Thus, Gypsy women do not realize that they deal with only a fraction of the Gajo population. In large cities, fortunetelling stores are often in underprivileged neighborhoods; few are seen in the affluent sections. Often the most faithful and lucrative customers are prostitutes; other women come in with love and sex problems; male homosexuals may spend many hours talking to Gypsies about their lovers. It is no wonder the Gypsies are convinced that all Americans are fools who are asking to be cheated.

The lack of respect for their customers affects the women's attitude toward gajo lifestyle and culture; they see little that is worthy of being taken over by their own people. Moreover, the structure of Gypsy society is such that women occupy a less important position than men as carriers of Gypsy culture, and therefore their influence upon adult members of the band is not felt in proportion to their numbers. Furthermore, traditionally, women were in no position to exert much influence over the children's development and training because they were away telling fortunes while the children remained in camp with the men. Maternal influence was also limited by the belief that the children belong to the husband and the husband's group. Tradi-tional child care patterns were continued even when the Gypsies came into the cities and lived in fortunetelling stores. The chil-dren, of course, could not be allowed to interrupt the women during readings, and it was the responsibility of the men and older children to keep the youngsters away from the business area. With the change to a separate locale used in conjunction with fortunetelling, the mothers again have become absent from their children for much of the time. This means that any acculturative influences experienced by the women in the course of their work cannot readily be passed on to the children.

The Gypsies believe themselves that it is possible to predict the future. They interpret dreams, and there are some who believe that mothers have a chance to find out their children's future during the first week after birth. In addition, individuals may have visions of the future either occasionally or frequently; but this gift is confined almost exclusively to Gypsy circles. Ordinarily, readings to gaje are considered entirely fallacious; should the seer believe during a reading that she has really foreseen a future event, she is disturbed; usually she does not reveal her vision to the customer.

In the early fifties, many members of the Arxentina Kalderaš devoted themselves to the xoxano baro, invading many business offices of Manhattan. In their boldness, some of the older women even attempted to prey upon the younger Mačvaja women. Their annoyance was aggravated by the embarrassing fact that they had nearly fallen victim to the trick, for the Arxentina had posed as poor, hapless Spanish women and had denied being Gypsies. A few of the girls had even given money to them out of sympathy. The Mačvaja girls were upset and angered by this unscrupulous behavior and brought their complaints to the older women of their own vitsas, requesting a kris. But the older women refused to take any action against the Arxentina, because of the many difficulties involved in setting up such a kris. They also believed the younger women should have been shrewd enough to see through any confidence games. The Arxentina were given due credit for their acting ability, and the Mačvaja were alerted to the existence of the danger.

The Economic Group

There are no permanent economic groups among the United States Gypsies.[14] All economic units are of a temporary nature,

[14]The European Lovara situation described in the writings of Jan Yoors (1967, 1971) seems to indicate much more permanent and important units integral to that tribe's economic unit.

ranging from a single one-day job to a whole summer season. The number of people entering into such a unit also varies, from a pair to the total male population of several extended families. The members of such a unit may belong to the same or to different vitsas; they may even belong to different tribes. The name of this unit is the *kumpanja*.

Sometimes an individual may find the opportunity to make some money that requires the cooperation of additional personnel for the completion of the project. This job-contractor then approaches friends or acquaintances for the needed assistance. In this type of kumpanja the original contractor is regarded as the absolute boss of the commission being undertaken. He has the right to determine all the arrangements of the job: decisions about membership in the kumpanja, the allocation of the work, the assignment of location of the work, the sharing of costs and profits. The contractor may not be honest with prospective employees about the nature of the business deal, but both parties are aware of it. Decisions are made not on the basis of whether the prospective employer is being honest or not, but solely upon whether they feel that the terms being offered them will make it worthwhile. Were the contractor to make a much larger profit on the enterprise than they, they bear him no grudge. The Gypsies will only regret the fact that they were not shrewd enough to negotiate a better deal for themselves.

The second type of kumpanja involves an arrangement among friends or relatives who become partners for a given period. This type of unit is based upon the tacit assumption that work, costs, and profits will be shared equally among all members. This type of kumpanja is preferred by the women. Women went out with partners during the Camping days; customers were not kept waiting too long, should the farm prove to have a number of individuals interested in having their fortunes told. The women were able to reinforce one another's "pitch." Moreover, the Romanies recognized that different personalities interact differently; certain customers are better served by one or another of the women present.

The business and social advantages of partnerships have been continued in the ofisa. During slack times, the women can chat and thus make the time pass quickly; during rush hours there are several readers on hand to tell fortunes. There is someone available to answer the telephone without interrupting a reading in progress or to welcome another customer. One of the women can go out to get refreshments without leaving the ofisa unattended. Women often participate in several partnerships at the same time. A woman who maintains several stores simultaneously can rely on her partners while she is away at another location.

In this type of kumpanja, the women are expected to share equally the costs of establishing the ofisa, including the money necessary to rent the store (usually the first month's rent in advance plus one or more monthly rentals as security), the furniture and materials needed for the store, the carpeting, a stove or heater or fan, and a television set. Daily incidental expenses for food and drink are shared on an equal basis as well. On the other hand, taxi fares to and from the store are an individual expense. All income is supposed to be shared equally as well. The only change from this egalitarian rule is where there has been a pre-arranged inequality in the distribution of work hours to be contributed to the partnership or in the original investment; these would involve differential profit-sharing.

Gypsies recognize the principle of capital investments returning a profit-interest. As a result, there is what may be regarded as a third type of partnership in relation to fortunetelling stores; only one of the partners invests money in the enterprise and then expects to share in the profits according to a fixed prior arrangement. Subsumed under this type of capital investment is the work (and often the money) entailed in obtaining a fortunetelling store because of the difficulty involved in getting it. Landlords and renting agents are usually reluctant to rent to Gypsies, and much ingenuity is required to devise a convincing and new story to use in seeking quarters. Since the landlords are very suspicious, it is often necessary to arrange for a non-Gypsy to do the renting for them. Thus, problems of finding and renting stores take up a significant amount of the time of many bands. Gypsies may end up by paying several hundred dollars to the gaje who has served as intermediary in obtaining the store.

What happens when the agent or landlord arrives to discover that instead of the expected bookstore or drapery store there is a fortunetelling parlor? The Romanies expect to be found out eventually, and they have devised a plan of action to cover this contingency. By the time they are discovered, the women have had a chance to estimate the potentials of the location. If the location is a profitable one, the Gypsies may engage an attorney to counter eviction proceedings with a delaying tactic. In the hands of an intelligent and knowledgeable lawyer eviction can be delayed for several months. By that time, the Gypsies have exhausted the possibilities of the location and are ready to move on. If the store's possibilities do not live up to expectations, the Romanies immediately allow the landlord to dispossess them. In the rare eventuality that no objection to their occupancy is raised and that the store is a steady money-producer, it is possible to sell or rent the ofisa to another partnership when the original partners are no longer interested in maintaining it.

Litigation Involving Economic Arrangements

Grievances arising from economic partnerships are settled by the *kris*, a sociopolitical institution with standard procedural rules and a body of customary law to draw upon. The kris includes a judge-arbitrator, the litigants, witnesses, and a group of adult men who function simultaneously as jury and *amici curiae*, for they question witnesses and have the right to speak up for the side they believe to be in the right. A whole segment of Gypsy justice is devoted to these frequent trials dealing with economic claims. Partners are often accused of being slackers and goldbrickers and therefore not deserving of a full share of the profits. Other cases involve a reneging upon the original agreement in terms of distribution of profits, such as the contractor failing to pay the full amount originally specified when the commission was completed.

Suits brought by women in connection with fortunetelling stores involve such matters as a partner failing to put in sufficient working hours while expecting to share in the profits equally or one of the partners incurring too many out-of-pocket expenses. This may arise because the women brought some of their children along, and this leads to higher daily food-and-drink expenses; or else the children disturbed the business. Allegations of actual dishonesty are more frequent among the women than among the men; a woman may claim that her partner has failed to report all income to the other partners. However, these allegations are rare.

Other legal procedures arise from territoriality. There is a limit to the number of stores any neighborhood can support profitably. Bands may establish claims to certain neighborhoods on the basis of prior possession. Other bands are supposed to stake out different neighborhoods. Furthermore, women already operating in the area have a right to object to the entry of too many additional stores in the immediate vicinity. Any arguments involving territories are brought to the kris.

The details of a kris are circulated far and wide. It is decidedly disadvantageous for the formation of future kumpanjas that an individual (or a family) develop a reputation for being dishonest or quarrelsome. Potential partners may refuse to deal with an individual whose reputation for lack of good faith or for habitually questioning the good faith of others has been established. The Romanies also learn what hidden pitfalls exist in any given procedural arrangement from listening to the accounts of other people's troubles, so that they may avoid similar trouble in the future themselves.

Food

Gypsy cuisine owes much to that of Europe, and Gypsy cooking methods have been adapted to the totality of living conditions under which they have operated in each period. When the Gypsies camped out, food was cooked by boiling, roasting (usually on a spit or in hot ashes), or frying. Each household had a huge iron cauldron in which stews and soups were made. Smaller pots were used for tea or for making Turkish or "hobo" coffee. Many families also owned large copper samovars. Chickens, turkeys, and large joints of meat were turned on a spit over a fire. A form of unleavened bread was baked on hot stoves. Steaks were fried. Potatoes were baked among hot ashes. Fish was boiled in a stew or fried. Broiling seems to have been unknown, and there was apparently no knowledge of cake-baking. Vegetables were boiled, sautéed, or made into salads.[15]

Meals consisted of meat or fish, large amounts of salad, sometimes more vegetables, soup, and bread. Large serving trays were spread out on a tablecloth, and individual trays or plates

[15]For Europe, cf. Block 1939: 104-112, Clébert 1963: 184-86; Petrovič 1939: 248.

were used for each diner. Forks were used only for cooking. Traditional Gypsy etiquette dictated an Oriental-like, dainty use of fingers and bread to convey food to the lips, the usual technique being to tear off a piece of bread of convenient size to surround the piece of food being eaten. Individual pocket knives were used to help cut off meat chunks.[16] Even today forks are not a necessity although they are commonly used. Sloppy eating habits are considered repulsive; nothing is allowed to fall upon the chin, and the food must enter the mouth without touching the lips. In a large gathering, the men eat first; the children eat separately lest they disgust the men with their improper eating habits; and the women eat after everyone else has finished, the younger daughters-in-law being the very last.

Coffee and tea are drunk often during the day. Gypsy etiquette prescribes that visitors be offered something to drink within a quarter-hour of arrival. If nothing is forthcoming during that time, the visitors take it to mean that their visit is ill-timed and they leave. This rule is enforced even in fortunetelling stores without facilities for food and drink; the hostess will either send (or go out herself) for some soda for lack of anything better.

In the Camp Period, two meals a day were the general rule. Everyone ate something upon arising in the morning, and then a large meal was served around four or five in the afternoon. In addition to the two main repasts, everyone was entitled to take something to eat whenever desired. Both men and women knew how to cook, and children either requested an adult to prepare something for them or else took care of it themselves; since a cauldron usually simmered over the campfire, this was not difficult. When they wanted to do so, the children also attempted their own cooking.

Most of the routine cooking was done by the women, but there were times when the men were the chefs. When a woman had her menstrual period, she was considered *marime* (ritually dangerous) and unable to prepare food for other people, especially for the men. If there were no other women around to take over the cooking chores, the men were required to substitute. For festivals, the men did all the cooking, thereby insuring acceptable ritual condition for the food.

---

[16]We know these eating habits have been perpetuated for several hundred years; cf. Grellman 1807:22-23.

When the Gypsies began to live in stores, cooking became a serious problem. Unless the Romanies brought in a stove themselves, there were no facilities for cooking. Most of the food had to be brought in, and major meals were frequently taken in restaurants. Prepared food products became staples, and some cooking techniques were lost.

But nowadays stoves are part of modern living conditions, and the Gypsies have returned to boiling and frying. The use of the oven is practically unknown, however. Spit-roasting is not practicable in an apartment, but for ceremonial occasions Gypsy groups arrange to have their turkeys or suckling pigs roasted by the local bakery. The Gypsies are also beginning to experiment with electric broilers, but the techniques are unfamiliar to many of them. They will probably do much better with rotisseries.

Gypsies are very permissive in their attitudes toward food, very few foods being taboo. There is a general proscription against snakes and another against flying birds, such as pigeons. In India and Europe, however, the Gypsies have been known for their predilection for *mulo mas* ("dead meat"); in fact, it is often suspected that livestock die too conveniently when Gypsies are about. Some foods are forbidden on some religious occasions, notably on Saint Nicholas Day, which requires the serving of fish but absolutely no meat. In addition, a person may take a personal vow to abstain from certain foods at specified times; most frequently, this takes the form of avoiding meat and/or sweets on Fridays. These vows, however, are binding only upon the people who make them voluntarily. They are respected by other people but they need not be followed in the presence of the person who has made the vow.

Gypsies will patronize a variety of restaurants in the cities. They are fond of Chinese food, but they upset waiters by demanding bread with the meal. They cannot understand why they are not welcome when they return to the same Chinese restaurant, attributing the attitude to the spread of anti-Gypsy feeling from the dominant group to the Chinese-Americans. Some of the Gypsies living on New York's Lower East Side are partial to such Jewish specialities as bagels and knishes. Some Mačvaja living in midtown New York City once asked me about the gefillte fish which they had seen in stores; they readily tried it when I brought some to them. Their dislike of the dish was occasioned solely by the unfamiliar taste and the fact that at any event they did not care for fish that much. Travel through Latin America, Texas, and California has made them familiar with chili and tamales, foods they often enjoy at home or in a restaurant. Spaghetti is eaten often, but Gypsy tomato sauce differs somewhat from the Italian sauces I have known; it tends to be more like the Spanish tomato-base sauces. They know and like Greek, Yugoslav, and other Balkan cooking as well as Russian foods.

Often the lack of any specific food upon the Romany table results from a lack of knowledge rather than a prohibition. For instance, at one feast held in 1954 there were a number of whole pineapples used to decorate the table. At the end of the meal, the pineapples remained on the table, and, as the young girls began to clear the dishes, I was asked if people "ate those things." I was requested to prepare the pineapples for them and they were offered to all present as a new and exciting dish.

The act of eating has important religious significance, for people are regarded as especially vulnerable to witchcraft and ceremonial pollution at this time. Like the Hindus, the Gypsies believe that supernatural contamination is spread readily through the medium of food.[17] People who are declared marime are not allowed to eat with others. Impure wishes and thoughts also can be transmitted to a victim while he is eating. Thus, Gypsies do not eat with strangers or with people they do not trust; sharing a meal together is a sign of trust and friendship, like the Arabic breaking of bread-and-salt.[18] Similarly, refusal to eat with a Gypsy is a sign of animosity and bad blood; anyone who does not wish to join a person or family at the dinner table must express the wish, *"xa sastimasa"* ("eat with health"), to show that no spell has been cast upon the diners. Even then care must be taken not to watch the eating process. This special Gypsy feeling toward the act of eating is most marked for the large meal of the day; then it diminishes as the meal diminishes in importance. Eating in a restaurant is not affected by this ban; apparently the Gypsies either equate a restaurant meal with eating a

[17]A good explanation of Hindu beliefs may be found in Mandelbaum 1970: I, 196-201.

[18]Many families also reserve certain cups for the exclusive use of outsiders; these cups and glasses are marime to Gypsies.

snack or else they feel that eating at different tables is the equivalent of eating in separate tents. On the other hand, when a catering hall is hired for a wedding feast, the Gypsies insist upon bringing the food already cooked themselves, and they set up a single large banquet table to accommodate all the married couples.

Clothing

Gypsy clothing, especially that of the men, is influenced by that encountered by them at the time they entered Western Europe. In rural Europe, great variety of dress exists, and men often adorned their clothing with large metal coins that served as buttons. In the United States, Gypsy men like to be dressed in the latest gaĵo style.[19] During the zoot suit era, for example, they wore zoot suits; more recently they have affected "mod" styles. The older men tend to be more conservative. However, the Big Men like to wear big, large-brimmed, light-colored hats similar to those seen in parts of the south and west. Although the European Lovara (Yoors 1967: 107) and the Canadian Rom (Lee 1972) apparently wear one suit for all occasions until it falls apart, the United States Rom like to have a variety of clothing from which to choose every day; they also keep one or two suits for special occasions.

The clothing of the women tends to be much more distinctive, particularly for business wear and for festivals. Romany women fashion their own dresses from materials bought in yard-goods stores. Most of the women either own a sewing machine or have access to one; they are also capable of hand-sewing their outfits. Nearly all the women have extensive wardrobes; some of the Mačvaja girls I have known own as many as one hundred different outfits, and Parry (1941: 19) reported that some of the Kalderaš girls have twenty-five to one hundred dresses.

Feminine undergarments consist of a simple slip with a plain bodice and skirt. Over this is worn a blouse and a number of skirts. The traditional skirt is a wrap-around with pleats, requiring nine to ten yards of material; it reaches to the floor, for women's ankles are not supposed to be seen. Today there has

[19]For earlier periods, consult the photographs in Brown 1924.

been a decrease both in the number of skirts worn simultaneously and in the yardage used in each skirt. The modern skirt may include as little as six yards of fabric, although seven or eight yards is more usual. Occasionally, some of the younger girls wear shorter skirts, with the hem roughly at the midpoint of the calf; even as I write, the hems seem to be creeping upward. For twenty years or more, slacks have been acceptable attire for the young girls under ten years of age, but for the last several years, some of the Kalderaš bands have allowed their older girls and young women to wear slacks in the home. This constitutes a radical change in Rom attitudes towards feminine attire.

One rule that has not changed is that married women cannot appear in public without a head scarf. This *diklo* is the equivalent of our wedding ring, and woman cannot be seen by men outside of her own family unless she is wearing one. In fact, one of the most characteristic gestures of Romany women is the impatient pulling at the diklo as it slides off the head—a frequent occurrence. A woman has several optional ways of tying her scarf, and many of my friends commented with great approval at the way I tied mine after I got married.

Formerly women wore a pocket-purse tied around their waists to carry the items now put into pocketbooks, but pocket-purses still are known and used as an alternative. They may be decorated with beads or sequins and a fringe.

The traditional woman's costume is quite practical; it can be changed quickly and easily in perfect modesty regardless of circumstances. With a number of different skirts being worn at the same time, it is also possible to effect a quick change to throw pursuers off the track. Gypsy clothing being very colorful, it acts as a form of camouflage. The gaĵe are not apt to notice a Gypsy woman's face when their eyes are bedazzled by the strange and striking outfits. If a Gypsy woman is caught pickpocketing or shoplifting, a change of skirt and the use of another as an improvised blouse can help deceive the victim as to the identity of the culprit; by the time the law arrives to make an arrest, the victim cannot identify the miscreant.

Still another advantage to Gypsy dress is the fact that wraparound skirts are usually without a side seam and thus expand automatically to accommodate the requirements of pregnancy. In this respect, Gypsy dresses were more sensible than American costumes before maternity clothing was invented. Even today Gypsies do not seem to care for maternity clothing. They do not know how to use store-bought patterns to make the dresses, and usually they do not like to try on dresses in stores.

Perhaps the most important advantage to the traditional woman's costume is the ease with which modesty can be kept. This is particularly important to them, for Gypsies are very prudish in their body attitudes. Any part of the anatomy above the belt-line is considered clean, and there is no embarrassment in having it seen by either sex. (This idea has somewhat changed among many bands over the last fifteen years; Gypsy women now tend to keep their breasts covered at all times and have taken to wearing brassieres. Formerly, there was no shame attached to showing the breasts, and blouses were changed in public view and children casually nursed. During the Transition Period, the Gypsies learned that the gaje objected to these practices, and nowadays they feel embarrassed if the upper parts of their body are seen by their own people. Young daughters-in-law now avoid having their fathers-in-law see them nurse their babies, just as they have traditionally avoided having the older men see them smoke.)

Body parts below the belt-line are unclean and must never be seen by anyone. Even brothers will not disrobe in one another's presence. In the crowded quarters in which the Romanies live, then, the women's clothes are a necessary requisite to modesty.

Gypsy women spend many happy hours in shoe stores. I suspect that part of the pleasure involves the fact that Gypsy males avoid feminine feet and footgear because they are considered marime. A Gypsy woman can threaten to render her husband ceremonially impure by stepping on his hat or throwing her shoe over his head in public. Thus, a non-Gypsy male actually handling their feet has all the titillation of a forbidden act; furthermore, the women believe they are making the hated non-Gypsies even more unclean than usual. Gypsies were delighted with platform soles when that fashion first was the rage in the forties; heels cannot come high enough to suit them. All new fads are adopted with alacrity, and price is never an obstacle.

Fur coats and jackets also are worn. The Romanies are well aware of the fact that furs depreciate in value with time, but they are a satisfactory item for emergency pawning. As a result, some women have several fur coats in their wardrobes.

Clothing styles for children have changed as radically as those of adults. During the Camp Period, Gypsy children up to five or six years of age wandered around without any clothing at all. Clothing fashioned after that of their elders was worn during festivals. The gaje regarded it as an indecency and as a cruelty to children to have the youngsters walk about naked during cold weather. To please gaje sensibilities, the Gypsies began to dress their offspring in a slip, regardless of sex. During the Crisis Period, they began to clothe their children; they also learned about diaper service for infants. Actually, for very young, active children, the traditional Gypsy costume of little or no clothing and frequent bathing is more hygienic. Gypsies do not rush toilet training, and they attach no shame to a child's body parts or excretions. The Romanies learned about panties when they began to use American dresses for the girls. The use of diapers and modern one-piece jumpers for babies led to the adoption of rubber pants and diapers. Now, Gypsy babies are experiencing diaper rash and other skin irritations.

Furniture

Gypsy furniture, like that of most nomads, was kept to a minimum and was geared to portability. Cushions or carpeting were the Romany equivalents of chairs. Featherbed quilts, known as *perina*, were both coverlets and mattresses; large trays, some of them on low stands, functioned as tables. All of the furniture and equipment of a household could be piled into a cart or wagon in one hour. In this way a camp could be struck rapidly, and the band was on its way, either to evade gaje pursuers or to obey the gajo command to "keep moving."

The Kalderaš used horsedrawn carts to move their belongings from one place to another, but they always camped in tents that could be pitched and struck quickly.[20] Other Gypsy groups were even more mobile; they had a *vardo*, a caravan trailer that was like a house on wheels in which the family lived both while

[20]For British Gypsies, cf. Huth 1945: 30-43.

traveling and while camping. For this reason, the Mačvaja, for instance, had an easy time making the transition to modern auto trailers.

A rather gradual transition to modern American furniture has been effected; the changes have presented some problems that remain unsolved. Some of the difficulties stem from the size of Gypsy families. For example, the question of seating is of no consequence when one sits on a carpet or on cushions that can be piled in a corner when not needed. On the other hand, our culture dictates that every member of the family must have a chair on which to sit, thereby creating a problem of space for a large family living in small quarters. Chairs must be kept on the living room floor and then must be carried to another location; the time involved in packing and unpacking is considerable. Furthermore, one can eat comfortably from a tray while sitting on a cushion, but not from a chair. Thus, tables must also be part of an apartment's furniture.

For a while, chairs were considered an item of prestige. Rules of etiquette were formulated whereby chairs were to be offered to honored guests and the important older men; extra chairs were to be offered to other men; then to older women. When I first started studying the Gypsies, I was instructed in the etiquette of sitting; it was the first sign that I had been accepted by my hosts. Chair priorities were outlined for me, and my new family gently explained to me that I would not be given a chair for I was no longer functioning in the role of honored guest. Now that I had become one of the unmarried daughters in the household, I would be expected to take my place on the floor. My Gypsy mother instructed me in the proper way to sit: with my legs folded tailor-fashion and my skirts wrapped neatly around me for the sake of modesty and to prevent the babies from tripping over them as they walked and crawled about. Today, nearly twenty years later, however, Gypsy acceptance of chairs is so complete that they are embarrassed to have me seen in this position by strangers. However, they do not prevent me from sitting on the floor for comfort's sake; in fact, older Gypsy women often adopt the cross-legged posture on wide chairs and sofas when there is sufficient room.

Beds are another item of furniture presenting space problems, but on a large scale, because of their intrinsically larger size. The Gypsy perina were spread out on the floor at night; then folded up and placed in a pile against the wall by day. Beds take considerable floor space and require blankets and pillows (hardly as comfortable and warm as those of the perina). Studio couches, daybeds, convertible sofas, and high-risers have solved part of the furniture problem for the Gypsies. Furthermore, replacement of perina is becoming necessary as the old quilts wear out; it is not possible to obtain new perina of good quality any more in the United States. Even if it were possible to purchase goosedown and feathers, the Gypsies do not know how to sew the quilts, for their traditional pattern has been to consider the perina heirlooms to be passed on to several generations before they wear out. Thus, change would have had to be effected through necessity in any event.

The current wholesale adoption of American furniture has disrupted the traditional Romany pattern to get up and move within a few hours. A correlation now exists between the amount of furniture in a place and the planned duration of residency. A partial solution to the problem of mobility is to sell all the furniture before making a move and then to buy new equipment at the new location. Still better, from the Gypsy viewpoint, is the discovery of installment buying; the Romanies use it as a form of furniture rental. They are aware that they are paying dearly, but the advantage of being able to move on short notice is thought to be worth the price differential. In addition, in some cases at least, the Gypsies would not want their new location on public record, a certainty through the use of hired movers and vans.

Shelter Patterns

The change from a tent or living-wagon to a modern apartment is very radical, but it has been done in a number of stages. The great initial leap was made during the Transition Period, when the living quarters in town were also used for fortunetelling purposes. However, the change was lessened by keeping some of the features regarded as most essential by the Gypsies themselves. For instance, since the Gypsies have preserved a strong feeling about the differential sanctity and importance of different parts of the body, they have avoided living in quarters in which other floors existed above theirs, to prevent people walking "over their heads." During the last five years, the Rom have begun to accept regular apartment dwellings and even fortunetelling locations, but for a long time the Gypsies favored living in "taxpayer stores" (i.e., those without additional stories overhead). Similar considerations also have kept the men from riding subway trains; for the Gypsies, it was a necessary part of their religious beliefs to have cars.

Gypsies often treat the walls of their homes as if they were the interior walls of tents. Instead of painting or wallpapering, they tack up fabric. Fabric also is used to partition off various sections of the store just as cloth sectioned off different areas of a tent. The Gypsies divide their stores into three basic sections. In the front of the store near the show-windows, the women sit to lure in potential customers. Often in a prominent place along one wall there is a table for candles and icons and sometimes incense burners, attesting to the Christian faith of the women in the store.

The middle section itself has three parts. In the middle is a clear isle on each side of which is a booth for private consultations between the reader and her customer. The back section, never open to the public (i.e., to non-Gypsies), is curtained off as the living quarters for the family.[21] Here we find the men and children, the bedding and sleeping area at night, the living section by day, and the cooking area. In order to obtain more space for the family, the front section is closed off at night, straight across the width of the store, and the middle section is then taken apart and becomes an adjunct of the back family quarters.[22]

Some of the stores are often rented in neighborhoods in which it is usual for the small businessowners to live in the stores themselves. In such cases, the back of the store has cooking and sanitation facilities. Elsewhere, stores may lack even a toilet. Thus, washing may become a major problem for a people accustomed to camping near running water so that they could bathe and wash clothes frequently.

[21]In 1973 one of the Kalderaš groups began using sliding Japanese *shoji* screens in place of curtains.

[22]Cf. Brown 1928: 159 for the early Transition Period in the United States; Moriarty 1929: 178 describes Canadian Kalderaš tents at the same time; Tillhagen 1947: 90 provides a comparison with Swedish Kalderaš.

Landlords may complain about Gypsy abuse of property; however, this seeming disregard for property is a characteristic of nomads (who are used to temporary living quarters, abandoned after use rather than subjected to any kind of upkeep). Techniques and utensils required to keep American housing clean were unknown to the Romanies: they knew nothing about vacuum cleaners or carpet sweepers. The Gypsies had to learn to sweep their carpets with a broom instead of hanging them up and beating them clean.

Some of the Gypsy's knowledge of housekeeping was acquired by hiring maids, a practice reported by Brown(1929) for the early twenties; some of it came from watching movies, and, later, television. From the same sources they also learned about lighting fixtures, venetian blinds, window shades, furniture, painting, and wallpaper.

In relatively easy stages, the Gypsies progressed to stores with overhead living quarters, then to "stores" in apartment houses (because of the lack of good locations), and finally to apartments used for their own housing. Recently houses have been rented for fortunetelling purposes in suburban areas in order to avoid the police. The Romanies like living in houses, particularly the Mačvaja, who have lived in motels out West. However, most New York Gypsies do not have the capital required for buying a house, and they fear that they would be more vulnerable to police arrest were they to settle in one.

Romanies have never been self-sufficient in such essentials as food, clothing, and furniture. They have always bartered or bought the necessary raw materials, and have depended on non-Gypsy goods just as much as non-Gypsies have needed their services and products. Because of this, the Gypsies have had always to obtain a good knowledge of the workings of a non-Gypsy economy and the economic system prevalent in a country.

4

SOCIOPOLITICAL ORGANIZATION OF THE NOMADS

We Americans are accustomed to differentiate rather strongly between our relatives, who may or may not live near us, and our neighbors, with whom we may cooperate on matters of mutual daily interest. Our neighborhoods we regard as part of our political structure, and the family often comes under the jurisdiction of a political unit and authority. For instance, schools educate our children and the police protects our family and our property. The Nomad Gypsies, on the other hand, tend to subsume many political activities under their kinship units, and, therefore, propinquity groups tend to be based on kinship relationships. Of these, the most important is the extended family; these in turn are grouped into vitsas.

The Extended Family: Bulwark of Gypsy Society

A Gypsy baby is born not into a small family unit of mother/father/sister/brother so typical of American families, but into a large grouping of relatives; they are pleased at his birth and ready to be concerned directly in his welfare. "Many children, much luck," runs the Gypsy proverb, and children are always welcomed.

The woman who gave birth to him, of course, welcomes him as her child; however, the baby also has a special value to his mother by changing her position within the group from *bori* (daughter-in-law) to mother-of-our-child. The baby belongs to his father's group; therefore, he is a member of the paternal unit

60

in which he will be raised. His patri-kin (relatives linked to him through his father and other male relatives) take an interest in his development because he will become a responsible member of their *vitsa* (band) and contribute to its future success. His maternal relatives also are interested in him because he is the child of one of their daughters and a potential future contact for economic endeavors, marriage arrangements, and political alliances. Thus, many people are concerned about his future welfare, directly or indirectly; however, the baby's most important circle of kin is his extended family.

The ideal Nomad Gypsy family consists of a man and his wife, their unmarried sub-adult children, and their married sons with their wives and children. Such a family is considerably larger than the American nuclear family and is referred to as an "extended family." Since a Gypsy couple may have six or more children, the Romany family can total 30 or 40 individuals.

Often the parents of a first-born child are only 15 or 16 years old, not much older. The young father has not learned entirely the full repertoire of adult male roles, and the young mother still is serving her apprenticeship under her mother-in-law. Full adult responsibility for the new baby rests with the young father's parents. The grandmother gives instructions on child-care to the mother, and, since the younger woman may be away most of the day fortunetelling, much of the physical care of the baby rests with her as well. The grandfather is responsible for the decisions made for the entire family, grandchildren included. Thus, Gypsy children are used to being cared for by many different people, and it is not altogether rare to find that the two-year-olds have difficulty in identifying their actual parents within the extended family. Any adult person will care for and express love for any of the children within the extended family without much distinction paid to the biological closeness of the relationship.

The extended family is the major functional unit of Gypsy society. Potentially, it is completely self-sufficient for all ordinary purposes, and, in fact, it can and sometimes does exist in isolation from other Gypsies. The extended family can succor and educate its young, protect its adult members, earn its own livelihood, function as a unit to celebrate religious rituals, care for its sick, bury its dead, etc. About the only activity the extended family cannot fulfill without assistance from another family is that of marriage since there is an interdiction against first cousin marriage (Cotten 1950: 152-53; Gropper 1967: 1051-52; Bonos 1942: 269).

Although a large extended family is in a better position to take care of itself than a small group, too many members in a single unit also present difficulties. Tactical problems of maneuverability are involved, for one thing. A large unit and its physical equipment cannot travel rapidly enough. In former times, during the period of outdoor camps, an extended family often occupied several tents, those of the married sons being grouped on each side of the parental tent, a residential pattern similar to that of the Mongol and Tibetan nomads (cf. Ekvall 1968: 25; Krader 1963: 148). The presence of many family members required many horses, and these, in turn, required new pastures periodically, forcing frequent changes in camp-sites as they ran out of pasturage. Furthermore, sanitation required that camps be periodically relocated, for the presence of many people led to a rapid accumulation of refuse. Each move entailed travel along main roads frequented by non-Gypsies, and a large party of Romanies seemed like a mass invasion, the sheer force of numbers frightening the gaje. This visibility was aggravated by the additional need to support a large group economically, thereby requiring contacts with outsiders. Besides, the more people in a unit, the greater the probability that disagreements will occur among its members. Furthermore, as the sons grew older and more experienced, they became increasingly restive under the direct control of an aging father. The Old One found his waning powers taxed more and more to maintain order and peace in a large unit.

Thus, conflicting pressures are brought to bear on the extended family, some of which encourage a larger size and others a smaller one. There is both a maximum size beyond which it is not feasible to grow and a minimum size beneath which it is impossible to remain independent and self-sufficient. The optimum size range strikes a felicitous balance between the upper and lower limits. (See Chart 4.1.)

Actually, the extended family functions as a single household only periodically. In our discussion of economic enterprises, we saw that smaller sub-units of the kumpanja-type may function

---

CHART 4.1

POPULATION SIZE IN THE EXTENDED FAMILY

Advantages of Small Size	*Advantages of Large Size*
Easier mobility	Natural population increase
Less pasturage needed	More adult males and thus more protection
Fewer sanitation problems	More work sharing
Less visibility	Better general self-sufficiency
Fewer disagreements	More important position in Gypsy affairs
Easier to find housing	

---

independently for limited periods of time.[1] But, more importantly, a family unit, like an individual, has a natural life-history, a developmental cycle.[2] It is created, grows and changes, and ultimately dies, having given birth to other such family units. Social scientists sometimes neglect the dynamics of the situation in favor of a static theoretical analysis of different family types, and we are left with the erroneous impression that there are clearcut boundaries separating family types and that families do not change over time. For the Gypsies, at least, social units tend to shade into one another, depending upon such factors as number of children born to a specific couple, ages of family members, and particular physical settings in which the families function at the moment.

When each boy marries, his bride comes to live in the same household as the boy's parents. Here the younger couple practices the new roles of husband and wife, and the bride, who usually comes from a different band and sometimes even a different tribe, is trained in the ways of her husband's people. Under the careful tutelage of the older couple, the young man and woman eventually add another dimension to their repertoire of social roles, and a third generation is incorporated into the extended family. The birth of a second child to the young couple often sets in motion pressures operating to encourage the

---

[1]According to Yoors 1967, the Lovara *kumpanja* existed for a much longer duration.

[2]For a general discussion of the developmental cycle of families, cf. Goody 1971.

establishment of a separate household for them. Another son probably has been married in the interim; the daughter-in-law has demonstrated satisfactorily her assimilation of the ways of her conjugal family, her abilities as a housekeeper and bread-winner, and her capability as a mother. Her links to her husband's group now are fairly strong since she knows that she would be forced to leave her children behind were the marriage to be dissolved. Her husband, too, has shown responsibility and steadiness within the group of adult men. The older people feel the new family constellation has had enough time to practice survival by itself, and the young people and their children are allowed to move out to establish their own independent house-hold and make room for the other families-coming-into-being within the paternal family (see Chart 4.2).

The new household maintains fairly close ties with the older unit. It can return to the protection and material assistance of the old people, and the senior male continues as the *baro* (Big Man), head of the extended family, and responsible for the actions of all its members. In former times, during the inactive winter months when encampments were larger, the various sub-units of the extended family customarily regrouped to-gether. This habit has been transferred to the urban situation, and the sub-groups of an extended family often try to find quarters near one another. On the other hand, during the sum-mer traveling months, the sub-units often spread out over the entire country, just as they did in the old days.

The transition from an outdoor camp to a city store imposed an additional deterrent on large family size. Landlords (and neighbors) objected to crowds of people occupying the same premises, and it was difficult to find sufficient housing close to the parents to provide an analogue to neighboring tents. Usually what happens now is that the older sons, with their wives and children, strike out on their own, leaving the younger sons at home with the parents. If they maintain regular close ties with their parents, they may still function as an extended family. If the older sons move far away or fail to visit frequently, the kin group may function as a stem family (old parents, plus one adult child with spouse and children). In fact, the Romany inheritance laws tend to favor stem-family formation rather than extended family.

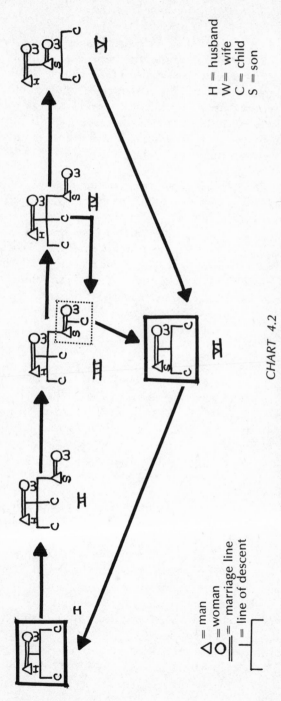

H = husband
W = wife
C = child
S = son

△ = man
○ = woman
= = marriage line
└─ = line of descent

CHART 4.2

THE NATURAL HISTORY OF A GYPSY EXTENDED FAMILY

The youngest son, ordinarily the last to marry, remains within his parents' household permanently; he is responsible for looking after his parents as they grow old. In return for this filial duty, the youngest son (and his own nuclear family) is entitled to inherit his parents' property; the older brothers do not share in the inheritance since they received their shares at the time they established their own households. The foregoing inheritance practices are also to be found in Central Asia (cf. Krader 1963: 144-46).

After the death of the baro, the brothers may continue to function as a single, large extended family (delegating one of the brothers to act as *pater familias*), or they may separate into as many smaller extended families as there are brothers. Even if the brothers elect to go their separate ways, they and their male descendants still belong to the same patrilineage (kinsmen related in the male line). Usually they remain in the same vitsa as well. In fact, these lineages often form the core of a Gypsy band.

The Vitsa or Band

The fully matured, extended family is the prototype of a vitsa (Cotten 1950: 152-55; Gropper 1967: 1051-52; Lee 1972: 72 refers to it as a "subfamily"; Maximoff 1947: 37 calls it a "clan"; Yoors 1967: 135 uses the Lovaritska *tzerha*). Anthropologists would refer to it as a patrilineal band. In principle, it consists of all males (and their wives and unmarried children) who are related to one another by a connecting male link: a man, his sons, his sons' sons, etc., but in actuality it may vary considerably from the ideal model.

Vitsa affiliation is subject to many factors (see Table 4.1); its members may change vitsa affiliation several times during its existence (the difficulties of this situation are discussed in Çoker 1966). Gypsies usually choose membership in a prestigious vitsa, one that has a large membership of adult males in their prime and is wealthy. A forceful, but benevolent, leadership is mutually beneficial to all members. The foregoing are the more important criteria for vitsa selection; geography, closeness of kin relationship, and the number of relatives of different types already in the vitsa are others. An individual feels more comfortable in a band in which he has kin, godparents, and friends (see Table 4.2).

TABLE 4.1

FACTORS TO BE CONSIDERED IN CHOOSING VITSA MEMBERSHIP

I. Kinship
   - A. Number of relatives already in vitsa
     The more, the better
   - B. Closeness of kinship tie to the closest connecting "link" relative
     The closer, the better

II. Protection
   - A. For protection against non-Gypsies
     The larger the vitsa, the more protection
     The more influential the leader, the better
   - B. For protection against other Gypsies
     The more prestigious the vitsa, the better

III. Leadership
   - A. Benevolence of leadership
     The more benevolent toward vitsa members, the better
   - B. Forcefulness of leadership
     The more forceful toward the outside, the better
   - C. Acquisition of leadership
     The more likely the chances for becoming leader oneself, the better

IV. Commercial
   - A. Business acumen of vitsa members
     The shrewder the business talents of the members, the more profitable the association
   - B. Wealth of vitsa
     The more capital available in the vitsa, the better the possibilities for economic aggrandizement for any member

V. Geographical
   - A. Distance from current base of operations
     The closer, the better known
   - B. Proximity to economic opportunities
     The closer to economic opportunity, the better
     The further from competition of other Gypsies, the better

---

TABLE 4.2

POSSIBLE BASES FOR VITSA MEMBERSHIP

Listed in descending order of preference:
   - A. Hereditary paternal right through male line
   - B. Hereditary maternal right through female line
   - C. Conjugal right through wife's lines
   - D. Affinal right through children's marital lines
   - E. Friendship alliance
   - F. Subordinate clientship

Does a vitsa ever reject a family aspiring to membership? Unless there are good reasons—such as a reputation as a troublemaker or untrustworthiness in business matters—a vitsa has nothing to lose by taking in a new member-family, and it profits by adding extra adult males. The new family might also have girls eligible for marriage and perhaps could be persuaded to arrange unions at a reduced brideprice to cement alliances within the band more firmly. The family's relative status in the band, however, may vary, depending upon such considerations as wealth, prestige, and closeness of kinship.

Many functions of the extended family are fulfilled by the vitsa, albeit on a larger scale. It cares for the children, furnishes economic opportunities and protection for its members, celebrates rituals, cares for the sick, and buries the dead.[3]

One of the rights of a vitsa is to claim a territory. A territory includes residences and storefront locations; it may be enlarged whenever possible. A territory may be occupied only seasonally, and, particularly in rural and other areas, only temporarily. For example, in New York City, the Coney Island area has an extensive Gypsy population that includes members of different vitsas; the unusual Gypsy density correlates with the non-Gypsy use of the area as a summer resort. In the winter, when the non-Gypsy population returns to its normally sparse numbers, Coney Island "belongs" exclusively to the members of one vitsa only.

A vitsa may cooperate with another vitsa in achieving a common goal. For instance, groups already resident in an area may wish to prevent other Gypsies from entering it; they can agree to pool their resources to make life uncomfortable for the newcomers, such as refusing hospitality, discouraging marriages, forming economic cartels, and instigating fights among the men. Or, if the leader of one vitsa is getting too powerful and despotic, they may try to influence other bands and their leaders in an effort to end his leadership. Alliance formation is not limited to any geographical area; several vitsas across the country, or even in different parts of the world, may form brotherhoods whereby

---

[3]In fact, as I noted in discussing the extended family, at least in theory vitsa-formation arises naturally from the developmental cycle of a normal extended family: the adult sons with established families of their own, including sons who are marrying and having children, automatically form an incipient vitsa if they continue to function together.

their members may travel freely in all the territories controlled by them. Such persons may participate in the economic, political, and social activities of their allies as if they were legitimate resident members. Such vitsas are expected to come to one another's assistance in times of emergency, including inter-vitsa battles.

Some twenty years ago, two New York vitsas started a feud over the birth of triplets. Over the years, animosity between the two bands accumulated; finally the paths of the groups crossed in Texas. A few minor skirmishes between small parties of men convinced the band leaders of the inevitability of armed confrontation (a rare event in the United States, but relatively common in Europe before World War II.)[4] Each side sent word out to its allied bands at once to send their men to Texas for the scheduled fight. It took a great deal of work by Rom leaders throughout the country to prevent a major battle.

The vitsa is also the unit that deals with the outside world. Local government officials prefer dealing with an equivalent structure to their own; on the Gypsy side, a vitsa acting as the contact unit simplifies and hastens negotiations with the gaĵe. The Police Department will look to the vitsa leader in case of trouble; the Welfare Department in the past used to clarify problems of eligibility with the vitsa. (The late Gypsy leader, Steve Kaslov, was able to to get W.P.A. assistance for his vitsa from the federal government in the thirties.) A vitsa leader may obtain benefits for his group by exerting a certain amount of pressure on gaĵe politicians around election time. Knowledge of local regulations controlling leases, stores, contracts, etc. is necessary information for all the members of a band; it makes more sense, therefore, for the band to retain a lawyer than for the families to negotiate individually in such matters. Data, then, can be shared and expenses pooled.

A major task of a vitsa is that of relocating when necessary. In the event that the vitsa finds itself in difficult times (such as the inability to make a living, increased harrassment by the constabulary, etc.) or finds out that some other part of the world holds greater promise, the group as a whole will explore alterna-

[4]Maximoff 1946 describes one in vivid terms.

tive areas for resettlement, sending members out to investigate and report back to the others. If the vitsa decides to move, the entire group can migrate, thereby buffering the unknown and giving mutual assistance and comfort to its members. Numerical strength is preserved, and all may benefit from the varied talents of individuals. The vitsa as the agent of extraordinary migration is well documented in Romany history. The European chronicles of the fifteenth century indicate that a single vitsa "opened up" Western Europe, entering as a single group, splitting into smaller units (perhaps extended families) for exploration, rejoining periodically for information-sharing and strategy plotting, redeploying in small groups, and reuniting. It is even possible that this original vitsa returned from whence it came, either in whole or part, to summon allied bands to the new area.

After World War II, many European Gypsies who survived the concentration camps decided to emigrate to the United States; to such end, they hoped to engage the support of their kin in American bands.[5] But immigrants must post bonds to assure the United States Government that they will not become a financial liability. The American Gypsies were willing to sponsor the European Rom only if the newcomers would agree to hand over their daughters as brides (without the usual brideprice, of course). The European groups chose to embark for South America instead, again in vitsa units. Most recently, some British Rom Gypsies have sent scouts to the United States to investigate the possibility of migrating to this country to escape a resurgence of anti-Gypsy feelings in England. So far, no English vitsa has arrived, much to the relief of the United States Rom, who are not happy at the prospect of economic competition.

Vitsa Leadership

The head of an extended family is called a "Big Man." The Big Man of the ruling family of a vitsa is the leader of that group. Gypsies often use the English term "king" to refer to their leader when talking to the gaje. However, an outsider coming to ask about "the king" may be informed that Romanies have no kings.

[5] A general summary can be found in Kenrick and Puxon 1972.

In at least one sense, both statements are true, for, inasmuch as Gypsy leadership tends to be hereditary—one of the sons of the former leader usually becomes leader in turn—as kingship is, one may say Gypsy leaders are kings; nevertheless, insofar as kings are assumed to be absolute rulers with the power of life and death over their subjects, Gypsies cannot be said to have kings. A better term, and one that is more accurate in an anthropological sense, is "chief."

Gypsy chiefs rule by persuasion more often than by coercion. A good leader must be able to think clearly and to persuade others about the rightness of his convictions. He also has the support of the adult males of his family and a successful history as a decision maker. However, a leader's wisdom is demonstrated by his keen sense of timing and by his ability to express when necessary the common, heretofore unspoken sentiment of the group.

The extended families comprising a vitsa have considerable independence of their own under the leadership of their individual Big Men, just as each adult male may have independence from his Big Man if he so desired. However, it is beneficial for all concerned to depend on and follow the leader's guidance.

A good leader takes care of his people much as a parent looks after his children. He functions as peacemaker in cases of disagreements, arbitrating and adjudicating wisely so that no resentment remains to erupt unpredictably at a future date. He makes the final decision on matters affecting the group as a whole. Benevolent leadership also involves a humane concern for the personal problems of group members, and good leaders must be ready to supply advice when requested to do so. They are expected to volunteer financial assistance to needy members and provide manpower in emergencies.

A vitsa chief, among the Rom I have met, is expected to function as contact man with the outside world; he represents the Rom when dealing with the police, welfare department, social agencies, political parties, etc. (Brown 1929: 159-60, 168-69; Mitchell 1945: 41-43; Parry 1941: 20 agree with my findings for the United States. Lee 1972 uses the felicitous term "patriarch" to describe a similar situation in Canada, and Starkie 1933: 285, 294 attests to a chief with equivalent roles for Transylvanian Kalderaš). Jan Yoors (1967:113-14), speaking for the

European Lovara, states that the contact man in Europe is an innocuous false-front position and that the chiefs are unknown to the gaje, but I have not found this to be so in the United States. However, often Gypsies will claim to be kings or queens when forced to deal with journalists and other outsiders. The visibility of the American chiefs requires that these individuals have an irreproachable reputation in the outside world—once a criminal record is obtained, that leader's usefulness to his group is over. He may be eminently respectable in Gypsy circles, but he can no longer represent the group to the hostile outside world. Unscrupulous Gypsy chiefs, in rivalry with one another, have not hesitated to convert this rule to their own purposes. Several Gypsy chiefs have been informed on to the police (and during World War II to the draft boards) in order to make them ineligible for political office among the Rom.

The vitsa chief is assisted and advised by a Council of Elders or *divano*, consisting of the Big Men, the heads of the member-extended families (Mitchell 1945: 47; Gropper 1967: 1051-52). A forceful and able leader may not feel the need to call upon the Council's aid; in fact, the Mačvaja chiefs do not usually convene a Council at all. Yet, no vitsa chief can safely ignore the consensus of his Big Men. The Council has a strong voice in the selection of a new vitsa chief, and it can withdraw its support en masse in the Romany equivalent of a vote of no confidence. Since no leader can exist without a following, the chief must maintain good relations with the Council. Furthermore, the Council functions as a clearinghouse; it processes information from the chief and from the separate extended families of the vitsa. The Council is an efficient political mechanism because according to Gypsy law each Big Man is responsible for all the members of his own extended family. (Similarly, the chief is responsible for all his vitsa followers in the eyes of other Gypsies, and each man is responsible for the behavior of his wife and children.)

Many expenses are incurred by a leader, some of which are unique to his position (such as lawyers' retaining fees, gifts and contributions to the police and other city officials). Household expenses are extraordinarily high because the leader's domicile is the official headquarters of the vitsa; his dwelling unit must be sufficiently large to accommodate many visitors—the male members of the vitsa frequently spend much time in their leader's home, and Gypsies from other groups are entertained here, too. Out-of-town guests often stay with the leader as well. Even the daily meetings require the offering of food, coffee, and beer. A good leader's generosity toward his followers is also expressed in his willingness to act as godparent (and contribute the attendant expenses), extend loans, and provide money in emergencies. No matter how wealthy a leader may be, he is always in need of cash.

The entire vitsa profits from the endeavors of their leader; indeed, in any society there are some political expenses, and not infrequently the component families (or individuals) are expected to share in the costs since they, too, benefit from the results. We are familiar with taxation, and that is precisely the mechanism used for sharing expenses among the Rom. The Gypsy tax base varies somewhat from ours, but it is roughly equivalent to an income tax: most extended families are expected to contribute a reasonable, often voluntary amount to the leader's treasury on a yearly basis. When there is an unusually high profit from an occasional economic endeavor, a surplus-profits tax, as it were, is requested. Apparently no set rule common to all the vitsas exists, for certain rulers have a reputation for requiring larger taxes than others. There are limits set by the total structure: thus, too large a "bite" encourages members to leave a vitsa and realign elsewhere, and too small a tax receipt prevents the ruler from functioning adequately for lack of resources.

From time to time, one reads in the newspapers about the Rom complaining that such a leader is a bandit who takes money away from his people in an extortion racket. But such statements say more about the Gypsies' knowledge of American ways (and their ability to manipulate the gaje) than about Romany methods of self-government.

Leadership Selection

Political ability, according to the Gypsies, results from a combination of innate shrewdness (itself God-given and also found in certain families) and experience gained in political situations, particularly in the context of the kris. Ability by itself is not sufficient to assure leadership, however. In order to succeed, a leader needs manpower and wealth. I know of one individual whose chieftainship was abortive because he did not have enough sons to assist him. Another family had the necessary wealth and manpower, but a campaign to obtain recognition was unsuccessful because the aspiring chief lacked the family prestige essential to the job.

It is usual for the chieftainship to remain within the same extended family, if not the same nuclear family. But that nuclear family may well have had five or six sons, and the extended family a dozen or more. Furthermore, a long-lived chief can continue to rule until his grandsons are old enough to succeed to leadership; thus, leadership may skip a generation if a more suitable candidate exists among the younger males. What may seem to an outsider as a limited choice of candidates for leadership—the successor being a member of the "royal family"—proves to be almost an overabundance. Another advantage to the vitsa members is the awareness of competition among the potential candidates, for it forces the less capable to bow out of the race early while it increases the motivation of the others to improve their skills assiduously. Those who would protest that the males of the royal family are compelled to outdo themselves constantly forget that leadership requires a strong personality, and, as the American saying goes, "Those who can't stand the heat should get out of the kitchen."

Leadership selection is a gradual process and a lengthy one, and so is leadership training; in fact, they are simultaneous and complementary in nature. The children are watched unobtrusively whenever vitsa members visit the chief's home: Are they poised or awkward? Are they respectful toward their elders, self-assertive with their equals, and protective toward younger children?

Much of the regular Gypsy child-training takes place in the playgroup, which usually consists of close relatives of different ages (and of both sexes in the early years). The royal playgroup differs only by virtue of having all the young eligibles in it. The boys are rated for such qualities as timidity (bad), strength (good), tenacity (also good), sense of humor (probably helpful if he does not develop into a clown), troublemaker (probably undesirable but at least an indication of originality), poor judgment (bad), and high self-esteem (good).

Gypsy youngsters participate in many of the activities of the adult members of their families. In this manner, they are exposed from an early age to the experiences of the adults. By just listening to the conversation of the adults, children can learn a great deal about daily matters. Furthermore, conversation at the chief's household centers mostly on political matters; the discussions tend to be more sophisticated and far-ranging in expressions of opinion, hypotheses of motivation, evaluation of character, and predictions of possible outcomes of current affairs than those heard elsewhere. Even the quiet, stay-at-home evenings normally devoted to storytelling have a different emphasis in the chief's family, for the youngsters are exposed to numerous tales of the exploits of their ancestors and to long narratives of their own group's past history. These tales are part of the oral traditions of the Rom and serve as unwritten training manuals and textbooks of politics in the education of the young students (Cotten 1954: 264-65).

All Gypsy boys are allowed to accompany their fathers and older brothers in their daily rounds; at first, the boys join male activities sporadically, but gradual incorporation into the adult world is stepped up as each individual youth demonstrates his ability and skills. The boys of the chief's family, too, are invited along when some of the men go out on business (but their business, of course, tends to be political in nature). The boys also begin to attend the kris at an earlier age than the other youths; perhaps the kris is the most important experience for the preparation of new leaders.

Thus far, I have discussed political leadership. However, one must not assume that political leadership is transferable to another domain of life; a political leader may not be a good economist, for example. There is no transferability of leadership among the Rom. Leadership must be earned in each area of life anew, and the Rom recognize that all-around excellence is hard to find. Gypsies believe that everybody has a special talent for a certain job and that no one is good at everything. This attitude is psychologically beneficial, for its converse—that no one is a total failure—allows a Gypsy to retain his self-respect, for surely the group will benefit from his particular talent at some point.

The Gypsy Kinship System

Nomad Gypsies emphasize patrilineal kin in their rules of residence, but their kinship system is similar to ours, recognizing equally both the father's and the mother's side of the family. For example, the Gypsy term for grandmother is the same for the maternal grandmother as for the paternal grandmother, and the term for uncle is applicable both to the mother's brother and to the father's brother.[6]

Anthropologists often say that a people's kinship system determines a set of attitudes toward those members of the system known by the same term. For instance, all the men known as "uncle" are expected to act in a certain way toward their "nephews" and "nieces"—the reciprocal terms. In those kinship systems in which the father's brothers are called "father" and the mother's brothers are called "uncle," it is usual to find that the men called "father" do act toward their "sons" in a way similar to that of the one man who actually sired the children, whereas the "uncles" behave quite differently toward their "nephews."

In the Gypsy kinship system different terms are used to refer to the affinal kin (in-laws): a woman refers to her husband's relatives under terms different from those referring to his in-laws. This is mirrored in the fact that the woman goes to live in her husband's group and establishes an intimate relationship with his relatives whereas the husband may have comparatively little daily contact with his wife's people. Terms of address vary considerably, and their use is often determined by circumstance. For instance, we may call someone Mr. Jones on occasion when we feel a certain social distance; at other, more relaxed times, we may call "Mr. Jones" simply "Bob." The choice of term may reflect a Gypsy's mood at a given time. For example, there is a special term, *xanamik*, for "parent of my child's spouse." There is no English equivalent for this term, perhaps because we do not readily associate with the parents of our daughters- and sons-in-law. However, among the Rom, such association is customary. The xanamik relationship is delicate and requires much tact. In

[6]Cohn 1969 discusses the kinship system as it compares with American English terms, and Cotten 1950: diagrams 16A and 16B show the traditional anthropological kinship chart study of kin terms.

one instance, I observed the "mother of the husband" trying to convince the "mother of the wife" (her xanamik) that she was warmly disposed toward her; she addressed the woman as "sister."

Among the Nomad Gypsies, the young wife is supposed to address her mother-in-law as "mother." The older woman is not only a mother-substitute responsible for the younger woman's training in living skills but also for her wellbeing. A good mother-in-law is concerned for her daughter-in-law's health and happiness. The father-in-law, by contrast, is referred to by a unique term (and he is not addressed at all); he is a distant figure to the young bride because she is required to practice a limited form of father-in-law avoidance. She tries to be as inconspicuous as possible when he is around although she is expected to serve him coffee and food. On his side of the relationship, he pretends not to notice her, rarely talking to her directly; he communicates to her through the mother-in-law. This is in marked contrast to the older man's affectionate and demonstrative behavior toward his daughters.

A woman uses a special term for her husband's brothers; but they address her as *bori* (the same term of reference used by the husband's parents and sisters; an accurate translation would be a "woman who has married into my family"). But two brothers-in-law will call each other "brother" to show that they are close to each other. Similarly, sisters-in-law will call one another "sister."

The term "bori" is particularly interesting. A new daughter-in-law must prove herself in her conjugal family; she is expected to perform services and demand little. All the members of her husband's group are entitled to ask her to help out. Being a bori is uncomfortable and stressful and many jokes are made about it in an attempt to lessen the strain involved (in the same manner that our mother-in-law jokes serve a similar purpose). For instance, married women of roughly the same age will laughingly preface a request for service by calling their peer "bori" ("Bori, close the door for me"), or a light refusal to do a favor will be phrased as, " I'm not your bori; do it yourself." Young girls have complained to me that "I'm working like a bori in my own family!" Especially happy households are complimented in the following terms: "You can't tell the bori from the *šej* (daughter) over there."

Fictive kinship in the form of godparent/godchild relationships somewhat loosens the kinship system. Godparenthood is not as important to the Rom as it is to Latin Americans, for example, possibly because Gypsy godparents are often away from each other. Often good friends of the family are chosen as godparents; this friendship element outweighs considerations of kinship, status, and even ethnic identity. In one Mačvaja group I know, the families often ask Greeks to act as godparents for the new babies because they claim that "Greeks enjoy being godparents and have a good heart toward babies." My Gypsy friends often express regret that I cannot be a godmother because I am not baptized. Godparents are supposed to provide some spiritual protection toward the baby and its family. The baptismal occasion may be used as a form of blood brotherhood among the adults involved; two unrelated families who are very friendly with each other will form one or more godparent links to cement the relationsip more firmly. The social status of the potential godparent is important: the chiefs have proportionately more godchildren than other men.

Adoption is an accepted procedure among the Nomad Gypsies, and it is used to equalize family size. Some families receive too large a blessing of children, and others are cursed by few children or sterility. Most adoptions occur between the families of brothers (i.e., within the same extended family); therefore, total numbers of people in the group remain the same, and an equitable distribution of children assures that they all get the necessary attention and financial support. An equal number of boys and girls in a family is helpful because the cost of buying brides for the sons is then balanced by the income received when the daughters leave the family as brides. Since the daughters are not permanent members of the family (unless one can arrange for a "male bride," as the Japanese call them), some sons are necessary to carry on the family.

In the event that twin boys are born, the Coppersmith Rom usually arrange to have one adopted into another family, preferably in a different city. They say this is done to protect the twins' father from bad luck.

Adoption is not shameful to any of the parties involved; consequently, the fact of adoption is not hidden (although it is polite not to mention it to the adoptive parents because it may remind them of their inability to have children). The children are aware that they are adopted and sometimes visit their natural parents. When the children are older, they may elect to return to their biological parents. In some cases, the original parents may ask for the return of their children. These requests are not denied.

Recently, other adoption sources have been used to compensate for losses incurred by the family when wives bearing children desert their husbands. According to Gypsy law, these unborn children belong to the husband's family; if the men knew about the pregnancy, they would fight for the return of the wife. The woman's family tries to keep the pregnancy secret by sending her to relatives or friends in another city and arranging for a quiet adoption into another vitsa and/or tribe.

The Gypsy kinship system's flexibility and bilaterality are suited to Romany needs. It furnishes the ability to change vitsa alliance and to seek aid and protection from both paternal and maternal kin. Lack of emphasis on seniority within a generation can be compensated for by use of terms of address more appropriate to two generations if extreme age differences (calling for formal address) exist. An uncle considerably older than one's father may be called "grandfather"; similarly a cousin much older may be addressed as "uncle." The tendency to merge all kinsmen in generations separated from one's own age group by more than one or two generations (by using fewer differentiating terms) not only realistically reflects the relatively short life spans (thus, there are fewer such relatives with whom to reckon) but also the dignified distance of the Old Ones and their impartiality toward all younger kinsmen within the lineages.

The Tribe

If one follows an ideal developmental cycle of the vitsa, one arrives at a stage where the vitsa splits because of size or factionalism. Descent from common ancestors would be remembered for a while; then, time is bound to blur some of the details. However, a sense of kinship would still remain. Hence, bands should be allies because they are distant brothers. In actual practice, however, feuds and rivalries exist among the vitsas of any one tribe, while friendship and business interests may crosscut tribal lines (albeit not as frequently as the former).

Tribal names change with time; the lists of tribes vary from one century to another among the Central Asiatic groups (where we have the benefit of written historical records [Krader 1963: 54-67]); and there is no reason to suppose that the Gypsy situation nowadays is any different. Rosters of tribes also vary and contradict one another from one country to another. Many tribal names make reference to traditional occupations; some seem to be geographic. In the New York City area, groups are sometimes referred to as vitsas and sometimes as tribes. Tribes do not share territory in common, but territorial rights are a prerogative of the vitsa. Tribes are not marriage-regulation units either; one may seek a mate within one's own tribe or outside of one's tribal affiliation.[7]

Obviously the tribe is not a functional unit among the Rom. The younger Gypsies are not always sure to which tribe they belong; but their vitsa affiliations and that of their mothers is learned early. Gypsies become conscious of the idea of tribe only during extreme emergencies.

"The Problem of the Tribe" (Helm 1968) has only recently begun to concern anthropologists to any great extent. The issue has a certain importance for historical reconstructions and dynamics of social change; but the Gypsies are not especially interested in it.

[7]Gropper 1967:1053-55 documents the New York City picture for the last thirty years.

5

THE KRIS

Nomad Gypsy bands are grouped into tribes; their number may change with time and place. The Gypsies themselves, however, are vague about what they call "tribe." Each tribe has its own customs, somewhat different from those of its neighbors.[1] Furthermore, a tribe's speech may differ slightly from that spoken by another one. But in spite of dissimilarities, all Nomad Gypsies agree on the definition of what constitutes the total Rom group—those speakers of Romany who participate and abide by the kris. An occasional marriage with a non-Gypsy woman may be accepted with aplomb; but no man is a true Rom unless he upholds the kris.

Kris Composition

The term "kris" refers both to the abstract concept of "justice" and to the institution responsible for settling disputes arising among different extended families (disputes within the extended family are settled by the Big Man of that family). Every case must be reviewed, and an impartial body capable of ensuring that the litigants will honor the terms of the final agreement acts as arbitrator. Impartiality is a necessary condition for justice, but there can be no justice without adequate evidence. Thus, the litigants are entitled to bring a group of favorably inclined wit-

---

[1] For example, in the 1950s, the Kalderaš allowed their young women to bleach their hair and use cosmetics whereas both were strictly forbidden by the Mačvaja.

nesses with them. The judge must be a man without affiliation to either side; he is responsible for running the trial properly and deciding which customary laws to apply. A group of neutral observers constitutes a form of jury, and many of the observers belong to the judge's own band; they may act as peacemakers as well.

The selection of a judge is predicated on a number of factors. The primary considerations are the judge's impartiality and his acceptability to both sides. Theoretically, then, any difference of opinion between members of two extended families belonging to the same band can be adjudicated before their own chief. Any differences between members of different bands can be argued before the chief of another band (but someone who can remain neutral to either side). In the second instance, there is no need to go beyond the tribe to find a judge. If disputes involve two different tribes, custom would suggest the use of a chief from a third tribe.

In actuality, however, some chiefs have a reputation for being outstanding judges, and they are in greater demand for their services than others; requests are not limited to their own tribes. On rare occasions, their services are requested even if their tribal affiliation is "wrong," because they are known for being impartial—a great compliment indeed! A kris judge with a national reputation whose services are in great demand is a highly respected person; his fame will be perpetuated in legend, and he will serve as a model for others to follow.

No Gypsy leader is obliged to act as judge; his decision is predicated upon a series of factors, most of which have direct bearing on, or are a result of, his own position among the Gypsies. No judge will accept a case unless both sides in the litigation promise to abide by the verdict of the kris; moreover, the participants must take a sworn oath to that effect. Even then, a judge must make a shrewd calculation about (a) the sincerity of the litigants; (b) his own ability to enforce the final verdict (he must have at hand the manpower required to prevent the loser from running away); and (c) the potential increment of his reputation if he successfully resolves a difficult case.

The litigants bring witnesses on their behalf as well as spokesmen/lawyers to the kris to plead their case for them. The Gypsies, like many Asiatic peoples, try to avoid an interpersonal situation in which one side would be forced to refuse a request directly or to defend itself publicly. In any potentially awkward or uncomfortable situation, the Rom will engage a person who will act as a courier, relaying messages from one side to the other, always acting with great tact and diplomacy in order not to offend either party. The spokesmen, however, are unabashedly partisan, like any other lawyers involved in a trial. Kris witnesses, on the contrary, are like witnesses in an American case; they are ostensibly neutral (unless they are brought in as character witnesses), but their "neutrality" may be open to doubt insofar as their understanding of the case may be faulty or their desire to help a kinsman or friend may tempt them into perjury.

The audience/jury consists of men who are related to the litigants or who belong to the judge's group. But no Gypsy would be denied admission to the kris, and any who are interested are free to attend. The jury hears the case with the judge and also shares with him the right to question witnesses and to express opinions. The judge himself is the final authority on customary law and its precedents, but members of the jury are also entitled to refer to these matters. While the case is in progress, jury members may ask for information, and, after both sides have been heard, they may present arguments in favor of one or the other litigant. All men present have a right to speak if they so desire, and each is entitled to equal attention, in order to debate the relative merits of each side. The judge acts to keep order in the court and to help obtain facts, but he may also interact with the jury in an attempt to arrive at the consensus of opinion necessary for a final decision. (If agreement is not reached, the situation is similar to an American "mistrial," and a new trial must be held.)[2]

The kris offers an opportunity for young men to practice their rhetorical skills, and it also serves as a testing ground for future leaders. A pretty speech is aesthetically pleasing to all; but future leaders are chosen for their ability to gain a following rather than for their skill at using Romany. Some men have charisma, a magnetic personality drawing and holding people by a little understood force that is not amenable to much conscious ma-

[2]Brown 1929:162-63; Mitchell 1945: 49; Parry 1941:40. The European counterpart is reported by Maximoff 1947b: 41-42 and Yoors 1967:172-74.

nipulation by the leader himself. Other men gain followers by their power to argue convincingly, using rational presentation and inexorable logic. Still others achieve leadership through a slow process of proven merit added to proven merit; they may be strong in mind and body, but rather inarticulate.[3]

The charismatic leader and the "one-who-knows" are both men with a mystique; they are "chosen" by fate. But charisma can wane: a still more charismatic man may come upon the scene, or the enchantment may wear off as mysteriously as it arose. The one-who-knows is a slow starter, but as his success score builds up consistently, people begin to respect him. Furthermore, his wisdom ripens with age; only senility threatens his powers.

The debator-orator type is least mysterious; he is merely a gifted individual, but he can develop some of the qualities of the other two. He can cultivate the show-business personality of the charismatic and the intelligence and experience of the one-who-knows. He can improve his rhetoric, and he can learn to blend reason, logic, and emotional appeal into his arguments.

Oratory

The speakers are expected to use an oratorical style as elegant as they can muster. Romany, an Indo-Aryan language, has a number of declensions of nouns and verbs, like Latin; this grammatical feature allows the speaker to combine word stems in complex and poetic new ways. A theme can be exploited forcefully using direct language or subtly through the use of metaphor. A good orator draws upon a vast collection of proverbs to introduce and support his points. Gypsies are language-conscious; they each speak at least two languages: their own Romany and English (often several more). Romany has incorporated many loan words from the languages of the countries through which these nomads have passed; this means that the Gypsy language has many alternate ways of saying the same thing. These choices (and the knowledge that some words are indigenous to the language and some are not) are made

[3]These three types are analytic extremes; they do no exist except as constructs.

consciously because Romany is used as a secret language to identify fellow Gypsies and to talk to one another freely in the presence of outsiders. Thus, a loanword from Italian would not be used in Italy although a German word would be acceptable. (A nicety of this linguistic situation is that a story-teller will pick his words appropriately in relating tales about various countries.)[4] Such inculcated sensitivity to individual words conditions the Rom to a highly sophisticated critical approach to speaking, and oratory is a well appreciated art among the Gypsies. Persons who talk easily, carefully choosing their vocabulary, enunciating clearly, projecting a pleasantly deep-toned, musical voice are highly appreciated.

I discovered this in an accidental, roundabout way. As an anthropologist, I had received training in linguistics and knew I must learn the Romany language to pursue my studies among the Gypsies. I began to teach myself Romany using some old monographs on the language. Since Romany is a "secret" language, I did not expect help from my future informants in learning it. But learning a language from books (or in most classrooms, for that matter) produces a stultified, semi-archaic style that must be loosened up through exposure to the normal, daily speech of native speakers. The older books could not tell me about the language currently spoken, and languages change constantly. So my Romany sounded rather "dated"—like foreigners in the United States who speak an English they have learned on the Continent. Luckily for me, the Gypsies found my speaking attempts reminiscent of the oratorical style, and they encouraged my efforts. My *hira* ("reputation stories," the collection of anecdotes documenting my behavior, character, and personal life) included my speech habits, and now Rom approach me and ask me to "say a little bit in Romany." It has become my hallmark, and I am stuck with it.

Types of Cases

Broken promises on the division of profits, unfair sharing of expenses, alleged stealing from partners, failure to work the

---

[4] I am indebted to Mr. Jan Yoors for these points.

requisite number of hours, etc.—any of these kumpanja problems can lead to a kris (Brown 1929: 162; Maximoff 1947b: 42;
Yoors 1967: 122, 174-76).[5]

Divorce cases occupy a large part of the kris calendar in any
one year and generate a lot of interest and discussion, some of
which shades into gossip. Marriages arranged between families
require that an amount of money be given to the bride's parents
by the groom's family; although this money traditionally is referred to both by Gypsies and anthropologists as a "brideprice,"
the true purpose of this transaction is to legitimize the future
offspring of the union and to establish the groom's side as the
children's family; thus, "progeny price" would be a more appropriate term. In the event that the marriage breaks up, a kris
often is necessary to determine how much of the original price (if
any) should be returned to the husband's family. Any family
involved in a divorce kris is concerned about its reputation: if the
man's family develops a name for being rough on a *bori*
(daughter-in-law), it will have trouble not only in getting another
wife for the newly divorced man but also for all the other males
in the family. After several unfavorable divorce decisions any
future cases would tend to go against the man's family on the
principle that the existence of so many unhappy women is more
than coincidence—as we would say, where there is smoke, there
is fire. Similarly, more than one or two unsatisfactory boris from
the same family lead the Rom to suspect that the family involved
lacks the ability to raise females properly.

Gypsy attitudes toward marriage vary in basic ways from those
held by us. Marriage for them is quite definitely more than a
union of husband and wife; it involves a lifetime alliance between two extended families. The marriage is arranged between
the parents of each spouse, who contract to enter into a xanamik
(in-law) relationship together. The boy's side gives money to the
bride's family to establish rights to the children, but the bride's
family not only returns part of this progeny price "to share in the
marriage," as the Rom phrase it, but also sends the bride to her
new home with a trousseau and with enough household equipment to get the new family started. The equivalence of this
dowry in dollars may be almost as much as that of the so-called

[5]Case histories may be found in Brown 1929: 163.

brideprice. I also suspect that returning part of the brideprice may symbolize the right of the woman's family to exercise some influence on the marriage's children.

After the wedding, the groom's family carries the burden of the success of the marriage. The bori is actually a stranger within her husband's family, but she is a human being after all and thus has certain rights that must be honored. For example, a bori is entitled to an adequate amount of food, clothing, and rest; etiquette requires that she pretend not to want them, but good manners and common decency also require that her mother-in-law should insist that she get all of them. This polite charade helps to draw mother-in-law and daughter-in-law together into an affectionate mother/daughter relationship. In an ideal family, the mother-in-law will say to her own daughters, "The bori has worked hard enough; you finish cleaning the house now." If the daughters buy shoes (Gypsy women are partial to expensive high-heeled shoes), the mother instructs them to get a pair for the bori. I remember entering a Gypsy household one Sunday to discover that the daughters were grumbling because their mother had just issued orders that they could not go to the movies that day; they had gone out several evenings during the preceding week without the bori, and now they must stay home so she could enjoy a show, too.

Thus, the woman's family will often argue at a divorce kris that their daughter has been made to work constantly, that her in-laws have begrudged her food, that they have never bought her anything, that they have made her stay home all the time. If these charges are true, the woman is entitled to a redress of grievances.

The bori's natal family prepares her for marriage. Her family raised her; therefore, her character and personality are molded by them.[6] She should be quiet, shy, cooperative, obedient, and chaste. She should be skilled at fortunetelling and sewing, and have a knowledge of housekeeping. Once married, the bori must change her ways to those of her husband's family; she will learn (or relearn) how to cook and clean under her mother-in-law's tutelage. Her own mother should have prepared her to expect and accept this.

[6]Gypsies believe that at least some character traits are inherited biologically.

If the woman's parents (or brothers) suspect that their kins-woman is being mistreated, they are entitled to discuss the matter with the xanamik. If the woman's family thinks she looks ill, they have the right to investigate. In fact, if a bori becomes sick, her parents-in-law usually inform her own parents to protect themselves against charges of neglect. (Were she to die, her husband's family would be held responsible.)

In a divorce kris, the woman's side of the family may be charged with giving into marriage a girl improperly prepared, interfering in the affairs of the xanamik, or making trouble for them. If the wife's family is found guilty of these charges, they must return a substantial amount of the brideprice.

Thus far, no reference to the relationship between husband and wife has been made. No Gypsy would be surprised at this method of exposition because he, too, would consider the husband-wife aspect of marriage least important. Aside from having a sex partner and someone beside his mother to fulfill his needs and give him money, the groom experiences little change in his lifestyle when he marries. His age-peers may joke about his sexual activities, and his mother and sisters may tell him to ask his wife for something because they are too busy. Gypsy marriage is not predicated on romantic love, and the Rom frown against any display of affection between husband and wife.[7] The husband wants his wife to perform services for him, but he continues to spend much of his time with brothers and cousins. Husband and wife rarely go out together. The wife could complain that she does not see her husband, but the statement would be regarded as mere carping unless she means to imply that he is running around with other women (and even that, unless excessive *and* flagrant, is a minor infringement). The only legitimate complaint allowable is that her husband (or his relatives) beat her hard and often, and, here, too, it is a matter of degree since a mild amount of corporal punishment is considered acceptable.

A divorce kris is a difficult affair; but an additional complication may now arise in the form of a racket whereby some families marry off their daughters and then order the girls to return home. Since the court never requires that the full brideprice be returned and the possibility exists that the court will decide in

---

[7]This rule is beginning to change in some Kalderaš groups.

favor of the bride's family, an unscrupulous family could derive a good income from this trickery, especially if they select as their victims those families whose prior marital records make them poor risks for a new marriage. But kris means "justice," and it would not be just to allow perpetrators of a racket to profit from their crimes. So the court must keep track of the marriages and divorces of all the Rom to prevent chicanery (Brown 1929: 163).[8]

A third kind of trial, very delicate in nature, concerns peacemaking between feuding bands.[9]   Ordinarily, feuds between large extended families and/or bands are not controllable by uninvolved Gypsies.   However, because of marital and political alliances among the bands, a long-standing feud of serious proportions could become a whirlpool sucking more and more groups into its center and leading them all to annihilation. If the feuding parties do not act promptly to resolve their differences, each side is tempted into increasingly amoral behavior, leading to the involvement of non-Gypsies in purely Gypsy affairs, and thereby jeopardizing all the Rom of an area. When their own protection is threatened, the Gypsy bands may force the hotheads to bring their differences before a kris. The contending factions are not easily persuaded to arbitrate in court; the peacemakers often find themselves resorting to threats. They may recall their women from the contentious bands and refuse to give additional daughters; they may stop inviting the conflicting groups to Gypsy events; they may exclude them from economic partnerships; and they may refuse them assistance in times of need and illness—in short, they make life as unbearable as possible for the miscreants.

Eventually, both sides reluctantly agree to come to the peace table if a mutually acceptable judge can be found who will agree to arbitrate. Unimpeachable character, intelligence, a forceful personality, knowledge of law and precedent, familiarity with both bands but a lack of partiality to either, and leadership of an adequate number of men to enforce the terms of the armistice are the qualities that somehow must be found in one chief; moreover, that man must be willing to accept the assignment and its attendant risks. Such a man already enjoys maximum reputation among the Rom or he would not be asked to take the case.

[8]Case histories are included in Bercovici 1928: 221-22 and Brown 1929: 163.
[9]A related group of cases deal with elopement, as described in a case history by Lee 1972: 45-53.

Should either party in the dispute decide that the judge is being unfair, it may withdraw abruptly. Either side may attempt to cajole or threaten vulnerable members of the judge's family. Why should a Big Man step into so dangerous a situation? Most chiefs do refuse; in such a case, a judge may be sought for in another country or tribe. Often a peacemaker cannot be found, and there is no way to solve the problem. The situation may get so bad that everyone gives up, and the problem eventually dies of itself.

Economic and divorce cases deal with conflicts between individual families; these are "civil" suits. But peacemaking implies the existence of a war between Gypsy groups and implies the potential involvement of all Rom Gypsies; these cases may be viewed as the Romany equivalent of international law.

There is a fourth type of kris, the equivalent of our own "criminal" cases (Brown 1929: 163-67; Maximoff 1947: 41).[10] The parallel fits well insofar as a crime may be committed against an individual (theft, rape, murder), but it is viewed as an offense against Gypsy society as a whole, not just against the immediate victim or his family. Our criminal law is secular, and consequently we Americans differentiate between "crime" and "sin." Sin is defined in a religious context and may be handled in an ecclesiastical court; it is regarded as a crime against God. With the separation of church and state, we Americans find ourselves in a position in which what is criminal may not be sinful (say, speeding) and what is sinful may not be criminal (say, blaspheming).

Gypsies are not faced with this anomaly; for them sins (in the sense of transgressions against the godly way, the Gypsy way) are crimes and are subject to the kris. Crimes against nature and the universe belong here; they were of greater importance in the days of outdoor camps, the urban environment not being regarded as natural (and, therefore, not godly). Modern readers may be surprised to learn that these infringements deal with pollution. To the Rom, pollution is a great sin because it upsets the harmony of the universe. We would say today that pouring wastes into a stream ruins the ecology for all living things who depend upon its fresh, clean waters; the Gypsies have always said

---

[10]Case histories may be found in Yoors 1967: 151, 164, 176-79.

that fresh, clean water is God-given, for plants and animals depend on it for their very existence. In former times, the Rom avoided contact with people who used a brook as a laundry tub or a toilet or a garbage pail. Pollution was investigated, and, if the culprits were Gypsies, they were warned that they must stop their sinful acts or face the kris. Careless use of the environment enrages man and God.

In a way, pollution may be said to underlie the *marime* (*maxrime*) cases as well, if we keep in mind that the Gypsy concept of pollution carries the idea of upsetting the harmony of the universe. The term "marime" has been translated as "uncleanliness" or "ritual pollution"; it is a concept easily misunderstood by Americans because we use "polluted" as a synonym for "dirty." A Gypsy will look at a sparklingly clean object (such as a kitchen sink) and announce that it is marime because the sink has been used by former, non-Gypsy occupants who probably not only washed dishes in it but also clothing. Similarly, something or someone may be dirty (say, an individual who has not had a bath) but not necessarily marime. Americans tend to be shocked at visible dirt, but Gypsies abhor invisible pollution. (Incidentally, this attitudinal difference may help to explain why we Americans are not willing to take action against ecological pollution until its dire results are clearly visible to the eye.)

To understand marime, one must talk about Romany philosophy and theology, particularly cosmology—the beliefs about the universe. Everything has its appropriate place in the universe. Stars belong in the sky, and flora and fauna belong on earth. This reasoning leads to the conclusion that, for example, a "shooting star" may indicate a break in harmony, a sign that something may be wrong with the cosmos. Inspection of the universe also reveals that some creatures characteristically occupy an overlapping zone between two otherwise disparate cosmological habitats. Birds are one such example, for they fly about in the sky as well as roost in trees, walk on the earth, and sometimes even swim and dive in the water. Thus, they are set apart as "special," having, as it were, a cosmological dispensation to exist in different zones of the universe without fear of cosmological sanctions for breaking the laws against invasion of other beings' space. The sky zone belongs to the stars and to such spiritual beings as angels and unborn souls; the celestial environment is the legitimate habitat for beings more powerful than mortals, or, to put it another way, it is more sacred. Flying birds are safe in the sky and therefore they must be furnished protection. Their contacts with the celestial beings "rub off" on them giving them greater power—they are infected with the contagiousness of sacredness, which they can pass on to other beings who lack their own sacred protection (we would say "natural immunity"). Therefore, they are marime, and the Rom usually will not eat wild birds like pigeons (chickens and other domesticated fowl do not fly well and are edible).

There is a temporal as well as a spatial dimension to cosmological harmony, and the space/time combination adds the dynamic component to the universe that results in developmental cycles. After all, he who is now a mortal in the terrestrial environment of secular space once was an unborn soul in the celestial environment of sacred space (to which he will return after death). This temporal/cyclical aspect introduces a further nuance to marime: just as birds overlap cosmological space with impunity, so man's life-cycle affords varying dispensations in accordance with temporal stages. A baby, so recently come from the unborn soul habitat, carries with him his original sacred immunity, which only gradually wears off. Thus, young children can safely do many things marime (forbidden) to adults—including the eating of flying birds.

Birds are marime because they fly; other beings are marime periodically because they function as portals between celestial and terrestrial space; for example, women in their childbearing age. A woman is marime during and after childbirth and during her monthly menstrual period. She is in contact with the unborn soul habitat and she is potentially dangerous to men, who lack the natural protection given to females. Also, feminine marime waxes and wanes imperceptibly in a short-term monthly cycle and in a long-term life cycle; understandably, men tend always to be a little cautious about these creatures. Marime ensures a safe distance between masculine and feminine space/time.

Women must not associate with men after childbirth and during menstruation, and this rule is extended to apply to anything belonging to men and women. A marime woman may not cook or serve food to men. She may not step over anything belonging to a man or allow her skirts to touch his things.

Women's clothing must be washed separately from men's. A husband may not sleep with his wife during the menstrual period, of course.[11]

The human body also has differentiated zones based on marime. The head is sacred and subject to pollution; nothing should be allowed to pass over it. On the other hand, the feet step on the ground, and the body wastes find their egress in the lower part of the trunk; thus, these regions are areas furnishing potential pollution. A convenient dividing boundary is the waist-belt: below it is marime, and above it is neutral, with the head and neck set off as sacred. One's own hands cannot touch one's head safely unless one blows on the fingers immediately thereafter (Bonos 1942: 262-64; Brown 1929: 163-65).[12]

None of these protections is followed by non-Gypsies, so the gaǰe are marime, and too close an association with them, especially sexual, is polluting.

Marime regulations pervade all of life, and it is difficult to honor all of them at all times, even if one so desires. Young Gypsies, imbued with the pulsating vitality of the everyday world and trained from infancy to self-reliance and self-pride, tend to be careless, not only about their own possible pollution but also that of their elders. It is not surprising, therefore, that the Rom realistically accept the infringement of marime rules as a fact of daily life.

Most ostensible marime cases actually hide other conflicts in Romany life that have not been resolved through the use of regular channels.[13] Desperation underlies these trials, and a permanently successful conclusion of a marime kris means that the court must diplomatically arbitrate the hidden issues. For instance, a bori, far from her own relatives, unable to get fair treatment from her husband and in-laws and reluctant to leave her children, will try to obtain justice by throwing her skirt over her husband's head during a large party with many witnesses

[11]This is confirmed for Kalderaš in Russia by Bercovici 1928: 22-23; other sources for Rom in Europe include Starkie 1937: 103 and Vesey-FitzGerald 1944: 46. For a comparison with English Gypsy beliefs and practices, refer to Thompson 1929: 33-39 and 1922: 15-43.

[12]A good description of Lovara beliefs may be found in Yoors 1967: 24, 150-51, 165. The formal kris declaration is given in Yoors 1971: 88-89.

[13]Brown 1929: 165 cites one example.

from several bands present. The elders cannot ignore the incident under these circumstances, and the unfortunate young woman is assured a public hearing.

I myself once had occasion to employ to my advantage the potential of a marime kris. A middle-aged man had persisted in paying me unwanted attention all afternoon at the chief's house where I am an adopted daughter. So, in order to discourage him, I began sweeping the rug and threatened to throw the broom over his head if he did not desist. Having contact with the floor on which feet tread, a broom is marime (this is the basis for the contention that Gypsies "fear" a broom); if the broom passes over one's head, one becomes marime, too. In the instance mentioned, my persecutor stopped short, thought a minute and with a studied lack of concern said he did not think that I, a non-Gypsy, could initiate a marime complaint. I replied that the legal issues were interesting and perhaps a new precedent could be set. The situation, I continued, had good dramatic potential and should provide days of gossip afterward—an innocent girl trying to defend herself against an older married man with daughters of his own. Unfortunately for the history of jurisprudence, the man left abruptly, and we shall never know what would have happened at the kris.

Marime charges may be filed against anyone who is intractable to the discipline and rules of his own family if the head of the extended family finds it necessary. Gypsy law does not recognize juvenile delinquency as a legal category; in fact, the idea would conflict with the dogma that the family head is responsible for the actions of all its members. Any misdeeds by even the junior members might lead to a trial of the Big Man. Consequently, if a recalcitrant youth persists in his crimes despite warnings and threats, the Big Man protects himself and the honor of the family by instituting marime proceedings against the culprit —manufacturing evidence if necessary.

When regular checks and balances between the prerogatives of leaders and the prerogatives of followers or the normal equilibrium among chiefs in a common area break down, so that the masses are burdened by a tyrannical ruler, marime may again come to the rescue. The offender is maneuvered into a polluting situation; when the case comes to trial, others come forward to testify to still other violations of marime. If the chief is convicted, he loses leadership, and he may never recover his loss of prestige.

A marime sentence is a severe punishment. As a matter of fact, it is too harsh on the culprit and too presumptuous of the Rom, who feel that, if a truly heinous sin has been committed, God Himself will see to the punishment in His own time.

One of the most famous Gypsy chiefs became a leader when he was only a thirteen-year-old youth. He was with a large and powerful band in Serbia headed by his father. The boy was intelligent but too ambitious to wait for his father to pass his leadership on to him. Thus, secretively, he approached some of the Big Men to suggest that they change their affiliation and form a new group under his leadership. Apparently, the youth was a convincing talker, and a number of families swore allegiance to him and broke away from the main band. The Rom were taken completely by surprise; according to the narrative I heard, the wily old chief knew nothing about these plans. The Gypsies were angered at the boy's actions and proposed to the grief-striken father that the boy be captured and held for a marime kris. The old chief refused to allow such a move and successfully used his great influence to prevent the Rom from finding his son. Word of the aborted plans having reached the new young chief, he decided to leave the area before a change of heart occurred, and he led his followers across the ocean to the New World. In the Americas, the band's fortunes thrived. The chief formed an alliance with a very powerful South American chief, who gave guidance and protection to the youth. When difficulties arose, the band made its way up to Mexico and then crossed the United States border, first locating in Chicago and then in New York City. Each move brought greater fame to the band and its chief and attracted more followers, but the group's reputation was predicated as much on its sharp practices as on its prosperity. It was respected because it was feared. Finally after World War II, the run of luck reversed: the chief had been imprisoned for draft evasion; the new chief was ineffectual and unable to control the large segment of the band that had joined up in South America; and other Gypsy bands and tribes were obtaining most of the financial profits available. The families that had deserted the old chief in Serbia were finding it increasingly hard to survive. When I commiserated with them, they shrugged their shoulders and said, "It is our punishment for all the bad things we have done. We never should have left our [old] chief, for he was a good as well as a wise man. We must atone for our sins."

Since God's universe can correct miscarriages of justice, Gypsies should concentrate on being helpful and understanding toward their fellow men. Therefore, there is a means whereby a permanent marime decree can be reversed. If a person under marime proscription can get some Rom to talk to him privately (it must be in secret; otherwise, the other Gypsy runs the risk of being declared marime by known association with a polluted one), he may convince him that he, the offender, deserves another trial. The man who promises to act as intermediary then talks to some of the influential men to see if they are willing to allow the outcast to return. If there is strong public feeling that the culprit has suffered enough, another kris is scheduled. This type of trial is very popular not only because of its nature but also because the defendant must pay for all the food and drink involved (however, he himself may not partake until and unless he wins his appeal—such sharing symbolizes his reincorporation into the group). Since several hearings sometimes are necessary before reinstatement is achieved, the defendant is paying dearly for the trial—and this, too, is considered part of the initial penalty.

The Procedure of the Kris

The personnel of the kris assemble at a prearranged time (announced sufficiently in advance to allow everyone to assemble, from different parts of the country if necessary) and at a prearranged place (either the home of the judge or a hall hired for the purpose). A kris involves a lot of talking, and talking is thirsty work; beer, wine, or liquor are legitimate courtroom supplies. In fact, if the trial promises to be lengthy, food must be procured for the participants. The expenses are paid by the guilty party at the conclusion of the trial (our courts, too, often require the guilty side to pay courtroom damages).

The plaintiff/accuser and his spokesman present their version of the case, followed by the defendant and his spokesman. Witnesses give their testimony, and the judge and jury may ask for clarification, additional data, and supporting evidence. All evidence must be carefully examined, and all who give testimony may be required to take oaths. Gypsies feel that lying to one's people in a serious situation such as a kris should not be a matter of mere human action, so Gypsy oaths carry supernatural sanctions for perjury. The Rom believe firmly in the efficacy of such oaths.

Indeed, oaths are so effective that they may substitute for a kris. Jan Yoors told me once of their use among the European Lovara tribe (1967:176-79): A woman found that her valuables had been stolen. The chief called all the people together and made them individually take an oath that they were innocent of the crime—they would die if they did not speak the truth. Within a few months, someone in the band sickened and died; the thief had been punished by God. Incidentally, this anecdote carries a postscript: the original victim of the theft regretted deeply that she had initiated the proceedings, for she felt responsible for the ensuing death. In her eyes, she was an indirect murderer.

Gypsy law also accepts in principle the ordeal as a form of justice, although I do not have personal knowledge of its use in the United States. Usually some substance is given to the plaintiff and defendant to swallow, and only the guilty party becomes ill.

Americans are often dubious about supernatural sanctions, but they will accept the results of lie detector tests. Lie detectors measure physiological changes which are subject to emotional states; in other words, these instruments indirectly measure feelings of guilt. Through suggestion, guilt feelings can produce psychosomatic symptoms in the culprit, and this knowledge serves as the basis for oaths and ordeals. Modern physicians are aware of the relationship between emotional and somatic reactions, and the eminent American physiologist Walter B. Cannon documented the existence of "Voodoo Death" in 1942 (1942: 169-81). Thus, we know the working of the human psyche can produce illness and even death if there is faith; therefore, oaths and ordeals can work if one believes in them as the Gypsies do.

After the facts of a particular case have been sorted out, the kris must consider the body of law that appertains. The Gypsies recognize a body of customary law, a series of edicts originally abstracted from the age-old practices of the people.[14] Romany not being a written language, formal codification cannot be demonstrated; but the Gypsies, like many of the possessors of unwritten languages, emphasize rote memorization of long verbal statements, and oral transmission must be letter-perfect. Oral material can be preserved and transmitted in this fashion, if the people consider it worthwhile. For example, Polynesians consider genealogy essential information for their way of life, for a man's status depends upon that of his ancestors. As a result, some Polynesians can not only recite long chains of ancestors for forty-odd generations but also such facts as the migration routes used to arrive at their particular island, together with navigational hazards, historical battles with other people encountered   along the way, and the sacred names of the canoes and their equipment.

Since customary law is so important to the Gypsies, many men have memorized much of it, and the youths of the chiefly families know that a thorough command of these laws is a necessary skill for aspirants to leadership. Hence, they devote much time and energy to kris law.

A legal system, to endure and serve its people, must be flexible—capable of innovation and responsive to changing needs. The Gypsy system has adapted, too. Some rules simply are overlooked when they no longer can be followed; for instance, the Gypsies today ignore the fact that apartments are stacked one on top of the other. The use of sanitary napkins now serves as an excuse to lessen the rigors of seclusion during menstruation, and the use of hospitals for childbirth means that parturients can return to normal responsibilities within days. As urban living caused increasing crowding for the Rom, their laws pertaining to territoriality have been revised. Fortunetelling locations that were rented from outsiders could be relocated without financial loss, and the rule that such places must be spaced three blocks apart worked no great hardship upon the bands even though close spacing tended to "use up" a neighbor-

[14]Yoors 1967: 147 refers to it as *"bayura"*; see also his 1947: 1-18.

hood more rapidly. However, some of the Rom in New York have invested in real estate, living and doing business in their own properties; they cannot afford to sell out and relocate, and territorial regulations now include the amendment that Gypsy places of business in property owned by Gypsies must be surrounded by a ten-block protective zone.

Making new laws by a formal proclamation shades imperceptibly into precedent law wherever there is no formal legislative body (the Council of Elders is a local group, having jurisdiction only over its own band). Precedent law is based on the record of decisions made in earlier trials. The participants argue that the circumstances of the current case are similar to or identical with at least one earlier case and imply that the kris at hand should have a similar outcome. Since no two situations in life ever are identical in all respects, arguing by precedent allows much difference of opinion. One need hardly add that no litigant will refer to earlier cases with final decisions contradicting his own hoped for verdict. Frequently, parallels to the immediate case exist in a number of precedent-setting cases, with conflicting outcomes. Precedent law is a safety valve, allowing a legal system to respond to change fairly rapidly, but at the cost of increasing the confusion in the system. (These conclusions will not surprise students of jurisprudence.)

Laws are meant to deal with an infinite number of legal problems, classified and arranged according to a finite number of principles and types. The underlying aim is to cut down the number of major decisions that must be made. But laws are like mass-produced clothing: they rarely fit any individual exactly without additional alteration. One way whereby a law can be changed to fit the circumstances is by applying the concept of extenuating circumstances. Gypsies place more value on extenuating circumstances than we do; they can afford to because they have a more detailed knowledge of their own people that is applicable in a kris. Our urban society has been characterized as "uninvolved"; we can live in the same apartment house for a decade and still have only a nodding acquaintance with our immediate neighbors. But Gypsy bands are smaller, and relationships are on a face-to-face basis. Everybody knows everybody else—or someone who does. Hence a participant in a kris is bound to know the litigants and their backgrounds. Pleas of extenuating circumstances may be validated immediately; someone in the jury may act as *amicus curiae* and furnish evidence of unbearable inequities, past unresolved grievances, and the like.

But wherein does justice reside? How does one make the wrong right again? The optimal solution would be to turn back the clock and prevent the harm from occurring; this being impossible, one may either concentrate on punishing the wrongdoer or trying to restore the loss to the victim. The first is the basis for punitive law; the punishment visited upon the culprit not only makes him suffer, thereby satisfying the vengeful desires of the victim's side, but also furnishes a warning of what will happen to anyone else who commits the same offense. Restitutive law, however, attempts to restore the loss to the victim. The biblical eye-for-an-eye is an example of punitive law, whereas the Plains Indian custom of having the murderer's family turn over one of its own members to replace the dead man is an example of restitutive law. In American law, capital punishment is punitive, but the payment of damages is restitutive. Gypsy justice emphasizes restitutive law in cases involving economic partnerships or divorce; money changes hands to redress "accounting mistakes" in the former instance or to equate with value received in the latter. Marime, rape, and murder come under the jurisdiction of punitive law. The verdict of marime declares the offender beyond the pale of Gypsy society; he is polluted and carries the danger of infectiousness. No one may mention his name, sleep with him, eat with him, or associate with him in any way—he is a pariah.

A permanent marime sentence is the most severe punishment; it is a living death in Gypsy eyes, and, if the outcast sees no way to win reinstatement into the society of Rom, he may well prefer ending his life by suicide. In fact, permanent marime sentences are regarded as the equivalent of death sentences. Would it not be easier and surer to kill the guilty party, then? The answer is yes, but it is much more of a risk to the executioner because of Gypsy beliefs in the *mule*, the ghosts of the dead. Not every marime, however, is permanent.

When a person dies, life departs from the corpse, which is then an empty hulk subject to putrefaction. But the individuality is not destroyed all at once. It separates gradually into several layers. Eventually, the soul component rejoins the habitat of unborn souls to await rebirth at some future time; this soul is a proper harmonic segment of the universe. Another layer of the individuality is the shadow or ghost; it is reluctant to leave its former dwelling, the body, and it is jealous of those who are still alive. It is also lonely in its anomalous half-world of being neither completely mortal nor immortal. The soul, being a legitimate part of the universe, consists of the beneficial elements of the deceased's personality; it retains that small portion of the omnipotent universe-force that is both life and divinity ("A little bit of God lives in all of us," my Gypsy friends explain to me). The soul, in its love of those left behind and its feeling of duty toward them is saddened to leave this world; but all souls will again meet their loved ones in the place of unborn souls. Now, at the time of death, they await reunion patiently. Rituals are performed to speed the soul on its way, as we shall see in the next chapter.

The ghost, on the other hand, will disintegrate, just as the body does, but more slowly and unpredictably. It is not a harmonic entity in the universe but a waste-product of psychospiritual living analogous to the body wastes given off by the flesh. The ghost retains all those aspects of individuality that are dislikable, in conflict with the laws of man and the universe. It is marime, disharmonic, unpleasant, and frightening. Most ghosts, luckily, are weak—powerless to do much harm—and subject to rapid disintegration. But someone who has met a violent end, whose life has been cut short before its proper time, has a powerful, vindictive ghost. It is as if everyone at birth were doled out a specified amount of vitality by the universe and if that vitality is not used up, the remainder stays with the ghost. Obviously, taking this belief as fact, one can see why Gypsies avoid killing people directly and have recourse to marime, which is an indirect form of executing them—without the chance of an angry ghost coming after one for revenge or company. As a result, Gypsies believe that a murderer will be punished by the ghost of his victim even if the Rom fail to do anything about the crime, or that a desperate Gypsy who cannot take advantage of marime as a form of escape may be driven to suicide so that he will become a powerful ghost and be able to take his revenge in that fashion. Suicide rates are very low among mature Gypsies in their thirties or older, but high among young people from fifteen to their early twenties. (Even so, suicide rates are not high as compared to other groups; in the 20-odd years that I have known the Rom, I have heard of only six instances.)

Young people threaten suicide; older people will threaten murder as capital punishment. In theory, if not in practice, there are only three types of situations that would elicit a death sentence: (1) A chief who ignored his own Big Men and, on his own initiative, violated Romany law could be killed by his people. When I first requested permission to study the Gypsies, I obtained approval from the chief. Two weeks thereafter, however, the chief's father (a former very powerful leader himself) told me that the Council of Elders would kill his son if I continued my work. Naturally I said I would stop until the Council gave its permission and I would be willing to come before the Big Men to answer any questions they might have and to let them get to know me. However, I was given the Council's permission in a few weeks. (2) A person considered to be a malevolent witch could be killed.[15] (3) A wife (or perhaps a daughter) who had committed a crime could be killed by her husband (father). In 1973, a Gypsy band threatened to kill a woman who had brought her baby into a hospital for surgery; the little boy had cancer and the mother's decision to risk whatever time her son had left to live by allowing an operation meant that she also risked her own life if he died on the operating table or as a result of the operation. The boy is still alive and so is she.

Should resort be made to capital punishment, the entire group making the decision must also share in the executioner's job to prevent revenge by the ghost. The Gypsies have a notion that there is safety in numbers, but as they are not sure of it, they seldom kill.

Lack of enforceability is a basic weakness of the kris system, and there is no mechanism within the culture to compensate for this. The whole institution is predicated upon an honor system whereby a man's word is a solemn pledge that must be fulfilled; it presupposes voluntary participation—otherwise, it falls apart. "What can be done with Gypsies who do not obey their own laws?" the Rom ask rhetorically and shrug their shoulders helplessly.[16]

[15]A novel in French by the Kalderaš Gypsy Matéo Maximoff, *The Ursitory*, includes a description of one such execution.

[16]Yoors 1967: 174 is in substantial agreement.

The Gypsy and Gaje Justice

The inability of Gypsy society to enforce kris law often forces the
Rom into taking advantage of the gajo penal system. Gypsies
have had long experience with gajo law, often being on the
receiving end as accused criminals of one kind or another.
Non-Gypsy law (in terms of recognized offenses and their attendant penalties) seems quite arbitrary to the Rom, and they
hardly respect the American legal system. But, like other aspects
of the non-Gypsy world, it is there to be exploited when necessary. "Unfair economic competition" may not be a recognized
crime in a local police station, but "predicting the future" is; just
inform on the other fortuneteller and sit back to await results.
Do you wish to get rid of another Gypsy chief in the area? All the
Rom know that the young men do most of the driving and have
the least money; therefore, many parking tickets on automobiles
registered in the name of a chief go unpaid (the youths hide
them to prevent being scolded). Let the police know about it, too,
and the rival chief becomes a scofflaw. He will be required to pay
the fines and with any luck at all he will be imprisoned for a
while.

Once having been driven to make gajo law serve Gypsy purposes, one easily goes a bit further and manufactures a little
evidence. A feud with another vitsa will probably lead to some
violence anyway, so how wrong is it to accuse them of jeopardizing the morals of minors by child marriage? Now, all Gypsies
know that respectable marriages among the Rom require an
economic transaction and a formal recognition *via* a Gypsy wedding; they do not require a marriage license. This means that
Gypsy marriages, in terms of non-Gypsy law, are technically
consensual unions, requiring the agreement of both parties, who
must be beyond the age of consent. Gypsies also know that at first
marriage the age of the bride and groom often is below 18 or
even 16. This information is neither common knowledge among
outsiders nor legally condonable by them. Both Gypsies and
non-Gypsies know the gaje attitudes toward making girls under
sixteen sexually available and encouraging young boys to have
sexual congress. Thus, the gaje unwittingly have provided a
marvelous opportunity for harrassing a Gypsy family; indig-
nantly one informs local authorities that a little boy and a little

girl are living together as man and wife with the full knowledge and approval of their parents. Or, one complains that a certain Gypsy man (who happens to be a chief, although this is not mentioned) is extorting protection money from Gypsy families (it is tax collection time for the vitsa treasury).

In the instances mentioned, the informer's statement is quite accurate literally; he merely takes advantage of the existence of conflict between Gypsy and non-Gypsy law. Such behavior goes against the interest of Gypsy society because it violates the rule against involving the outside world in Gypsy affairs. But little can be done about it since the informer is protected by gajo law. On the principle of fighting fire with fire, a cycle of informing and counter-informing may be initiated. Once non-Gypsies are allowed into the lives of Gypsies, they tend to probe deeper and deeper. They learn considerably more than is safe for them to know, and the inevitable result is that every Gypsy family in the vicinity, originally involved in the argument or not, becomes a casualty of the warfare (i.e., at least one member of each family is accused of some non-Gypsy crime).

This situation has several possible solutions, most of which are fairly extreme. One alternative is for everyone to leave town until things cool down again. In addition to the difficulty of relocation itself, this may entail a major reshuffling of vitsa affiliations with the possible loss of some of one's hard-won status and the danger that another group may move in and take over in one's absence. Another choice is for the Big Men of all of the bands to meet and resolve the internal conflicts in a kris; then they all work together to move the gaje out of the picture by pooling resources and greasing non-Gypsy palms liberally. This alternative is the preferable one—if (a large if) they all behave like honorable men and keep their bargain and if they can manage to control all the factions under them. The first course of action is a desperate last resort, and the second often is too idealistic to be practical. By default, a third move may be made: all endure the situation as manfully as possible and wait for human nature to do the rest. Sooner or later, someone will cross the boundary line from a half-truth to a complete lie, both from the Gypsy and the gajo points of view. Recently, for example, a Gypsy accused another one of kidnapping. The truth was established easily; the accuser had sent his wife and children to another city. The gajo authorities, becoming as weary of the whole situation as the majority of the Gypsies, began to ignore the complaints and counter-complaints, and the entire affair died under its own weight.

The Gypsies and Gajo Crime

Gypsies are often involved as defendants in gaje criminal proceedings because they have no regard for non-Gypsy law even while they are aware that they are breaking it. Fortunetelling, *per se*, is a crime in many states; this is accepted as an occupational hazard. Some groups will work confidence games, pick pockets, steal, and rob; the victims are always non-Gypsies, for a Rom must not perpetrate these acts on other Rom. Gypsies may occasionally use strong-arm methods, but they are never hired killers. Perhaps their reluctance to murder explains why they never become members of national crime syndicates. Some twenty years ago, the few who dabbled in small-scale narcotics operations voluntarily withdrew (smuggling other contraband is still acceptable; in fact smuggling has long been a traditional Romany pursuit). Thus, stretching or breaking the law is part of the Gypsy way of life.

The Gypsies protect themselves in the same fashion as other lawbreakers. They bribe local officials. Most of their crimes are relatively petty and quite nonviolent, and cash and valuables may be lost but the victim retains life, limb, and sanity. The police are well aware of this and ordinarily prefer to go after other types of criminals on the basis of higher priority. Furthermore, the Gypsy fortunetelling clientele includes many marginal types; in the course of fortunetelling readings much information is gleaned which is of little import to the Gypsies themselves but highly useful to the police. . . and "One hand washes the other," teaches our proverb. Tradeoff of information for protection is abetted by the structure of the law enforcement agencies, where one division has little communication with and no control over the others. For instance, I went to help out in a fortunetelling location one evening and found a pleasant-looking man sitting and relaxing in the front. No introductions were offered, and I asked for none. Several times, people came in for readings, which were given, and we returned to our rather desultory conversation with the visitor. When he left, my Gypsy sister mentioned casually that he was a detective on the Narcotics Squad. She was quite amused at my reaction.

Other Relations with the Gajo World

The Gypsies have only a slight acquaintance with non-Gypsy ways, despite their need to know more about the gaje's way of life. They rarely enter non-Gypsy homes, and they have only a vague idea about many non-Gypsy occupations. They must know about gaje law, the local political structure (official and informal), transportation routes, communication methods. To tell fortunes successfully, they must understand the usual problems faced by their customers, their frustrations, their deepset worries, and their secret hopes.

However, those people who become steady customers are not representative of the total American population. Well-adjusted, happy, successful people do not spend their time behind a fortuneteller's curtains; disturbed, lonely, rejected people with psychopathologies often do. The Gypsies are also familiar with people "on the take" who accept Gypsy bribes and hang around for more favors. Other people with whom Gypsies interact habitually are tradespeople. The first two groups are slightly unsavory. The third entertains prejudices against the Rom, expecting them to steal; to compensate, they overcharge the Rom, act suspiciously, and treat them roughly. We who live fully within the American culture know that Gypsies are most apt to meet and interact with a special stratum of the population, not with a representative sample. We know it, but the Gypsies do not. They are convinced that the people with whom they come into frequent contact are typical of all gaje. They do not like what they see, and they generalize the faults they find to all gaje and reach the conclusion that non-Gypsies are unclean, despicable, subhuman creatures who should be avoided as much as possible.

The prejudices held by the Rom against the gaje are reciprocated by the non-Gypsies. In this way, Merton's self-fulfilling hypothesis (1957: *passim*) comes into play. The Gypsy approaches the non-Gypsy expecting trouble, and the non-Gypsy approaches the Gypsy suspiciously, expecting double-dealing. A clash is probable under the circumstances, and both will leave the encounter fully reinforced in their prejudices. For example, a physician was called in to attend a very sick Gypsy baby; he was not the first doctor called, but he was the first willing to come. We escorted him toward the back bedroom, but he stopped short of the threshold of the patient's room. "This visit will be fifteen dollars, and you owe me five dollars from the last time. Pay me the twenty dollars before I see the patient," he demanded. "Okay, okay, you'll get it—just look at the baby now," the Gypsies pleaded. Several more go-arounds occurred before I intervened. Ten dollars changed hands, and the doctor examined the patient. After the visit, I discovered the Gypsies, in revenge, did not intend to pay the other ten dollars. Each new experience adds to the general feeling of resentment: the many times sheriffs came by and made the band break camp and move to the next county while a woman was in the middle of childbirth; the places where the local people would not allow the Gypsies into food stores but insisted that the Rom pay dearly for foodstuffs they could neither choose nor see (the food was rotten); and so on.

Any positive interactions with non-Gypsies are considered to be atypical. They are forgotten rapidly if the personal exchange was a casual and temporary one. On the other hand, once having been convinced that a specific non-Gypsy is as much a decent human being as they, Gypsies do not forget it easily and show their gratitude. My friendship with the Gypsies puzzles them, for I accept no recompense for any services I can render, and my relaxed, approving attitude in allowing my children to interact with them is a subject for thought. I do not fit the facts of non-Gypsy behavior and so I must be explained. Some of the Rom believe I am part Gypsy. I demurred, pointing out that my people are as stringent about marriages only within the group as the Rom themselves. Another hypothesis, the one to which I suspect most now subscribe, is that I was a Gypsy in a former incarnation.

Distrust and suspicion are the keynotes of relations with non-Gypsies. These attitudes act as a distortion lens through which the Gypsies view the outside world. They also function effectively to isolate the Rom from intensive, intimate contact, and hence from many possibilities at sociocultural borrowing.

6

GYPSY RELIGION AND PHILOSOPHY

American culture often sets religion apart from the rest of life's activities; for instance, we differentiate between the "sacred" and the "profane" or "secular." We go to church on Sunday and on special holy days, but often religion does not enter our lives on the other six days of the week. We view life and the universe as divided between the common, everyday, "natural" on the one hand and the special, occasional, "supernatural" on the other. In fact, this distinction is so basic to our thinking that even anthropologists, who should know better, often use "supernatural" as a synonym for "religion" and imply that it is set off from the mundane world because it is "above-natural." However, there are many cultures in the world, such as that of the Gypsies, where spirits and powers are considered an integral part of the natural world and are part of everyday life. For such groups, religion and philosophy tend to merge, as we have seen in the discussions of the kris.

Established Religion and the Gypsies

To survive, the Gypsies tended to accept the dominant religion of the area in which they lived.

This was one way to avoid religious persecution, of course, and the non-Gypsy was content to assume the Gypsies' conversion at face value. Conversion was rapid but superficial. This suited the Gypsies (as it had some American Indian and African groups as well), who incorporated the established religion into their preexistent practices and beliefs. Traditionally tolerant and respectful toward all religions, the Rom readily have absorbed practices around them. So, in Spain, Italy, and France, they become Roman Catholic; in England usually Protestant; and in southeast Europe (occupied for so long by Muslim conquerors) they are either Muslim or Greek Orthodox (Grellman 1807: 79-80; Clébert 1963: 133-34; Maximoff 1946b: 108-09; Yoors 1967: 6). Here in the United States, the Rom usually follow the Eastern Rites of the Catholic Church, mainly because so many of them came to this country from areas of Europe in which they were practiced (Brown 1929: 170; Mitchell 1945: 48; Parry 1941: 20; Wright 1947: 132; for Canada, Moriarty 1929: 180).

A rather special situation exists in Europe where the Festival of Saint Sarah is held every summer. Saint Sarah is supposed to have been a Gypsy who volunteered to attend the Virgin Mary and Mary Magdalene after the Crucifixion. These saints are said to have landed on the coast of southwest France, accompanied by a faithful, dark Gypsy handmaiden. There is an underground chapel at Saintes Marie de la Mer, France, with a statue of a swarthy lady, Saint Sarah, and Gypsies make a pilgrimage to her. The Sedentary Gypsies, especially those of Spain and France, attend the festival frequently, and some of the Rom participate in fulfillment of a personal vow. The festival combines sincere religious fervor and gay carnival spirit; and in recent years, it has attracted many tourists from all over the world and drawn other Gypsies to the area for business purposes (Cowles 1948: 19-33; Clébert 1963: 141-44; Esty 1969:78-89; Starkie 1953).

The Rom proverb "A Gypsy goes to church twice in his lifetime—once to be baptized and once to be buried" is a cynical if somewhat misleading statement. The Rom are fascinated by all religions, and the subject interests them as a topic for philosophical discourse and debate. But the men usually leave the religious duties to the women. I suspect that they feel they are practicing the Gypsy religion constantly by participating in the kris, although they do not actually say so. The women, on the other hand, have no such decision-making role in the kris, but they are active in the arrangement and maintenance of an altar area in their homes and stores. They set up icons, decorate them

with figurines and artificial flowers, light candles, and sometimes burn incense.

Most of the icons show either the Infant Jesus or Saint Anne.
There are surprisingly few pictures of the adult Christ or of the
Virgin Mary (unless She is holding the Babe). These preferences
are consistent with other Romany values and beliefs. For instance, Gypsy fear of ghosts probably explains the apparent
antipathy toward crucifixes and the Crucifixion scene. The
Romany pleasure in babies, however, and their belief in the
spiritual proximity between infants and angels probably explains the universal appeal of the Holy Infant. Icons of the adult
Christ are rarely displayed; the Gypsies feel little awe for a
grown man in the prime of life. The Rom feel that that particular
stage of life has the least connection with godly pursuits; it is the
Gypsy equivalent of the Hindu "householder" phase of life, that
period when a man is most involved with earthly affairs. Mary as
Mother affords an easy identification with the young married
women, but they, like their husbands, are concentrating their
attentions on economic pursuits. Thus, most icons of the Virgin
Mary are found in the fortunetelling stores in which the young
women spend most of their time, and they turn to the Holy
Virgin for comfort when they are having problems of adjustment to their in-laws or want a child. The older women also tend
to regard Mary as a bori and, therefore, feel little affinity toward
Her. Since the dwelling units are in the care of the mothers-in-
law, fewer icons of the Virgin appear there (except for the
Meksikaja and Arxentina groups, whose older members spent so
much time in Latin America, where the Virgin cults figure
prominently). The older women favor icons of Saint Anne,
considering her a logical saint for them in their capacity as
grandmother and mother-in-law, to whom they can turn for
help with their own problems.

Although the men are not interested in icon-worship, they do
participate in the religious fêtes. A number of saints' days are
honored with special meals and plenty to drink, arranging for
singing and dancing, and inviting relatives and friends to join
them. St. Nicholas Day may serve as an illustration (compare
with the Greek Nomads' Saska's Feast [Myers 1945: 92-93]). This
festival is held in the middle of December, and it is distinguished
by the absence of all meat. In addition to salads, vegetables, and

fruits, all kinds of fish are served—fish soups, fish stews, baked whole fish. Each participating household prepares a feast and decorates the room with artificial flowers, crêpe-paper ornaments, candles, etc. Whisky punch is readied, and the members dress in new clothing. The arrival of visitors is the cue for the hostess to greet each person by pouring a soup-ladleful of punch into his or her mouth. When everyone has had at least one drink, the older couples sit down to eat and drink while the younger people provide the entertainment. Then the others eat, and the older people leave to attend the other parties to which they have been invited; the younger girls and women of the household clean up and then they, too, leave for the next party. Occasionally, some families hire a catering hall for their segment of the movable feast because their own homes are not large enough to accommodate all the guests. Thus, the entire day, starting around eleven o'clock in the morning and continuing late into the next morning, is devoted to a wholehearted celebration of St. Nicholas Day.

The Rom also celebrate the name days of the older men. Mature Gypsies do not usually remember their birthdates and therefore cannot celebrate birthdays even if they wish to do so. Instead, a baro's wife and children will hold an annual party for him on his name day—the day of the religious calendar reserved for the saint whose name he shares (Brown 1929: 171; Mitchell 1945: 47-48). Name day celebrations are private affairs, held at the home of the celebrant and with a limited guest list. Like most parties, the integral elements are food, drink, and music. (The name days of women, if celebrated at all, are modest versions of the men's, and the guests tend to be older female relatives and friends.) Nowadays, however, it is customary to celebrate the birthday of children.

The Gypsies enjoy parties of all kinds, and any excuse for a celebration seems acceptable. So the Rom honor Christmas and Easter twice—once following the American calendar and again according to the Orthodox calendar. Similarly, United States Gypsies have enthusiastically adopted Thanksgiving and New Year's (Cohn 1973: 33-35; Parry 1941: 40; Wright 1947: 132-33).

The Gypsy also takes an interest in miracles. He reacts to them with respect but also with reserve. Some sixteen years ago,

Philadelphians became excited over the reported appearance of the image of the Virgin Mary in some local trees. The Rom of Philadelphia spread the word to those of New York City, some of whom traveled to the site and returned with photographic "evidence" purporting to show Her form in the foliage. The possibility that one could actually see St. Mary in the photographs was the subject of heated discussion, those who took the pictures averring that She appeared more clearly in the foliage when one was present in person. A debate then developed between those who considered photographs more reliable evidence than sense-data (on the basis that a form of group hysteria could be at work) and those who felt that spirits would not necessarily register on photographic film. Word came that the Virgin had revealed to some children that She would reappear on a Sunday, and some New York Rom met to determine if they would organize motor caravans to Philadelphia. The group I attended finally decided not to make a pilgrimage on the grounds that (1) others would be on hand to act as witnesses; (2) it might be a farce, and the trip would be long and dangerous because of the presence of so many strangers, Gypsy and non-Gypsy; and (3) if the Virgin did appear, She would announce what it was She wanted people to do, and the Rom would eventually participate. The majority opinion was that a vow to fulfill Her wishes would be more important than any other possible behavior. The Philadelphia incident came to nothing; the Rom were not surprised, but they *were* regretful.

The Gypsies may be skeptical of some aspects of Christianity; they do not like priests and nuns. For one, the Rom believe that celibacy is unnatural, because it runs counter to the rules of the universe. They feel there must be something "wrong" with adults who never marry, especially females, for they are not fulfilling the destiny of their bodies. Gypsy celibates are very rare indeed; in all the years I have known Gypsies, I have come across less than a handful. Males who have never married are usually feebleminded (there were two such cases I knew of, and their parents nevertheless tried desperately to find brides for them); where a young man refuses to marry and there is no evidence that his refusal stems from a stubborn determination to select his own mate, the Gypsies suspect him of homosexual tendencies. Of course, a young girl is supposed to be reluctant to marry; virgins are expected to fear, or at least to be embarrassed by the thought of coitus. But virtuousness should only be carried so far; a lifelong refusal is indicative of pathology.

When I was an unmarried girl among them, my Gypsy mother sermonized me frequently about the inevitability of marriage; in fact, she had tried to find me a husband herself. Later, she suggested that I spend a little less time with them and devote a little more of my energies to finding a husband (since that was the way of my people, as I had explained). Her own daughter, several years younger than I, also refused marriage, and a third young girl of approximately the same age was the unmarried daughter of a family on very close terms with ours. We three girls were the old spinsters of the band, known collectively as "The Three Musketeers." The nickname was affectionate, but its inappropriateness was well recognized by all and implied strong disapproval of our behavior. Of course, to them I always appeared somewhat of a screwball, for having been born a non-Gypsy, I nevertheless chose to associate with Gypsies. The daughter of the other family was a very attractive girl and an excellent money-maker, but she was a cripple; this in itself was not much of a bar to marriage since her ailment was not hereditary but the result of an accident in infancy. The Gypsies suspected that her mother was loath to give up her financial services to the family, and so she was regarded as the most normal of the triumvirate. My Gypsy sister was considered very beautiful but overindulged by her parents because she was the only true child, the others all having been adopted.

I was the first of the trio to become engaged, and I wondered how the Rom would react. The younger ones teased me gently, and the older people approved when I explained that the young man was a close friend of my uncle and that I had been finding it increasingly troublesome to be nagged at by all my Gypsy and non-Gypsy relatives. My fiancé was introduced to my Gypsy relatives, and my father put the final stamp of approval on the union by these words: "He's all right. Now teach him Romany!" The crippled Musketeer got married less than a year later—by running off with her jewelry and furs. Her husband was a respectable young Gypsy man of good family. Much to my surprise, opinion was on her side. I had expected the Gypsies to express shock and disgust on the basis that a virtuous unmarried girl is not supposed to want to get married, but the Rom decided that the girl had been driven to desperate measures because her parents mistakenly and selfishly prevented her from fulfilling her natural destiny. In this instance, the consensus was that upholding the harmony of the universe was more important than maintaining the polite fiction of a grown female's reluctance to cohabit sexually or of respecting her parents. My Gypsy sister never did get married, but she is fulfilling her destiny by adopting and raising a baby.

Thus, nuns and priests are suspect. That they are servants of God does not make the situation any more acceptable to the Rom, for the underlying concept of human beings especially dedicated to the service of God is foreign to their thinking. The Gypsies believe all adult human beings are equal before God and should serve Him, and they see no reason to accord special respect to the status of priests and nuns. (Perhaps one of the reasons the Rom prefer the Orthodox Church is because of the married priests.) However, on the other side of the human equation, the Gypsies are equally alien and inexplicable to the priests. Their actions seem inappropriate and even callous to outsiders. A young priest newly assigned to a church used by New York Mačvaja Gypsies found himself officiating at a funeral service. Following tradition, the Gypsies had brought liquor and musicians, and they were drinking, dancing, and laughing. The young priest became increasingly agitated and finally plunged into a long harangue about indecorous behavior in a house of God and in the presence of the dead. Some of the Gypsies edged him to one side and clearly announced that he was being paid to deliver the funeral oration but that the rest of the rites were in the hands of the Rom. "He doesn't know our ways. He'll have to learn," was the verdict.

Gypsy Religious Beliefs

Gypsy religious beliefs are relatively unstructured. The term for God (*del*) is not a loan word, and He always is referred to in the singular person. Gypsies frequently make reference to God in talking, but the allusions are to His omniscience and omnipotence. That He exists is indubitable, but the impression is that most Gypsies feel He is remote from daily human concerns. It is as if, having set up the universe and programmed it to maintain its own harmonic balance, He now can relax and let events flow. Only rarely and capriciously does He reassert His presence among the Rom. Thus, one may call upon God, but one does not necessarily expect an immediate response.

The word for "devil" is not of Romany origin, and the concept itself is not particularly well incorporated into the total structure of Gypsy beliefs even though a number of folk stories deal with "The Devil." Of course, the devil appears daily in terms of curses ("the devil take that stinking car; it's broken again"), but apparently less frequently in Romany than in English. Other Gypsy usages and attitudes tend to imply that more than one devil exists—"He's got *a* devil on his neck," not *"The* devil is on his back"—and the idea of "devil" tends to blend with Gypsy ideas of lesser, somewhat malevolent spirits.

Gypsies recognize a category of beings that I call "nature-spirits." These creatures are alive but they are not human. The Gypsies are vague on their specific characteristics, but the impression is that they are incorporeal (although they may sometimes temporarily assume a visible body). Some Rom feel these spirits are either male or female, and thus they can form an emotional attachment to a human of the opposite sex. Other Gypsies feel they are really asexual because traditional stories do not describe how they reproduce—if they reproduce at all. The need to replace nature-spirits apparently does not arise frequently. They are neither immortal nor invincible, but their lifespans are indefinitely long and their powers far beyond human capacity.

Among the nature-spirits recognized by the Gypsies are water-spirits and tree- and/or forest-spirits. Some European sources also refer to earth-spirits, but I have not come across them (Block 1939; Leland 1891; von Wlislocki 1891, 1892). In fact, the only spirits to whom the American Rom pay any attention are those of the water. They are neither good nor evil and tend to remain away from human affairs. But they are entitled to respect from humans; if respectful behavior is not forthcoming, they will wreak vengeance upon the careless mortal involved. These water beings punish those who pollute running water with illness and misfortune; the part water plays in the world's ecology must also be acknowledged.

As it is characteristic of other pastoral nomads, the Gypsies attribute no will to vegetation (trees not being grouped with other members of the plant kingdom, like grasses and vegetables) and do not acknowledge the role it plays in the support of life. The credit goes to the action of the elements—to rain, water, and wind. Every spring the Rom go to a forested place with a running brook to perform a "first-fruits ceremony" at the water's edge during which representative specimens of vegetables and fruits are thrown into the water as an offering. The Rom are not permitted to eat any of the newly grown plants of the season before the ceremony takes place.

Nature-spirits are capricious; they may take a dislike toward some individual or an equally unjustified affection for someone, and either torment or indulge him at their whim.

Another group of beings, the sky-spirits or angels, seem to bridge the gap between nature-spirits and God. Unlike the former, they function as God's servants and delegates and thus do not act from whim or selfish motivation. Besides acting as overseers of human affairs they are also the custodians of unborn souls.

Considerably less vague to the Kalderaš (the Mačvaja do not seem to place as much importance on them, and Jan Yoors, in a personal communication, totally denies them for the Lovara) are the *ursitori* or Fates (Maximoff 1946). These are spirits controlling the destiny of human beings, deciding the fate of each individual three days after birth. On that day, a Gypsy mother dresses the baby in special new clothes and addresses a prayer for the baby's future health, happiness, and prosperity. According to Maximoff, there are three ursitori: one who is tenderhearted toward humans and, therefore, inclined to assign a good fate; another who is misanthropic and consequently apt to demand an unhappy fate; and the leader, who is neutral and tends to work out a compromise between the two extreme positions. The final decision of the ursitori determines with how much luck a person starts out life. The amount of luck is contingent partially on a concept similar to that of the Hindu *karma*, the accumulation of merit from former existences. The Gypsy thinking is not as clearly defined as that of the Hindu, but it includes a belief that one's position in life is in part the result of one's past incarnations. If a man or woman led a virtuous existence in a former lifetime, merit would accrue therefrom and be rewarded in the current life. On the other hand, misdeeds in former lives are debits, to be repaid by suffering misfortune in the new incarnation. Furthermore, some of the debits of ancestors may have to be repaid as well. These additions and subtractions of luck are weighed, and the leader of the Fates arrives at a compromise. However, the sum total of luck allocated to an individual waxes and wanes according to particular circumstances; a particularly meritorious person may be granted additional good fortune or an especially evil person may be punished repeatedly.

Fate-plus-luck is a convenient explanatory device in Gypsy thinking. A Gypsy is expected to be competent, self-reliant, and independent. He should possess enough of the skills necessary for living to survive adequately, and he should work at improving minimal skills and acquiring additional ones in order to lead a comfortable, worry-free life. To put it another way, a Gypsy in large measure is held responsible for what he does with his own life. However, there are some talented individuals who work hard and conscientiously without ever fulfilling their goals, and others whose abilities are limited and who do not exert themselves unduly but who nevertheless always seem to get what they want. Both extremes, of course, are viewed as undeserved and are explainable only in terms of fate and/or luck.

Some Americans entertain preconceived notions about the supposed fatalistic attitude of other groups; they think it is used as an excuse for inaction. This may be true for some individuals or families with psychopathology, but Gypsy fatalism seems to work toward the amelioration of unbearable frustration in times of adversity and the preservation of the moral code. Where the value system of a culture inculcates the feeling of personal responsibility for oneself, an individual will experience strong guilt feelings in case of failure. These guilt feelings may undermine the individual's ego and lead to a lack of self-respect. The resultant demoralization may disrupt the habitual living patterns and foster self-defeating attitudes. Fate/luck, on the other hand, preserves the ego structure and the inherent human dignity of the individual at the same time that it affords a culturally approved mechanism for redirecting energies; the evaluation of the individual's skills remains unshaken, for they are merely held in temporary abeyance, ready to be called upon with confidence in the future. Similarly, a value system based on reward and punishment is threatened by the occurrence of cases in which the laudable seems to be penalized and the heinous blessed. Here, too, fate/luck serves to explain away the exceptions and even offers the promise of eventual correction of the "bookkeeping." (Christianity, like Hindu and Buddhist karma, balances the overpayment of credits and the underpayment of debits after the death of the individual—Christianity by promising an appropriate afterlife and Hinduism and Buddhism an appropriate rebirth.)

Another set of spirits recognized by the Gypsies are the ancestor spirits. The ultimate relationship between the ancestral spirits and the unborn souls remains vague, although there is some implicit connection, since the souls of the dead eventually return to the reservoir of unborn souls to await rebirth on earth. I have already dealt with the belief of a gradual separation after death of the soul from the body. The funerary rites are designed to hasten the initial separation, and special memorial feasts are held during the first *post mortem* year because the soul retains a separate identity. During this period, the soul should be feasted and entertained at proper intervals; after the first year, the soul merges its once-individual identity with the collectivity of ancestral souls, who are themselves honored annually with a feast. All ancestors dwell with the angelic sky-spirits, who are God's agents and maintain an interest in the welfare of the Gypsies; they are thought to be able to help the Rom in time of need and to penalize offenders of Gypsy law (i.e., those who disrupt the harmony of the universe).

The only truly malevolent beings recognized by Gypsy cosmology are the ghosts of the dead, who are thought of as embodying all the hostility, jealousy, selfishness, and cunning of which humans are capable. The sole aim of these *mule* is to entice living Gypsies to form an emotional attachment to one of their kind; this love serves as a fatal trap, causing a lingering death with dreadful psychological symptoms. Characteristically, the victim—always a male—encounters a band of strange Gypsies, who welcome him cordially and offer him a generous hospitality—feasting, drinking, dancing. Sometimes, he is invited to stay overnight or to revisit. In any event, the Rom falls in love with a beautiful young girl, whom he is allowed to court freely (this in itself being contrary to usual customs). If the man is virtuous, he approaches her parents and makes arrangements for a formal visit by his parents and a go-between to discuss possible marriage; in other cases, the young couple clandestinely plot to run away together. But whether a Gypsy conducts himself properly or not, the end result is the same; he discovers that he has been consorting with the dead, and the knowledge causes profound psychological trauma. He returns to his people, pale, incoherent, and shaken. He is unable to eat or to sleep; he may be so depressed that he cannot talk at all or he may spend his days between manic-depressive states of babbling and screaming. He loses weight rapidly, his tissues wasting away from inactivity and lack of nourishment. Only with great difficulty can his people extract the story; he dies slowly while his family watches, impotent against the inexorable.

Reversal of the damages caused by exposure to the mule is possible only in cases in which the victim suspects the true nature of mule before much contact occurs, i.e., very little conversation has taken place and no physical contact or eating has transpired. The mule are clever and persistent in their attempts to lure the victim into their midst, and as a last resort they may even give chase to the victim to prevent escape. However, if the victim can disengage himself, the prognosis is hopeful, although he may still suffer a temporary psychotic interlude.

Cosmic Principles: A Review

The ghosts of the dead are the closest approximation to evil the Gypsies recognize in the universe. Indeed, the good-versus-evil theme, so common in the Western world, is a poor analogue to Gypsy philosophy. The Rom differentiate between right and wrong, but "right" is that which is in harmony with (consistent with) the general dynamics of the universe; this view includes both a creative and a destructive phase. Appropriateness is the criterion they consistently apply. All those characteristics that are natural, in the sense of appropriate and/or prevalent, are right and proper. For example, there is nothing evil about a

snake biting a man, for it is its appropriate behavior and therefore right. Inappropriateness and/or rarity are suspect and
probably wrong. Thus, Gypsies believe that animals that have
coats of a solid color (such as all black or all white, unlike the
variegated coats of most mammals) are malignant. Melanic, or
black, squirrels encountered by the Rom are referred to as "the
devil's squirrel." Similarly, as chickens are birds that do not fly
properly, the Gypsies contend that eating chicken is not as satisfying as eating other meats—they complain that chicken does
not "stick to the ribs," as we would say, that one becomes hungry
again within several hours after a meal.[1]

The Gypsy emphasis upon the rightness of that which is
natural predisposes them toward greater toleration of variability
in the world, for what is natural for one group of people may not
be natural for another. The particular type of group invoked in
explanation, however, varies as the occasion demands. For instance, Gypsies and non-Gypsies are different groups, but sometimes the crucial group membership criterion, for the sake of
discussion, may be sex ("all men are demanding") or age ("young
people are impatient"), rather than ethnicity. Philosophically,
superimposition of membership in a number of groups leads to
the probable conclusion that each is unique. The logical extension of this attitude is that Gypsies accept variations in customs
and lifestyles more readily than we Americans, who tend to insist
upon conformity. My personal idiosyncracies are more easily
accepted by my Gypsy friends than by my American ones; the
former will shrug them off with a very easy-going,
"that's-just-her-way" attitude whereas the latter will warn me
about the social sanctions that may be used against me. Furthermore, the private inner voice of conscience is given much more
credence and respect by the Rom. Like the Hindus and Buddh-
ists, the Gypsies believe that each living creature contains a small
portion of the primordial energy-mass of the universe. This
Ur-seed, planted in each man, can flourish if nurtured with love
by its possessor, or it can go protectively dormant if neglected. A
person, then, carries within himself the potential for knowledge
of the universe and its pulsations. No one can understand or
respond to the microcosmic universe in someone else, for each is

[1] I am much indebted to numerous conversations with Jan Yoors for clarification of some of the points made herein.

unique, and only taken altogether does it constitute the totality of the macrocosm. Logically, therefore, there is no certain way for people to judge whether a person is obeying his rightful function in the world; what may seem like improper behavior actually may be fulfilling the greater purpose of the universe. Any human interference thus may upset the divine plan and provoke the wrath of the universe.

The small bit of the universe in every human enables him to enjoy immediate rapport with God—if only he has the sense to listen and respond. Whatever the inner voice commands one should obey, whether it is a warning to desist from an action or an urging to commence a new behavior. Therefore, the Rom believe firmly in personal vows, and many of them do make and follow such sacred promises individually. Friends and relatives may know of a person's vow, although they do not feel compelled to assist him in keeping it or to object if he is seen breaking it. For example, a Gypsy woman may promise to abstain from meat and sweets on Fridays. Such a vow does not prevent the family or friends from serving and eating such foods in front of the adherent to such a promise. If the abstainer partakes, no comment is passed, for it is nobody's business to do so. Moreover, no guilt feelings are held if the vow is broken. I remember the evening I took some Gypsy girls to Columbia University. They had been anxious to see what a college looked like, and a rather warm spring Friday afternoon seemed like a good time for me to furnish a guided tour. I mentioned that the fountains provided a cool respite that we could reinforce by patronizing a neighborhood ice cream parlor. "But, Raino," objected one of the girls, "today's *Friday*." When I looked puzzled, another girl laughed and explained, "She's made a vow not to eat sweet things like ice cream on Friday. But the rest of us can, so let's go." I protested that it would not be fair and said I thought we should postpone the trip to another day. However, Gypsy enthusiasm was keen and our friend decided to break her vow for this one day. I seemed to be the only one who was upset. Later I mentioned my misgivings to my Gypsy sister, who laughed away my unhappiness. "She can make it up some other day. Besides, if she feels it's okay, that's up to her." My attempt to explain that I had been guilty of putting temptation in the girl's path was met with a brusque, "You didn't do nothing wrong—so forget it."

It is this emphasis on inner guidance, this belief that what is good for Mr. Jones is not necessarily good for Mr. Brown, that makes the Rom philosophically tolerant of other people's beliefs and ways of life. Romany ideals and practices, of course, do not necessarily coincide any more than ours do. They feel that truth comes in many shapes and may not necessarily be the same for all of us. A logical (and fervently endorsed) extension of this principle is that what is right for Americans is not necessarily right for Gypsies.

7
GYPSY CHILDHOOD

Behavioral scientists are especially interested in the way people raise their children because the period of childhood is looked upon as the "formative years," the time when individuals are developing the major characteristics of their personalities and learning the basic rules of their society and culture. The various cultures of the world are very different in respect to their contents, but still they all start out each generation with the same raw material, the newborn human baby, and convert it into a member of a specific, unique society and culture. Not all individuals are able to respond adequately to the norms of a culture (such people are referred to as "deviants") nor do all individuals display the same skills within their cultures (those particularly skilled are considered the epitome of their cultural norms). However, a satisfactory mutual adjustment between individual and group seems to be usual.

In some cultures, the balance is tipped slightly in favor of the group, for the cultural ideals inculcate a readiness to place the group's benefit above the wishes of the individual. In other cultures, the individual seems to take precedence over the group. The Rom have, to a large extent, an individualistically oriented culture, but nevertheless the Gypsy group manages to persevere through time. We can obtain an understanding of this seeming contradiction by examining the life cycle of the Gypsy individual.

Pregnancy and Birth

The sexual act and pregnancy are topics of some embarrassment to Gypsies; but the birth of a baby is an occasion for great joy, and a first baby is an especially important event for a couple. As soon as the young bori is aware of her condition, she is expected to let her mother-in-law know; however, if she is young and inexperienced or feels embarrassed, she probably will expect her mother-in-law to approach her first. (I have known a number of cases in which the young woman was not aware of her pregnancy.) Responsibility for the health of the bori belongs to the mother-in-law. She may inform the bori's parents about the pregnancy, but she is not obligated to do so unless there is a serious medical problem.

Within the last three years, I have heard increasingly of young women complaining to their husbands of sundry aches and pains during pregnancy. Not long ago, young Gypsy women accepted any discomfort connected with pregnancy as both inevitable and unworthy of mention. Discussing pregnancy with one's husband is shocking enough to an old-fashioned Gypsy; but, worse yet, nowadays the young men expect that their mothers treat the daughters-in-law as if they were ill—by lessening their wives' work load and by allowing them to rest in bed as often as they wish. Some husbands go as far as to suggest that a doctor should be consulted.

Some Gypsy bands have recently become interested in prenatal care for the young women. The older people are often willing to ignore Gypsy rules of modesty because of the increasing prevalence of medical difficulties encountered during late pregnancy and immediately postnatally. Some of the Old Ones believe that the birth rate has been decreasing since the Rom have adopted urban living.[1] They feel that conceptions do not occur as readily now as in former times and that miscarriages have become more frequent. But researches into the genealogies of the Rom do not confirm their statements. Most Gypsies, however, still regard pregnancy and birth as natural conditions for females in the childbearing ages.

[1] Apparently this belief arose in the forties since Mitchell 1945: 58 refers to it.

Morning-sickness in the early months is accepted as part of normal pregnancy; it is treated by the ingestion of raw white potato. If the woman's food intake remains low after the first trimester there is cause for worry; and any food craved by the pregnant woman must be satisfied. Otherwise, it is believed she runs the risk of miscarrying. My Gypsy mother was adamant on this point, insisting that I must, for the sake of the baby, overcome my embarrassment at eating in quantity in the presence of my in-laws and my reluctance to call attention to myself (a bori should be shy and retiring) by requesting special foods. She told me that, when she was expecting, she and her young husband boarded a train. She noticed a large, beautiful pear on the floor, and she wanted to pick it up to save for later consumption. But her husband was disturbed at the prospect of non-Gypsies seeing her do so. That night, she miscarried, and she attributes the loss to her neglected food craving.

Gypsy women fear that if they see something hideous while pregnant, the foetus may exhibit the same characteristics, and be born with a "mark." An expectant mother should be exposed to beautiful stimuli if at all possible. I recall my Gypsy sister discussing with us a movie she had just seen; it was called "The Bad Seed" and dealt with a child who had murderous inclinations. She said she had enjoyed it very much, and, looking at my husband, she said, "Be sure to see it." Then, turning to me, she added, "But you stay home."

In the last trimester of pregnancy, the woman withdraws gradually from active social life although she may still remain active around the house or at the store. Birth is marime; therefore, going into labor at a social gathering would be most awkward for all (and, incidentally, the presence of many people at a birth would increase the risk of infection to the woman and child).

Nowadays, out of convenience the women go to a hospital for delivery; this in itself is a recent development, the result of urban living. Formerly, a woman retired to a separate tent or wagon when her time came; if it were convenient, her mother-in-law or some of the other women might assist in the delivery of a first child, but it was expected from all that a healthy woman could deliver her child unassisted without any difficulty.[2]

[2]Cf. Yoors 1967: 108-09 for a Lovara case history of birth. Lee 1972: 125 confirms marime beliefs for Canadian Rom.

The first six weeks after birth is also a period of marime, mother and child being only recently removed from contact with the realm of unborn souls; contact with them could be dangerous for others, especially for adult males. After the first few days, during which only women closely related can see them, the mother and baby are visited by some of the married women of the band. Today, the marime period has been shortened on the basis of the hospital stay, and some of the young men even visit their wives during the period of confinement.

The six-week isolation period of mother and baby affords a well-needed vacation for the woman from the demands of her roles as wife and daughter-in-law. She is free to relax and to think only of herself and her infant, and she can anticipate the spate of attention and approval she will receive from her husband's group when she returns to normal life. The first-time mother (and father) gains in status within the band, and each child thereafter augments her position. Should the family size increase beyond their financial resources, the baby could be adopted within its extended family. Indeed, giving birth is a joyous occasion, except for mothers who are already grandmothers—then birth is considered inappropriate and perhaps a little obscene, to judge from the snickers accompanying its mention.

The birth of twins of opposite sex is considered a happy bonus, and both babies are brought up by their parents. Among the Kalderaš, however, the birth of twins of the same sex, especially male, requires that one of them be adopted into a different nuclear family and away from the traveling unit of the natural parents. The Gypsies say this is done to safeguard the health of the father. No attempt is made to hide the facts from the boys, and the one who is not raised by his progenitor may visit his parents' household freely. He may even elect to return to his natal family upon reaching maturity. I could not obtain an explanation for this custom, but I suspect that it may reflect a fear that two boys, preternaturally linked, could supersede their father precociously. A youth may challenge his father's authority when he feels sufficiently self-reliant and independent; his strength and ability increase as the older man's wanes. A father is increasingly hard put to remain in authority; eventually and inevitably he loses the contest, and this sequence is in keeping with the nature of life and is accepted by all. But twin boys, growing up together, might upset the balance of the group by throwing off the proper timing of events.

I know of only one birth of triplets, all boys, and the event (in the late forties) precipitated a crisis between the husband's family and that of the wife. Apparently the union had been arranged as a way of patching up past disagreements between the two families, and the birth of triplets undid all the initial peacemaking. Ultimately, a widespread feud broke out and was resolved only by great effort on the part of various Rom leaders.

Adoption

Barrenness in a woman is pitied, but, unlike other Oriental peoples, a barren woman is neither censured nor divorced. Gypsies acknowledge that childlessness may be the result of either the woman's or the man's sterility. Even though only the sons remain within a family, the Rom welcome the arrival of daughters, the ideal family including an equal number of girls and boys. The biological mechanism of sex determination of the baby is either unknown or unrecognized by the Gypsies. So neither parent is held responsible if the family fails to produce an even balance of males and females.[3]

The Gypsies prefer to have in a completed family (i.e., one in which the woman is past childbearing age) six or seven fullgrown sons. Part of the importance of an extended family depends on its manpower; a family with a paucity of strong males is at a disadvantage. However, raising many sons places a burden upon the family both financially and in expenditure of parental energy. Each of the sons must be provided with a wife and enough capital to start the nucleus of another family. Thus, if the family consists exclusively of sons, the treasury may be depleted severely. In a family in which there are sons, the birth of daughters means the arrival of individuals who will share in the housekeeping duties and contribute a modicum of steady income from fortunetelling; more importantly, each daughter

[3]Compare this to the Eastern European Jewish beliefs, for example, in which Orthodox Jewish law permits a man to divorce his wife if she fails to produce a son.

represents available future capital with which to finance a bori. So a good balance of sons and daughters is as much a necessity to a Gypsy family as having children at all.

Some families are too small, and others have too many members. Adoption serves as a stabilizing mechanism. The Rom consider adoption a particularly felicitous solution, and they do not hide the fact of adoption from the world. Children know they are adopted and may visit their biological parents at will. Since the adopted child often is a close collateral relative, he is usually a kinsman anyway. Neither the adopted child nor the Gypsies feel that the biological parents have deserted or rejected the baby. It is simply that the event of biological parenthood fades into insignificance compared to that of sustained social parenthood. In other words, one may be predisposed to love one's own children, but this love is actualized and nurtured through the daily interactions with them.

Adoptions can be arranged at any time in the life cycle, even during the adulthood of the adopted child. However, preference is for as early an adoption as possible. Sometimes, the adoption is arranged prior to the birth of the baby. A similar arrangement may be worked out during pregnancy, whereby the fathers agree that the child may be adopted immediately upon birth. (In such cases, the Kalderaš ceremonies on the third day after birth are performed by the social, not the biological, parents.)

A somewhat different idea was proposed by one of my Gypsy brothers during my first pregnancy. He and his wife had already had two sons and she was expecting another baby. While we were all sitting and joking together in the fashion of fully but only recently mature Gypsy couples, uninhibited by the presence of the Old Ones in the room, my brother suggested that he and my husband agree to switch children. "My wife will give birth before yours, and you'll have your baby by that much sooner," said he. I teased him, saying that I had every intention of having a boy myself, and I asked what he would do if his own baby were a girl. As luck would have it, my sister-in-law presented her husband with a third boy around Thanksgiving, and I delivered a daughter in February. To this day, my Gypsy brother half-seriously says my firstborn should have been his even though they had several daughters subsequently.

Baptism

The baby should be baptized six weeks after birth; thereafter it is considered officially a new member of the group. At this point, the mother may resume normal activities. Baptism may be postponed if the godparents selected have not been contacted or if difficulties arise in arranging itineraries for meeting together for the requisite church service. It is more important to choose the right godparents than to hold baptism promptly. I have known truly long delays; the longest postponement of which I have a record is a case in which a sixteen-year-old groom was baptized on his wedding day. However, the child's acceptance into Gypsy society is accomplished, at any event, by a formal announcement of the birth by the father to the assembled company of Rom, followed by a drinking party at which the men toast the child's future and congratulate the parents.[4]

Godparents are chosen (Table 7.1) on the basis of the same religious sect, preferring influential people or those belonging to families of high status, asking rich people rather than poor ones, selecting individuals who do not already have a large number of godchildren, and using godparenthood to cement a friendship. Foremost is to choose people "who have a good heart toward the baby." This is so important that Gypsy families sometimes will select non-Gypsies over Gypsies as godparents. In one Mačvaja family I know, there is a predilection for choosing Greek-Americans "because Greeks enjoy being godparents so much." It is believed that a godparent who enters into the rela-

TABLE 7.1

SELECTION OF GODPARENTS—CHOICE CONTINGENT UPON THE FOLLOWING FACTORS:

Less Acceptable	*More Acceptable*
Commoner family	Family of high status
	Influential person
Poor individual	Well-to-do individual
Many godchildren already	Few godchildren
Reluctant acquiescence	Close friend of parents
	Wholehearted acceptance
Ordinary person	Particularly lucky individual
	Person with spiritual strength

[4]Cf. Yoors 1967: 108-09 for the Lovara customs.

tionship in a joyous and sincere fashion somehow establishes a strong spiritual link with his godchild, so that his personal luck and favor with the universe can be tapped for the child's needs. The adult's accumulation of sacred strength rubs off onto his spiritual son, as it were. Since infant mortality rates among the Gypsies were once as high as elsewhere in the non-Western world—as much as 50 percent in some areas—the ability to pull a baby through his first years of life was crucial; godparenthood was most important in this respect. In fact, a sickly baby's baptism is hastened, not for the usual Christian reason of ensuring that his little soul be saved were he to die, but to try to forestall that death.

Childcare Philosophy

Babies, according to Gypsy beliefs, are born with definite temperaments and personalities; hence, each baby is a distinct individual. The older people in the family may influence the development of the growing child, and certain characteristics may tend to run in families, but adults are incapable of remolding a baby's personality completely.

This pediatric philosophy, although not unique to the Rom, is far from universal—we Americans frequently tend to think that a baby's personality is shaped almost exclusively by his environment. Thus, Americans tend to hold the parents and other significant adults responsible for the individual's ultimate development, whereas the Romany philosophy leads to the conclusion that a disappointing development very well may be the result of inherent factors. Gypsies, consequently, keenly observe the new baby in an effort to discover his disposition and inclinations.

Children are considered miniature versions of adults, lacking only the motor strength and skill of adults and, of course, lacking experience in life. But willpower and desires, emotions and potential intelligence are all inborn and are functional immediately. It follows, therefore, that their rights are also the same as those of adults. Their wishes should be respected to the same extent as the wishes of other human beings. For example, I remember watching a young mother put her four-month-old on the rug and sit down to play with him. The baby started to cry after just a minute or two. "Can't you see that he doesn't want to play now?" scolded the woman's mother-in-law. Similarly, anything given to a baby (or anything he takes) belongs to him; one does not wrest it away by brute force. One may ask for it, beg for it, offer a substitute; but, if the child still refuses to give it up, a roomful of adults will stand by helplessly until the little one tires of the object and releases it voluntarily.

Since babies are greatly desired and are regarded as being just recently in contact with the angels, they are indulged until they are superceded by another new baby in the group. Thus, a Gypsy group usually has a little tyrant in residence, but the specific individual changes every two years or so. We Americans would expect Gypsy youngsters to be spoiled brats as a result of this practice, but such is not the case. The warm, loving acceptance characteristic of the earliest period of development seems to act as an initial security-engendering mechanism that is echoed in other aspects of childrearing.

That the method works is something to which I can attest, having watched a succession of little terrors grow to responsible adulthood. My favorite example is one of my Gypsy nephews: he had a reputation even among the Rom for being unmanageable, and some of the younger adults were reluctant to visit when Larry was around. Larry at three years of age should have been displaced as youngest; but his parents had not had a baby as yet, and they traveled alone as a small family unit so there were no other babies in the immediate vicinity. At one party which I attended, Larry grabbed a huge breadknife, which he refused to surrender, particularly since he was enjoying the experience of walking around the room intimidating everyone. I observed the scene for about fifteen minutes and then abandoned whatever anthropological objectivity I had (it was minimal at best, for I was drawn strongly to this bright little fellow) and walked over to him, peremptorily offering him the choice of either giving me the knife immediately or having it taken away from him by virtue of my superior strength. Larry chose the contest, but a small chase around the room and a minor cut on my finger got the knife returned to the kitchen. Some seven years later, I was visiting Larry's father with my own little daughter. Larry had earned some money shining shoes and with it had bought himself a hot dog and a soda, which he took into the kitchen. In the middle of our conversation with my brother and sister-in-law, I realized that my little daughter had been out of the room for several minutes. Curiosity more than concern motivated me to see what she was doing: in the kitchen, my darling was happily eating Larry's hot dog and demanding his soda while Larry (who had been known as the "Terror of the East Coast" to all Mačvaja) sheepishly hovered nearby, ready to protect her from falling off the kitchen stool.

Infancy

The intimate contact between baby and mother is expanded to include other members of the family after the six-week seclusion period. Babies are rarely more than four feet away from some older person, and most often they are being held or carried. (Carriages and cribs are now popular among some Gypsies.) American-style nurseries have no place in Gypsy life, and the babies are kept in the midst of daily activities, exposed to a continuous stimulation of sights, sounds, and smells. Additional stimulation is furnished by the habitual patterns of passing the baby around from person to person, talking and playing with him for extended periods, and allowing him to see and handle whatever strikes his fancy. Not surprisingly, the babies develop into alert, active youngsters filled with curiosity and a zest for exploring and testing their social and physical environments.

Gypsy babies are well coordinated, and the Rom expect a rapid physical development (sitting up at six months, crawling at nine months, and walking at one year—as well as dancing by eighteen months!). But they will not force a baby or become worried if a particular baby lags behind. The infant who takes the initiative and tries to achieve some independence does so with the approval of his elders. Each small advance is exaggerated into a major triumph by all present. On the other hand, any backward slide or failure simply is ignored (Cotten 1950: 228). Alert eyes watch babies and toddlers to prevent serious mishaps; an older person casually removes the little one from harm's reach without saying anything. Thus, serious accidents are prevented without discouraging attempts to explore the environment or to master new motor behavior skills; for the adults do not communicate by word or deed that there is anything to be feared.

Contrast the Romany situation with that prevailing among overprotective middle-class American mothers who bombard their babies with the constant reiteration of warnings—"Be careful, or you'll hurt yourself, darling." The American baby gets the double message that experimenting is dangerous and that avoiding pain is preferable to learning something new. The Gypsy child, on the other hand, is taught that physical independence is valued and worth the price of a little pain; minor hurts pass unnoticed by those same observant adult eyes. A toddler who loses his footing and suffers a bump is left to his own devices; he must pick himself up and decide whether he will try again, for none will rush over to express concern and give comfort and encouragement. An older child who trips and cries may even be rebuked for being inept.

Gradualness is also the keynote of toilet-training and modesty despite adult prudery about themselves and other adults. Babies are exempted from rules of marime, and their physiological requirements are not considered polluting. It is taken for granted that babies will soil whoever holds them, and no one fusses when it happens. Even important Old Ones will announce calmly, without moving any muscles but the ones required to talk, that a baby has urinated on them, then quietly summon a daughter-in-law to change the diaper—if the child is wearing one. Ordinarily, Gypsies are very casual about keeping babies dressed; in the privacy of the Gypsy home, babies may begin the day by being dressed in a shirt, diaper, and pants, but continuous redressing throughout the day requires more patience than most Rom have. It is much easier to keep the baby uncovered —and it prevents diaper rash.

Little girls begin to remain fully clothed around three years of age, but boys are given several more years of leeway. My impression is that until the early secondary sexual characteristics begin to appear, accidental uncovering is ignored. Toilet-training, however, once children have learned it, is expected to be honored in full (it is a subject that should not be discussed anymore); I know of no cases of bedwetting continuing as a symptom of emotional problems among older children.

Knowledge of sexual matters comes early to the Gypsies. This is partially correlated with the former occupations involving animal-handling: like all pastoralists, the Gypsies discuss the sexual behavior of animals and take it for granted. Youngsters tending the animals may watch coitus. In part, too, the youngsters' knowledge of sex stems from the Gypsy living conditions. Babies sleep in the same bed as their parents for several years, at least until the time of full weaning from breast feeding (up to three years of age usually). After that, they may share a bed with an older sibling; but all bedding, including that of the parents, may be in the same room.

Beyond waiting until it is dark and everyone has retired for the night, the adults can do nothing to ensure privacy during coitus. The sexuality of children is taken for granted by the Gypsies, and between birth and the age of eight it is even encouraged. A squalling baby girl is asked with mock concern if she wishes a husband, and a baby boy may be offered a wife. In some groups, the penis of a little boy is pulled gently during play with the women; little girls are flirted with by the grown men and encouraged to walk provocatively. Girls just barely able to walk are urged to dance, and they get the greatest attention and approval when they shake their shoulders and chests in imitation of their elders.

The Playgroup

The playgroup, consisting of all children of an extended family, provides an excellent training-ground for the development of future skills; membership therein starts as soon as a Gypsy child can walk and talk. The Gypsy peer group emphasizes similarity of ages to a much less extent that its American equivalent, but it tends to insist more rigorously upon kinship and same-sex groupings, the youngest members entering the playgroup without respect to sex, but the older boys tending to separate out into their own sub-group. However, separation according to sex is gradual and unobtrusive, for it is the direct result of the greater freedom of movement and lessened accountability afforded to males.

Youngsters between three and eight spend much of their time in these groups, venturing out to join the adults, tolerated only as long as they do not impede the older people's activities and sent back to the playgroup when they become an annoyance. In this milieu, they amuse themselves by rough-housing and playing games, many of which are imitative of adult pursuits. The girls play at baby-tending and weddings; sometimes they have parties modeled after adult festivals. They play such games as ball, jacks, and skiprope. The boys' activities have always been more active and physical; today, they play baseball and football whereas formerly the emphasis was on horseback riding and pugilism. My impression is that the boys' imitative games (horse-trading, smithing) together with their sporadic hunting endeavors have disappeared and that proportionately more time is devoted today to earning a living.[5]

Thus, in the playgroup, the children practice their skills, learning to assert themselves against those who are older, stronger, and more experienced; benefiting from the learning model the older children provide; utilizing the group as a haven into which to retire after experimental forays into the outside world.

The child is usually not taught to avoid danger before he is two and beginning to talk himself. "Stay away from that cigarette; it is hot," may be repeated once or twice, but no more. The child who decides to disobey is allowed to take the consequences of his choice.

Individual choice is a constant leitmotif throughout childhood and beyond, and the choice is quite genuine because many options are open to children. Being a member of a large extended family, a Gypsy child has many relatives to whom he can turn. Thus, a child who, in the heat of an argument, threatens to leave home is not making an empty gesture—he really can ask to live elsewhere; it would be considered to be within his rights, and, unless they could effect a change of mind, the adults would have to honor his wishes. (A child can also expect a welcome reception at a godparent's home.)[6]

---

[5]Yoors 1967: 29 provides a short description of activities of the young Lovara of playgroup age.

[6]Contrast this to the spurious choice offered to youngsters in some segments of American society—"If you don't like it here, you can leave," is not to be considered a serious option, for where would an eight-year-old from an isolated nuclear family go?

Theoretically and simplistically, a parent owes a child protection, nourishment, shelter, clothing, etc., and the child has a reciprocal debt of obedience, respect, and cooperation. If either of the contracting parties reneges on his obligations, the other side is no longer required to honor the debt. In other words, the Judeo-Christian commandment, "Honor thy father and thy mother" ("no matter what," being implied) is not the equivalent of the Romany command, "Give your parents the honor they deserve." Of course, both groups assume that parents will want to be devoted and will love their offspring and provide for them, and so in actual practice, the two positions seem identical.

This attitude of voluntary contractual obligation extends to all parental injunctions. Both the child and parent know that obedience is a price paid for services rendered; defiance is interpreted as an expression of readiness for independence. During the early years, the parents have the additional advantage of reminding the child that they will provide for a marriage; however, other kinsmen stand ready to help because the entire group benefits through the acquisition of more members.

Incidentally, the interpretation of the nature of human relationships as a voluntary social contract from which all contracting parties derive some benefit is learned in childhood but carried over into adult life. A Gypsy freely continues a relationship with someone because he expects to benefit from it in some way. He also believes that the other person should derive good from the interaction as well, and he worries only when he cannot see wherein the profit lies for the other individual. A one-sided exchange is beyond his ken; more accurately, perhaps, one should say it is considered "unnatural." Thus, if I cannot see immediately what the other fellow is getting out of it, I may be getting a much shorter end of the stick than I know. An ostensibly altruistic act is most suspect to a Rom.

The psychological ramifications of this "voluntary choice" philosophy are such that Gypsies as a whole tend to be assertive, secure, and free in their relationships. "I make my own decisions whenever I wish"; "I can bide my time and improve myself, if I lack capacities now"; etc. The fact that fellow human beings can do the same fosters a sensitivity to the psychological dynamics of others and a realization of their free will. Cooperation and compromise become more advisable than competition and arbitrariness. Interpersonal relations cannot be taken for granted on the assumption that, once achieved, they will be permanent; dynamic give-and-take, readjustments and reassessments are inevitable as people and circumstances change.

Acceptance of physical pain, which starts as the baby begins to explore his environment, is expected of Gypsies. Therefore, they are not opposed to spanking children. However, the administration of corporal punishment characteristically follows the sequence of (1) slapping the child and then (2) sweeping him into the arms of the disciplinarian for a warm embrace. Apparently, the message being communicated is that the pain is a concomitant of the child's own behavior, the giver of the punishment being forced to execute the rules but doing so reluctantly.

A child who hits an adult in anger or who directs verbal abuse against someone is not punished (but, following the Gypsy law of equal treatment for both child and adult, neither is an adult). In fact, what we Americans consider "fresh" behavior is encouraged actively. Youngsters are urged to stand up for their rights and to defend their prerogatives against all comers, no matter how much bigger or more important the opponents may be.

Being fearful and intimidated are behavioral characteristics disliked by the Rom, and practice sessions in learning how to conquer these emotions are contrived by the adults. What happens typically is this: an older person sets himself up as the villain of the piece, and another adult functions as the child's ally and emotional support. (The mentor usually holds a higher position in the social hierarchy, for only an acknowledged influential person can urge the child convincingly to face up to an adult with determination and for an extended period of time.) The "villain" initiates an attack, or more usually, the youngster is told to speak of the villain in abusive terms. Exaggerated umbrage is taken, and the villain counterattacks with seemingly great anger. If the youngster shows signs of retreating, he is exhorted to hurl a retort, or his partner does it for him. These exchanges continue for some time, including light slapping, the duration contingent upon the child's age and ability. The child is allowed the final word and then all the participants make peace and joke together.[7]

[7]Yoors 1967: 161-62 discusses this situation among the Lovara.

From the age of eight to ten, depending upon the child's demonstrated abilities and inclinations, the adults increasingly include the youngster in the ordinary adult routines. Boys are invited to accompany their fathers and male relatives on economic enterprises, initially as observers and then as participants. They also attend the kris and other male gatherings. In a similar vein, the girls take over household duties and begin to observe and participate in fortunetelling. Training continues to be mostly unpressured and positive. The neophyte progresses at his own pace, and improvement is commended liberally. Mistakes may, however, be drawn to the learner's attention. There is no compelling reason to hasten the process since men usually work in groups, and girls will need to be supervised and retrained by their mothers-in-law. Leisurely incorporation and gradually augmenting skills produce competent adults in due course.

8

MARRIAGE

As the challenge of learning life's skills decreases and the physiological process of maturation contributes its own set of needs and drives, the boys become restive and harder to control. This is taken by the Gypsies as a clear indication that the time for marriage is quickening. Ordinarily, marriages are arranged in a sequence according to age, the second son being married after the espousal of the first, etc.; but exceptions are made in terms of such factors as relative developmental age, need to control a particularly unruly boy, matching personalities with an eligible girl. Similar considerations may affect the daughters' sequence of marriages (see Tables 8.1 and 8.2).

Formerly, the ideal Kalderaš pattern prescribed that a thirteen-year-old boy marry a sixteen-year-old girl; today, the age range for a boy may be from 13 to 20, with most falling around 16. Girls may be anywhere from 10 to 18 (no marriage being consummated before biological puberty, however), but mostly around 14 or 15. One can see that there has been a slight shift away from older wife/younger husband to a union where both spouses are the same age or at most extreme where the husband is a year or so older.

Selecting a Spouse

Marriage plays an important role in the life of a Gypsy. The young peoples' development is closely watched, and their marriage potential carefully evaluated; their *hiras* ("tales of reputa-

TABLE 8.1

AGE AT MARRIAGE OF BOY

Decisions based on the following factors:

Early Marriage	*Late Marriage*
Early physiological maturation	Late physiological maturation
All older brothers already married	Some older brothers not yet married
Financial circumstances of family good	Financial circumstances strained
Suitable girl readily available	No suitable girl available
Sister available for exchange	No sister
Boy becomes restless and uncooperative	Boy refuses the idea of marriage
Desire to end feud with another family	
Boy threatens suicide if parents do not arrange a specific union for him	

TABLE 8.2

AGE AT MARRIAGE OF GIRL

Decisions based on the following factors:

Early Marriage	*Late Marriage*
All older sisters already married	Some older sisters still unwed
Younger sisters still at home	Last daughter left at home
Need for money	Girl threatens to run away if wed
No mother to care for child	
Desire to end feud with another family	
Exchange marriage a possibility for son	

tion," anecdotes relating their personal attributes and characteristic behaviors) become a favorite topic of conversation. Gypsy marriages unite not only a girl and a boy but also the extended families of each, and not infrequently the union serves to reinforce ties between bands. Adults who have formed close friendships look forward to uniting their lineages through the marriages of their children, betrothals sometimes being arranged even before the children are born. The resolution of past disagreements often includes the arrangement of several marriages between the formerly antagonistic sides.

Spouse selection involves the issue of family suitability, particularly in relation to grooms. Gypsies tend to practice hypergamy, a custom whereby girls marry into statuses higher than or at a level with their own (whereas a man takes his bride from a family of equal or lower status). In other words, insofar as marriage is concerned, women practice upward social mobility. Since the children resulting from such unions belong to the groom's family (because of the brideprice paid), they gain in status. I suspect that hypergamy correlates with the importance of the woman in maintaining the honor and spiritual integrity of the group. The Rom are quite class conscious among themselves and are familiar with the current status of other families, lineages, and bands. Only non-Gypsies are considered unsuitable for marriage. Occasionally, however, a non-Gypsy girl is taken as a bride. Three such marriages among the Kalderaš of New York have occurred within the last ten years, a comparatively high number. I only realized recently that my Mačvaja friends had proposed indirectly that I marry into their group when I was single. Intertribal unions also occur, and the Kalderaš frequently give daughters in marriage to the Mačvaja; the Mačvaja seldom reciprocate, however. The fact that the Kalderaš also outnumber the Mačvaja by more than three to one may be significant in this respect, but the Mačvaja are proud that the majority of their girls marry within their own bands. Those that marry into the Kalderaš do so with the most aristocratic lineages of that tribe.[1] Other factors affect marriage between Gypsies as well (see Table 8.3).

The wish to be able to visit as often as possible the family which receives the bride is strong, for the Gypsies feel it serves to protect the girl. An unannounced visit provides a handy checkup on her conjugal family. Does she look well? Has she lost weight? Does she seem overworked and tired? Is she wearing good clothing? These questions are better answered by a quick visit than by a telephone call. A girl is expected to have a rather

[1] A similar attitude is reported by Maximoff (1946b: 109) for his people (who, however, are Kalderaš).

difficult adjustment period when she marries, and she displays her worth in part by not complaining. Furthermore, since marriages are arranged, any complaints on her part could be interpreted as criticisms of her parents' choice. Thus, love for her parents and respect for their wishes pressure her into hiding her feelings from them. The duty to shield her parents from her problems in turn obligates them to find out for themselves if she is in trouble, and this requirement is best fulfilled by frequent visits.

The girl's family also prefers to marry her into a family in comfortable financial circumstances not only because of hypergamy but also because that family can afford to offer a higher price. A concomitant advantage to marrying into a well-to-do family, however, is that the bori may have no need to earn large sums of money quickly, the immediate financial needs being satisfied. (A family with a penny-pinching, money-hungry reputation is undesirable.)

As for the youth's personal qualifications: the Rom prefer a bachelor to a divorced man on the basis that he or his family must have been doing something wrong if a previous bride left him (the more frequently married he has been, the poorer the risk he is now). Despite knowledge of the divorce kris, even a favorable kris decision, some doubt always remains in people's minds, and the Gypsies prefer to gamble on a young bachelor from a good family. The boy's physical characteristics are of no importance to the girl's parents, but they will not knowingly marry their daughter to someone who is mentally retarded or psychotic. A boy with a known bad temper is avoided, too. The girl's parents will prefer a youth who seems to have a high potential for self-improvement, for an older woman's status, to a very large extent, is contingent upon that of her husband. Beyond that, the Gypsies try to estimate whether the individual personalities will be congenial. A shy girl may do well with an extroverted husband leading her; but an outgoing girl who enjoys talking to people may be poorly received by a shy, retiring husband, for instance.

Thus far, we have been discussing the choices open to the girl's family; but these involve only yes-or-no decisions. This is because the boy's family has the prerogative of initiating marriage proceedings (Table 8.4). His family will favor an inexperienced

---

TABLE 8.3
DEGREE OF ELIGIBILITY OF A YOUTH

Less Desirable	*Preferable*
Low family and band status	High family and band status
Family hard on daughters-in-law	Family good to daughters-in-law
Family poor	Family rich
Little or no overlap of seasonal routes with that of girl's family	Family well-known and friendly with girl's family
Previously married	First marriage
Poor brideprice offer	High brideprice offer
Poor prognosis for youth's future development	Good prognosis for youth's future development
Poor temperamental match for girl	Good temperamental match for girl
Mental retardate	
Non-Mačvaja (if girl is Mačvaja)	

TABLE 8.4
ELIGIBILITY OF GIRL

Less Desirable	*Preferable*
Poor family reputation for female virtue	Excellent reputation for female virtue
Low family fecundity record	High family fecundity record
High brideprice	Low brideprice
Poor money-maker	Good money-maker
Previously married	First marriage
Low intelligence	High intelligence
Bad temper	Quiet and obedient
Poor physical health	
Demand that youth live with girl's band	

young girl to one previously married, although there is no longer an insistence upon virginity, except in the case of a first marriage (Myers 1945: 90). The family background of the girl is important because the Rom feel that female virtue and ability to produce healthy children run in families. The Gypsies believe that a broad-hipped girl who walks gracefully is bound to be fecund and the mother of numerous offspring.

The girl's personal qualifications are more important than those of the boy, probably because the responsibility for maintaining the new family successfully will be mostly hers. She must make the initial adjustments to alien surroundings whereas the groom remains in the bosom of his kin group. The bride is expected to take on housekeeping and breadwinning duties from the outset, but the groom continues the same gradual incorporation into the group of adult males that he had experienced prior to his marriage. Whereas physical appearance is not very important, it is important that the girl should be in good health. An intelligent bride is valued not only because of her intellect but also because she is expected to be an able moneymaker. As far as the Gypsies are concerned, however, high intelligence often correlates with a bad temper and unruly disposition, both of which are negative features in a bride. Finally, the boy's family would prefer paying a low brideprice, all other things being equal.[2]

Assuming that all other conditions were satisfied, there is one demand by the girl's family that would usually drive away a suitor—the stipulation that the youth must relocate into the bride's family—for this is a direct reversal of the normal marital situation and virtually places the boy in the position of bori. Only under two sets of circumstances would a boy's family agree: (1) great prestige of the girl's family or (2) great desperation on the part of the boy's family to marry him.

Premarital Arrangements

Having selected a possible bride for their son, the youth's family then chooses a trusted friend or relative to act as intermediary in

[2]Cf. Yoors 1967: 181-83 for a detailed discussion of spouse selection among the European Lovara.

the betrothal. The go-between must be known to both families; by preference he should be prestigious, respected as a man of honor and power, articulate so that he may plead the boy's case well, and sufficiently intelligent and self-disciplined so that he may function as just arbitrator between the demands of the two families. The boy's family may have already been in direct contact with the girl's family. Such preliminary contact is not a formal affair; any visit by the boy's group is conducted in a seemingly casual way. But the visit is important because it provides an opportunity to get to know how the family lives and to observe the girl herself in her daily environment.

Even without such preliminary contacts by the boy's family, news that the family is looking for a bride would have spread among the Rom. Thus, the purpose of the formal visit by the intermediary ordinarily is well known. Nevertheless, circumspection and ritual surround the proceedings; it would be a serious breach of etiquette for either side to quicken the pace in any way. Direct allusion to marriage is a *faux pas*, and the inventiveness of the go-between in dealing with the situation poetically is appreciated as an aesthetic experience. "A little cow is needed," or "A wagon is lacking a wheel," might start things off. The girl's father and his relatives and friends take up the allusion and find ways of expressing their points in an appropriately subtle way. There is no haste, and the company of men may drink and talk without once alluding directly to the subject at hand, much to everyone's pleasure. The game is more enjoyable if the outcome is expected to be positive on the part of the girl's family; in most cases, men will refuse to act as go-between if they feel the boy's family has no chance of succeeding.

A different approach is required if the girl's people wish to deny the marriage request (see Table 8.5). A direct approach is inexcusable; rudeness may engender sufficient resentment to initiate a feud between the two families. If the girl's people anticipate an unwelcome marriage proposal, they may decide to postpone a confrontation by going on the road for a while. They may even arrange a quick engagement to someone else. If the visitor catches them unprepared, he will be made to wait until the family procures a go-between of their own. The situation may be astutely manipulated in order to confuse the boy's family; for example, the brideprice may be raised, so that the re-

---

TABLE 8.5

POSSIBLE WAYS TO PREVENT AN UNDESIRABLE MARRIAGE

I. Total avoidance of confrontation

II.

Objections	Solution
Girl's fear of marriage	Inevitability of marriage
Girl's training incomplete	Training to be completed by mother-in-law
Girl too young	Immediate betrothal but delayed wedding
Only girl left at home to work	Substitution of a daughter-in-law
Mother ill	Immediate betrothal but delayed wedding

III. Hasty betrothal to someone else

IV. Demand for a preposterously high brideprice

V. Insistence that boy join girl's family

---

quired discretion on the part of the intermediary will make it difficult for him to figure out if the girl's people are unwilling to agree to a marriage altogether or if they are merely trying to bargain for a higher brideprice. Furthermore, the intermediary cannot accuse the girl's family of lying even if he suspects it to be the case. His options, therefore, are limited even if the boy's family is determined to obtain this particular girl. The boy's spokesman may suggest that the youth stay with the girl's people; this, as previously indicated, is unusual and may be a move to call the bluff of the other side. If the same suggestion were initiated by the girl's family, it, too, might well be a poker move. If the boy's side expresses a willingness to accede to all the demands of the girl's family and continues to press for a marriage, the only recourse open to the girl's parents is to name an exorbitant brideprice, gambling that the boy's people will then withdraw their suit.

Among the Gypsies, as in any other human group, social interaction is governed by tacit assumptions mutually upheld. However, such assumptions may not be honored by all parties, and this leads to a confrontation without ground rules upon which to fall back. Usually, the side that ignores the assumptions has the advantage in such a gambit because their behavior is completely unexpected. This element of surprise confuses the opponents, and, without the resources of traditional options from which to choose a course of action, they fail to produce an effective countermove. Frequently, they panic and do nothing at all aside from accusing the deviants of criminality.

Thus, instances of Gypsy "bandits" demanding and obtaining girls at minimal brideprices and threatening bodily harm to the families if the suitors were refused are known. Outright capture of the girls has also been documented; Ronald Lee (1972) describes a modern instance among the Canadian Rom culminating in a kris and an eventual *post hoc* agreement on brideprice. (The marriage ceremony of some Gypsy bands also includes a mock bride-capture ritual.) However, these examples of rulebreaking, although much feared, to judge by the frequency with which they are discussed, are apparently quite rare in actuality. Moreover, bride capture and intimidation are now regarded as possible options that may be adopted by the boy's family; so counter-strategies can be formulated ahead of time. For example, the once frequent bride capture no longer holds. Formerly, my informants explained, a non-virginal woman was not acceptable as a bride for a youth;[3] today many brides have already been previously married. Therefore, the modern girl's family can bring her back home and arrange another marriage for her. The new groom's family will protect her and her family from the wrath of the former husband's people. Indeed, she may marry into a family whose seasonal migration routes do not overlap with those of the former husband's family and whose location is unknown to them.

[3]My informants were adamant on the former tradition of virgin brides; Jan Yoors, with whom I have discussed this matter, agrees. However, as far back as 1929, Brown (1929: 166) reported that Romany marriages at least in the United States were very brittle and that remarriage was frequent. Possibly some of the Kalderaš were less opposed to marrying first-time grooms to previously married brides, and they were the initiators of the change in attitude for all the Rom. Certainly, it remains true that the Gypsies, especially the Mačvaja upper class, prefer to avoid broken marriages for their daughters. On the other hand, Brown (1929: 166) refers to wife-stealing as an occasional, non-clandestine phenomenon and asserts that it is regarded as a private matter between the two men involved, the most likely resolution being "indemnification." I have heard of wife-stealing among the Rom, but most of the arguments discussed at social gatherings involve women accusing one another of husband-stealing.

1. 1951. A married woman of the Mačvaja group posing inside a fortunetelling store. Note the liberal use of fabrics as wall-coverings.

2. 1951. A married woman of the Mačvaja group in a typical hand-on-hip pose. She wears a bracelet cuff. The window display includes used dreambooks.

3. 1954. A family portrait of a Mačvaja father and his three sons. Note the large collection of photographs on the mantel piece behind them.

4. 1954. Two young unmarried Mačvaja girls dressed for a wedding celebration.

5. 1974. A first-floor ofisa that has been in steady use for more than three years. The location is ideal because it is on a major shopping street.

6. 1974. A street-level ofisa showing the elaborate signs first adopted in New York City in the 1950s. Note the display items in the window and the young girl looking out.

7. 1974. A street-level ofisa of the Arxentina group. This spacious ofisa is used both as living quarters and as a fortunetelling location.

8. 1974. A first-floor ofisa with an elaborate sign catering to the current American interests in astrology and tarot cards. Three Gypsy youngsters who wanted to be included in the photograph peer through the window.

A Note on Brideprice

Before we discuss the formal betrothal visit, let us gather together what we have said thus far on the brideprice. Brideprices fluctuate in response to the general economic circumstances of the Rom, being larger in prosperous times than in depressions. Local and national rates display variations, too, and sometimes it pays to get a bride from a different country. Some girls command a higher price than others, contingent upon such factors as the relative status of the bride's family; a girl from a prestigious family commands a higher price than a commoner. A trustworthy rule-of-thumb is that the more desirable the girl is as a bride, the higher the price she will command (see Table 8.6 for a recapitulation of this subject.) On the other hand, if the groom's family aspires to rise socially, it will offer a higher brideprice than is truly necessary to arrange the marriage.

TABLE 8.6
BRIDEPRICE COST
Decisions based on the following factors:

Lower Prices	*Higher Prices*
Low status of bride's family	High status of bride's family
Bride already married several times	Virgin bride
Close friendship between families	Desire of groom's family to increase prestige
General economic depression	Time of economic prosperity
No experience as fortuneteller	Good money-maker
Not intelligent	High intelligence
Narrow-hipped	Wide hips
Bad tempered	Docile
	Unusual physical characteristics: e.g., natural blonde

NO MONEY INVOLVED
Bride exchange
Non-Gypsy bride

This is a case of conspicuous consumption, for brideprices are matters of public record and are discussed and remembered by the Rom. Therefore, the family's willingness to splurge is interpreted as an announcement of their affluence. I also have a case history of a marriage being arranged for a boy no older than ten just to prove to the Rom that, contrary to the rumors then circulating, his family could afford to buy a bride and finance an elaborate wedding. The strategy worked well, and the family's prestige was safeguarded.

The social and behavioral attributes of the bride are considerably more important than her physical characteristics, with two exceptions. If her body build gives indications that she may have difficulty bearing many healthy children, the Rom feel justified in paying less for her, for one of the primary functions of a woman is to bear sons for her husband's group. On the other hand, an unusual and aesthetically admired physical attribute considered inheritable may produce a higher price. A Gypsy girl with naturally blonde hair was brought into a New York Kalderaš band for $7,000[4] at a time when the going rate among them was about $2,000. Opinion was divided about this event; some of the Rom were a little envious, but many felt that the groom's family had not acted wisely and might have "broken their luck" by an un-Romany emphasis on something as trivial as feminine pulchritude, which as everyone knows is bound to fade.

The highest price paid within the last thirty years in New York City has been $10,000; the lowest, $250. During the Depression, the median was about $500; in the prosperous forties, it was around $3,500.

In some instances, no money at all is involved, for the Rom may practice bride exchange; a daughter on each side becomes a bride of the other side, implying that both girls are of equal value. Bride exchange has two advantages besides the circumvention of cash expenditure. A doubly strong tie between families occurs, and, since a single wedding banquet may be held for the double wedding with both families sharing costs, the attendant wedding expenses are reduced.

A potential disadvantage inherent in bride exhange lies in the possibility of divorce. One might think that bride exchange is

[4]I do not know whether this is the same case as that reported by Parry (1941: 40); he quotes a brideprice of $10,000.

common among the Rom, but it is not. In fact, Gypsies dislike the system and say that it is unlucky, that one or the other of the marriages is certain to fail. The infrequency of exchange marriages prevents valid statistical study of these claims because contemporary marriages have been notoriously short-lived regardless of their origin.

Should a marriage based on bride exchange break up, the *xanamik* (in-laws) are faced with a serious problem (see Table 8.7). One possibility is to dissolve both marriages, but obviously it would be regrettable to break up a marriage that is viable and in which children may be involved. Furthermore, insisting that the

---

TABLE 8.7
DISSOLVING AN EXCHANGE MARRIAGE

Possible Solution
Dissolution of both marriages
Substitution of another sister
Hold regular divorce trial

Disadvantages	*Advantages*
Other marriage may be successful and with children	No kris required
Broken tie may lead to animosity between families	No kris
Husband or his family already unsatisfactory	No money
Sister may be reluctant	Preservation of second marriage
Must hold *post hoc* brideprice bargaining for both wives	Preservation of alliance with in-laws

---

other wife leave her husband for no reason intrinsic to that marriage may foster additional resentment at a moment of existent psychological stress. The continuation of the sister's marriage would be tantamount to a mutual statement of continuing good faith between the xanamik and a willingness to work things out amicably. Another possibility is to arrange for a sister to substitute for the returning wife; but this is very rare. Thus, the preferred alternative usually is to process the divorce in the usual manner, via a kris.

But in exchange marriages no brideprice sum is ever mentioned, and now the other wife's marriage and progeny require legitimization through payment as will any children resulting from the broken marriage. Furthermore, the kris requires that the brideprice returned be proportional to the blame. Thus, there must be brideprice bargaining after the fact of marriage—a much more difficult situation, for both sides may be tempted to slander each other during such negotiations, and the usual "fun" aspect of the bargaining is spoiled by the knowledge that one of the marriages has gone bad.

A non-Gypsy bride requires no brideprice; but the groom's parents will do well to give her a token payment in order to legitimatize the children.

The Betrothal Visit

Assuming that the suggested union is acceptable to both sides, the boy's intermediary arranges for the next step in the marriage proceedings; this is a formal call upon the girl's parents by the intermediary and the boy's parents. Other kinsmen from both sides are free also to participate in this interaction. The purpose of the visit, arranging the final details of brideprice and setting up a tentative wedding date, is signaled by the fact that the groom's faction brings with them and displays ostentatiously a bottle of brandy wrapped in red ribbons and further decorated with gold coins.[5]

The groom's intermediary opens the discussions by praising both families and auguring a happy future for the couple. The girl's family demurs, expressing their reluctance to lose such a beloved member. The girl's mother appears especially loath to countenance a marriage, and the father is urged to take his wife to one side and talk to her in an effort to convince her of the desirability of the marriage. In a leisurely fashion, the boy's side offers a low brideprice, implying that the honor of the marital alliance is valuable enough. The girl's side may counter by claiming that the girl's activities have been an important contribution

---

[5] The literature well confirms this custom; e.g., Brown (1929: 167) attests to it for the United States Rom, and Bercovici (1928: 223) for the Russian Kalderaš.

to the family treasury; they may suggest an exorbitant bride-price. The groom's spokesman may then perhaps describe the blissful existence and magnanimous treatment the girl will have as a bori; he may also raise his offer a little. The girl's spokesman may reply by further lauding the girl's virtues; he may also reduce his asking price somewhat. Thus the negotiations proceed, freely accompanied by drinking, eating, and socializing. Eventually a sum is agreed upon amidst great rejoicing, and the entire gathering is now devoted to enjoying a good night's entertainment.

After the brideprice is agreed upon, her future mother-in-law puts *galbe* (the necklace of gold coins) around the girl's neck and gives her other jewelry and ribbons as a sign of her engagement and of her new allegiance to her future conjugal family. From that moment on, the girl wears the jewelry and a ribbon in her hair to indicate that she has been spoken for (a single girl is bareheaded, and a married woman always wears a headscarf in public.)

Living in the household where the betrothal arrangements are occurring, of course, the bride-to-be is aware of the engagement proceedings and must participate in the final steps of donning the necklace and putting the ribbon in her hair. The groom-to-be may not even be aware that he is getting married; in the past, he may have found out indirectly through the gossiping of other bandmembers. Today, the young man may insist upon being consulted; some may even approach their parents, asking them to arrange marriage to a specific girl. As recently as thirty years ago, this behavior would have been unconscionable (love marriages definitely were not allowed); however, youths often pressured their elders by threatening to commit suicide. Even today, a young girl cannot indicate her preference for a particular spouse. She can only object to her parents' wishes by threatening either to kill herself before the wedding or else to run away after the marriage.

The Wedding

The date for the wedding is set at the end of the betrothal meeting. Usually the ceremonial payment of the brideprice precedes the wedding by several days; the payment is made at the home of the bride's parents and thus is held most conveniently when the groom's people come to escort the bridal party to the wedding. A party is held at the time of the monetary exchange for the bride's band; the band acts as witnesses who can attest to the adequacy of the payment. A bottle of brandy wrapped in a red scarf is a necessary component of the etiquette.

The party celebrating the payment of the brideprice is financed by the bride's parents whereas the wedding expenses are borne by the groom's. Money in the form of cash attractively wrapped in a red scarf and decorated with ribbons, flowers, and gold coins is given to the bride's father by the groom's father, accompanied by a properly solemn speech. (The young man himself usually remains at home.) The girl's father acknowledges receipt of the money with a speech, opens the package, and counts the money. Several of the older men on the girl's side (including the Old One of the group), acting as godfather-witnesses, also count the money to confirm the validity of the transaction.

The girl now is a part of the groom's family, but her parents show their desire to continue to participate in her welfare and that of their son-in-law by returning part of the brideprice money "to help get the young couple started." They also donate housekeeping equipment (bedding, furniture, brass trays, samovars, etc.) and provide their daughter with a trousseau (which may include furs, diamonds, and gold jewelry) that should take care of her needs for the first year of marriage. All in all, the bride's side contributes a large dowry that may even match in value the brideprice. The bride's parents are free to give as little as they choose, provided that some token return of cash occurs. They may also give as much as they wish, but etiquette requires that they do not exceed the value of the brideprice (anything additionally given can be done quietly and informally outside of the official ritual). Oddly enough, the Gypsies themselves do not often speak about the dowry, although they will about the brideprice. In fact, some of the Gypsy men who have written on the customs of the Rom (Yoors, Maximoff, Lee) do not mention a dowry at all; but my Kalderaš and Mačvaja informants confirm its existence without exception.

The groom's parents usually stay overnight in their xanamik's household. Then a traveling party is assembled to accompany the bride and her dowry to the place where the wedding is to be performed. The bride's parents and perhaps her paternal grandparents are usually in the entourage, as are the groom's parents and any of their kin who have come along to assist them with the baggage.

News of the impending wedding travels quickly by word of mouth. A formal invitation to attend is unnecessary. The wedding is held in the groom's home territory and whoever lives within it is welcome to come. Gypsies from outside the area may wish to attend because they are related to the couple or because the families being united are important members of Rom society. A large catering hall may be rented for the occasion, and hired musicians provide the entertainment.

The groom's relatives are expected to arrive around ten o'clock in the morning; they bring all the food with them, prepared in strict accord with Gypsy dietary law. The banquet tables and hall are decorated with artificial flowers, crêpe paper, and anything else that strikes the fancy. The only constant feature is a large red wedding-banner decorated with gold coins (and sometimes small bells) and mounted on a large stick.

Close relatives and friends are expected to arrive around eleven o'clock. The young girls of the groom's band are in charge of dressing the bride; only the unmarried girls are present. This is often the bride's first introduction to her new relatives; it is often an unnerving experience. The girls criticize the groom, the groom's mother, the state of matrimony in general, and the bride's appearance; they are expected to ask many personal questions. The bride emerges beautiful outside but shaky and miserable inside. The more upset she appears, the more the guests are impressed with her virtue. The ideal bride should spend most of her wedding day huddled in a corner, weeping; her mother is there to ensure that her daughter appears as miserable as possible, often pinching the girl to make her cry.

After the bride has been dressed, the bridal crown is placed on her head by a woman acting as her godmother. The wedding godmother is the personification of the wishes that the marriage be permanent, fruitful, of long duration, and happy. Therefore, the woman must be selected from among the ranks of older women who have been married only once, whose husbands are still alive, who have numerous children, and whose marriages are considered happy. In fact, all women who are widowed or divorced are supposed to avoid physical contact with the bride, and the groom's mother is to make sure that this interdiction is enforced.

The bride now is properly dressed (nowadays she may be dressed in a regular American wedding gown), and she is led to the center of the hall, where her groom and mother-in-law await her. She is then placed between them, and the three hold hands, forming an inner circle, the rest of the Rom acting as a large outer circle with the Old One of the groom's family holding the wedding banner. A circle dance, resembling the southeastern European *kola* or Israeli *hora* commences, the two circles facing each other but moving in opposite directions.

The scene is impressive: symbolically, the bride is being incorporated into a new social grouping, the members of which face her, acknowledging her presence and bidding her welcome by their encirclement. Since the bride is in the middle of the inner triad, the more she tries to pull away from her groom out of shyness, the closer she is drawn to her mother-in-law. The harder she tries to avoid her mother-in-law, the closer she gets to her groom. In this way, she is made forcibly aware of the two most significant people in her new life.

Once the dance is over, the older married people sit down to the banquet; the other guests may dance. From time to time, the young men form their own private circle, some providing rhythmic accompaniment by beating on chairs or clapping while their age-mates perform a crouching dance in the center of the ring. Only the young men participate in these dances because they are reputed to be obscene.

Among the Kalderaš, a friend of the groom's father acts as the master of ceremonies, after the elders have eaten. (Like his feminine counterpart, this man should be once-married, and happily at that.) He takes a large loaf of Italian or French bread and hollows it out. "We have a house to build," he announces; then he walks around the banquet table, approaching in turn each of the seated guests who gives him a cash present. The godfather will hold the money over each contributor's head, announcing the denomination of the bill (often exaggerating the amount by adding 100 to the actual value). The money then is placed in the loaf, and the donor is given a red scarf or a flower to wear.

At some Mačvaja weddings, the guests are offered flowers before the banquet; accepting and wearing them is a pledge to contribute during the banquet. From time to time, the godfather counts the money in the loaf and informs the assembly of the total thus far. At his discretion, he may spur the guests on by such statements as "Well, we have the walls built, but we still need a roof." When finally he is satisfied, he presents the loaf and money to the groom's father with great flourish.

Wedding parties are no different from other large social gatherings insofar as rules of sobriety are concerned: in each family grouping, one of the young men (more if the family is large) is designated to remain sober throughout the festivities; the others may drink as much as they please. Not many members of the band are happy to act as the "sober" one, so the Old One alternates the duty among his relatives in an equitable fashion. But one member must always remain sober; it is considered an offense for everyone to get drunk. The sober one has two major responsibilities. During the party, he is there to help the others if they become ill from drinking too much or if they grow overly aggressive and argumentative; after the party, to act as chauffeur to get the family home safely.

At some time between the end of the banquet and the end of the party, the bride is taken into a private room by the older women of the man's group, and her body is inspected to determine if she is a virgin. Today this ritual is almost meaningless, for many brides have been married several times; but seventy years ago, this part of the wedding ceremony was crucial. The godfather is then told of the bride's status; thereafter, he signals the band for a fanfare, and raising his hands, shouts: "We have seen the tokens of virginity." The audience then yells and applauds and forms itself into a large chain to weave its way around the ballroom floor in another circle dance.

The party may continue for several more hours (until four or five o'clock in the afternoon), but the bridal couple and immediate family leave as soon as the bride's virginity has been announced. Their departure sometimes takes the form of a mock marriage-by-capture; that is, the girl's relatives surround her, and the groom's friends are supposed to wrest her away by force.[6]

Post-Nuptial Behavior

Among the Kalderaš, the bride and groom do not cohabit for three days after the wedding. I have been told that this gives the girl time to adjust to her new family and surroundings before the shock of first coitus. Other Gypsy tribes, however, do not require this waiting-period; nor is it required in cases of previously married brides.[7] In some groups, blood stains must be shown to a number of band members, and so today in the instances of remarriages they are faked by using chicken blood or cutting one's finger. Some bands follow the custom of requiring the bridal couple to inform both sets of parents of the nuptial night; this report is made only when the bride is being married for the first time. The bride and groom make a courtesy call on his parents, and the groom reports that the sexual act has been successful; then, the couple pays a formal call on her parents to repeat the announcement. Many young grooms find it necessary to bolster their courage from a bottle before they can face their fathers-in-law to deliver the report.

Duty having been done, the young couple settles into married life immediately. There is no honeymoon; but if at all possible, a certain amount of sleeping privacy is granted out of deference to the embarrassment both should feel at this early stage of marriage. Psychological privacy is not considered desirable; the groom's parents consider it their duty to keep a discrete eye on the neophytes to ascertain if there are any problems (sexual or

[6]During the camping days, however, wedding festivals required special wedding encampments, with many tents set up in a large circle in a forest clearing. The camp was decorated with red banners (of which the current wedding banner is the sole survivor), and many campfires were needed to roast the pigs and turkeys to be consumed in the two-week ceremony. People ate and drank and danced and sang throughout the period, snatching sleep periodically as they desired. The bridal couple was given a separate tent, and after first intercourse the hymenal stains were hoisted on a pole in the center of the camp. Today, of course, none of this is possible.

[7]Brown (1929: 169) specified a one-day abstention period. Yoors (personal communication) says the Lovara lack this custom.

otherwise) in the union. In discussing the matter with me, some of the older people remarked that they thought American honeymoon customs were cruel: "Two young people are cast out to try their luck in a new situation without the means to get loving advice from those who are experienced in these matters."

The groom now has a wife who caters to his needs and whom he orders about, so his mother and sisters may devote less time to him. The bride, on the other hand, is now a bori, to be ordered around by all. She is expected to be the first one to awake in the morning and the last one to go to bed. She should do much of the housework as well as work as a fortuneteller, giving her earnings to her husband and mother-in-law; she should eat sparingly and only after everyone else has finished; she must ask neither for clothing nor for an opportunity to go out; she should be grateful if she gets either. She is too embarrassed to talk to her father-in-law, who is supposed to ignore her presence for the most part; her mother-in-law talks to the girl frequently, but these dialogues resemble a series of commands and remonstrances more than social intercourse.

At least since the 1920s, Gypsy marriages have been short-lived (Brown 1929: 167-69); most young people seem unable to achieve a permanent union without several attempts at marriage. When I began my research in the 1940s, at least 60 percent had been married more than once; but the 1970s have seen an improvement in the rate of stable first marriages. These changes are best understood by examining the concomitant attitudinal changes. The original marriage pattern dictated a stable union until it was broken by the demise of either spouse. The rule that married women had to remain with their husbands was strictly enforced even by the woman's kin, who would refuse to accept her back into their group if she ran away from her husband. My informants mentioned that parents would try to give a runaway to any man who would accept her; they also said such a man was hard to find since marriage to a non-virgin "spoiled his chances" to obtain a virgin bride in the future.

These statements seem to indicate that running away/remarriage was a possible, albeit rare, alternative. We must also consider the fact that the no-remarriage rule was an almost unattainable ideal more honored in the breach than in actuality.

Be that as it may, the universally negative feelings toward remarriage acted as a strong deterrent to easy remarriage and prevented many women from leaving an unhappy union. Another deterrent, of course, was and is the rule that a woman cannot take her children with her.

I cannot ascertain either from research into the literature or from discussions with the Gypsies themselves when running away and remarrying became frequent. But the change in attitude which not only made remarriage frequent but also granted the parents the right to hold another public wedding celebration acted to encourage unhappy wives to leave their husbands, especially if no children had been produced by the union. We have seen that the young bori is subjected to much psychological strain in the early years of her marriage; consequently, most women are dissatisfied with or even despondent about their marriages until they become mothers. Without any custom to dissuade them from doing so, they have a strong tendency to run back home.

A remarkable change is occurring in the connubial relationship; although marriages still are arranged, the young people are less inhibited in expressing their emotions in public and in receiving emotional support from their spouses. Many seem genuinely to fall in love. The young wives feel free to complain to their husbands, and the young men are willing to defend their wives against their mothers. The husbands are especially solicitous during pregnancy.

This unsuppressed emotionality has helped to counteract the former strains built into the marital relationship. The new shift toward marriages emphasizing a postmarital love bond between the partners that can be expressed in public without shame is an innovation for the Rom, replacing the traditional rules of public avoidance of one's spouse and the maintenance of the husband's absolute loyalty to his parents. I believe that the innovation has become feasible because of the older age at which youths now marry; older boys are more psychologically prepared to cut the parental bonds needed by young boys. I also think that there is a good chance that Gypsy marital stability will continue to increase over the next several decades.

All the Gypsies I know are monogamous, one man marrying

one woman at a time. But I know of two cases in which a man had two wives. In each of these instances exceptional circumstances prevailed: a very young boy was married to a woman of his mother's age because his own (widowed) mother was mortally ill. This "wife" then raised the youth until he was of marriageable age and bought him a young bride, who functioned as his real wife whereas the older woman remained as a mother surrogate. Some of the literature (e.g., Brown 1929: 168) on the Gypsies indicates that polygyny (several wives at the same time) was or is occasionally practiced; but I have never encountered it in my experience. Nor have I any evidence whatsoever that youths' fathers were temporary husbands to young brides (op. cit.: 166). I suspect that such reports either were unfactual or else were examples of psychopathological conditions.

9

MATURITY, DECLINE, AND DEATH

A man fully achieves his place in Gypsy society when he becomes the father of several children. His wife, now a mother, is regarded as a permanent member of the band, and her movements are much less in question. She now arranges her own *ofisa* (fortunetelling store) partnerships, and she runs her own household free from the interference and supervision of her mother-in-law. Such a husband-wife team is free to travel by itself, achieving increasing autonomy and leadership.

A Man's Prime

A man's physical and social prime overlap to a great extent. His ascendancy begins after he has sired several sons, and as his children grow, so does his status. He will reach the peak of his powers when he starts marrying them off; with the help of his family, he will go as far as his ambition and capacity will take him. The higher his status, the longer he can remain there, for his usefulness to Gypsy society shifts gradually as he ages. As a youth, his contribution will be mostly physical; as he matures, his contribution will be mostly intellectual. Having lived a long and successful life, he will be listened to and followed. He will be called upon to solve problems, give advice, settle disagreements. He will also be called upon to act as a repository for and as a safeguard of Romany traditions and law. These manifold duties increasingly force him to concentrate his time and energies on the affairs of the band rather than on those of his own immediate family. He is becoming an Old One and a Big Man.

A Woman's Prime

As the man begins to relinquish his role as family supervisor, his wife takes over. Her physical capabilities, aside from the ability to bear children, are never very important in establishing her status. Initially, her ranking within her conjugal band is based on her brideprice. Her status then moves up according to that of her husband. Business acumen is an important factor affecting social mobility, and the overall financial success of the couple is mutually rewarding. Thus, if a woman is a good money-maker, her husband has capital available for business ventures; if she is also shrewd and can make her husband listen to her advice, her husband may become successful on the basis of her shrewdness. However, a gifted wife married to a man who is lazy or incapable cannot go very far because of her status as a woman. The band may agree tacitly that she is smarter or a harder worker than her mate, but official commendation goes only to the man, as head of his family unit. An unsuccessful man is still responsible for his own family affairs, and his wife remains relegated to a secondary position.

Assuming that the husband's position among the Rom rises continuously, his wife is expected to take on some of his duties within the immediate family group. Knowing his wishes and how he would react, she becomes his lieutenant. There is more leeway in this situation than is formally recognized, and in large measure a woman can run the affairs of the family to suit herself. Her daughters-in-law have been taking orders from her from the time they entered the household; her sons listen to her, partly out of habit, partly out of love and respect. Their obedience neither demeans them in the eyes of other Gypsies nor threatens their male egos, since theoretically they are following the leadership of their father, whose commands are being conveyed through the mother. Adult men do go to their mothers for guidance, and the older women also freely offer unsolicited advice (Wright 1946: 117-18).

The woman's ascendancy in her own conjugal family is contingent upon her native intelligence, strength of will, and experience. In many bands, the women are the ones who do most of the business with the gaǰe. Every day they meet non-Gypsies in their fortunetelling; hence, they learn about gaǰe hopes and fears, motivations, and weaknesses. They also deal with the tradespeople who supply their household needs. Their sons and husbands can draw upon this knowledge. If the test of experience shows that the woman's counsel has been good, the men return for more, and she can build up a formidable reputation as advisor.

Another advantage in her favor stems from the Gypsy feeling that living past the age of forty requires a reservoir of superhuman (Americans would say "supernatural") power and influence in the universe. Therefore, older people, especially women, are said to control forces that they can use to further their ends.

Witches

The Rom believe in witchcraft. They are aware that the outside world often sees them as witches and sorcerers, and they encourage this attitude, since it is not only good for business but also acts as protection for the Rom. When questioned, however, Gypsies tend to be noncommital or somewhat skeptical about their role in witchcraft. They do believe in the power of words —that a wish verbalized may come true—but they do not speculate on the reasons therefore. They also feel that a strong belief in something brings about its own fulfillment. Some believe in the power of revelation; the future could be divined, for example, by someone with a special kind of intuition. But they seem to believe most strongly in what Robert Merton has called the "self-fulfilling hypothesis" (1957: 128-29, 421-36): once a person has a strong belief in something, he inadvertently makes it come to fruition through an unconscious screening process. That individual is predisposed to observe and remember what he expects to; thus, his behavior is governed by his expectations. Anticipating success, he acts with confidence and self-assurance. His motor coordination is good; he is psychologically receptive and is alert to opportunities. Anticipating failure, on the other hand, he acts timidly and half-heartedly; his motor coordination is poor, and he is psychologically defensive and withdrawn.

Most Rom, however, believe that in the past and perhaps even now there are some Gypsy women who have studied under sorcerers and deliberately can cause things to happen by ritual (magical) procedures. Such women are called "witches"; they may be suspect, but there is rarely evidence to prove that they engage in sorcery.

Yet there is another type of witch, one who has inherent powers to make things come to pass merely by wishing them; these desired events are frequently harmful to someone else. Gypsies believe that any strong negative emotion, such as hate or envy, generates a disharmonic force field in the universe that attracts more disharmony (Americans would say "evil"). This power can become concentrated so that it can then be directed toward an object, especially a human being. This idea is akin to that of the "evil eye." For example, someone inadvertently allows a feeling of jealousy to express itself in his thought or speech, and the object of jealousy becomes the victim of misfortune or illness. Since all of us harbor negative emotions from time to time, it follows that we all are capable of causing the evil eye, or, to put it another way, each of us is a potential "witch."

This potential power to do evil is taken for granted by the Rom. No one is totally free of negative emotions; but if something unlucky were to happen to a Gypsy with whom one is temporarily at odds, one is not to blame because the victim simply may be reaping the just deserts of past misdeeds. However, if someone notices, for example, that people I dislike have more bad luck than most, that when I get angry bad things happen to others, then he may begin to suspect that I am a witch. If, in addition, I do not seem to suffer my fair share of life's adversities (my luck is consistently good; my business prospers; my loved ones are thriving; my health is excellent), then a suspicion may turn to a conviction. Furthermore, the older I get without too many hard knocks (while my age-mates are suffering increased adversity), the more I show that I am a witch. (If we recall that a man's social position depends in part on his physical capabilities, then we can understand why fewer men are thought to be witches. They usually begin to experience a "loss of luck" as they go into physical decline.)

A witch's power increases through time; again, the reasons are unclear. Perhaps a form of "practice makes perfect" is involved, and the concentration of disharmonic force fields becomes faster and more efficient. For whatever reason, some old women are thought to be formidable witches and are feared by most of the Rom. However, the witch cannot be held morally responsible for any evil she causes since she is both unaware of the possession of her powers and also incapable of divesting herself of them. People simply tend to avoid her lest they anger her in some unforeseen way; if they must interact with her or if she seeks them out and makes some request of them, they are careful to please her insofar as possible, catering to her desires and speaking flatteringly of her.

Women whose senility takes the form of perpetual irascibility are a great strain to have around. The Gypsies recount the killing of some of these women (Maximoff 1949). Such witch executions were extreme acts, resorted to only in desperation and after much consultation among the Big Men. Complete unanimity of opinion was required, and all members of the band had to participate in the final act. This rule was designed to ensure that all shared equal blame in the taking of a life and thus all ran equal risks in the eventuality of vengeance either by the witch's family or, more dangerously, by the witch's ghost.

The Declining Years

As intellectual capacity diminishes, so does a man's position within Gypsy society. One man who is hale and hearty in his sixties may continue as the Big Man of his extended family, chief of his band, and respected judge at the kris; another man whose health begins to fail in his thirties may rapidly lose status so that he is a social nonentity by the time he is forty.

Loss of status is a gradual process, and this fact in itself spares the ego of the man going into decline, for he may be unaware of it. At first, fewer families will seek to join his kumpanja; later, some of his followers will realign elsewhere. The change is not announced—some families simply fail to reappear after the routine summer dispersions. Fewer men visit him to seek his counsel or to ask him to participate in the kris. But his presence at these meetings is still accepted, and, if he chooses to speak, he is given a hearing, although his advice may no longer be considered seriously. At social gatherings, he is treated with deference, being among the first to be offered food and drink; the other men may consider it their duty to spend some time with him. The older and more infirm he becomes, the more outwardly deferential the Gypsies act toward him. Imperceptibly, the younger people gently weave a protective cocoon around him, sparing him anxiety and affording him an opportunity to live out his life uneventfully and with dignity.

Truly old people are still relatively rare among the Rom, and forty is considered to be the beginning of old age. Few men survive into their sixties and seventies. Old women, too, are far from common among the Gypsies. After they enjoy their period of domination within their own extended families—approximately from the time of the marriages of their sons to the maturation of their grandchildren—older women tend to become exceedingly reticent and antisocial. They sit quietly, and their everyday life is one of observing but not participating. Many of them smoke a large white Turkish meerschaum pipe incessantly. This lack of activity and uncommunicativeness is threatening to the other members of their groups, for there is no way to know what these old people are thinking. Furthermore, since Gypsies tend to be very active, spirited, highly verbal people, the contrast with the wordless, solemn, motionless, old women tends to be unsettling. However, those old women who retain their mental faculties receive the complete attention of all those present when, on rare occasions, they deign to say something. Everyone strains to hear the pronouncement, and the opinion or advice is followed unquestioningly.

Dying and Death

The process of building a protective human wall around the aging intensifies when illness threatens. Pain and trouble are taken for granted as inevitable, but an effort is made to alleviate discomfort and to distract a person's attention from what ails him. Neither the aged one nor the family expects or desires a sudden death. Gypsies think one should prepare for death in a rational and dignified way. The psychological debts of a lifetime should be paid; those who still harbor negative feelings toward the dying man should divest themselves of such thoughts and emotions. Similarly, the dying should not leave this life still encumbered with negative psychic energy. Dying should be a dignified completion of life; thus, the seriously ill are made as comfortable as possible, and a ritual exchange of mutual forgiveness should occur. In some instances, an attempt is made to prolong life a little longer so that as many relatives and friends as possible can meet the dying person. A younger, stronger individual grasps the hands of the dying person in the hope that the more vital life force will flow temporarily into the enfeebled body, or contact with the life-giving earth is attempted through an object that can be simultaneously gripped by the individual and still touch the ground (such as a chair or a stick driven into the soil) or by laying the person directly on the earth. All of these methods utilize a principle akin to electrical conduction; the human body or the object is a conductor of the forces of life.

When death comes, Gypsies abandon themselves to intense expressions of grief, weeping and screaming and beating themselves. All reflecting surfaces are covered (mirrors, stagnant water, etc.) so that no one can see himself. Washing, combing, shaving, and eating cease until after the funeral. The corpse is laid out, and a vigil is held near the body. In some groups, everyone drinks liquor to get himself through his initial ordeal. News of the death travels by word of mouth and by telephone- and telegram-chains, and relatives and friends are expected to come to pay their respects and to speak the ritual of forgiveness. The more important the deceased and the more unexpected his death, the longer the interval to the funeral. The deceased's soul is believed to remain in the corpse until burial. Burial releases both the permanent soul and also the temporary ghost from the body.

Apparently, Gypsies once practiced cremation and the burning of the deceased's possessions. Today, Gypsy funerals are held in a church, and the priest is expected to conduct services and deliver an eulogy. Thereafter, the total grief to which the Rom have surrendered themselves thus far must be attenuated and replaced by a feeling of gladness that the deceased has left this human world to return to the land of his ancestors and of unborn souls. This is necessary not only to restore normal functioning to the living but also to help the deceased make the transition. So drinking, singing, and dancing are an integral part of the Gypsy ritual, and the Rom bring liquor and music into the church to carry out the Gypsy part of the funeral services. In this fashion, they fulfill the need to entertain the dead soul of their kinsman, to reassure him that his obligations to the living have been fulfilled, to demonstrate that they are reconciled to the separation, and to urge him to begin his final journey back to his place of origin.

Burial service at the gravesite usually is an all-Gypsy ritual. A final farewell is said at the open grave by all present, and individuals pour wine or whisky and cast offerings into the grave while the drinking, singing, and dancing continues. Then a speech is made to the dead in which the ritual of forgiveness is repeated; he is told he must sever his emotional connections with the living and return to the place of the souls. Each kinsman files past the grave, stopping to address the deceased by name and solemnly repeating, "So-and-so, I leave you to God," and then walking away quickly without looking back.

Remembrance feasts are held during the first year after death to honor the deceased, whose soul and ghost still remain partially attached to the living. Most groups hold such celebrations on the third day and the ninth day after death, six weeks after death, on the six-month anniversary, and finally on the year anniversary. The parties fulfill some of the same functions as the funeral celebration. An individual of the same sex as the deceased is given new clothes to wear and functions as the guest of honor. He acts as a substitute for the dead person at the party, and whatever he wears and eats and drinks and enjoys is paralleled in the world of the dead by the deceased. During these parties, the deceased is addressed by name and invited to participate with his living kinsmen and friends. Apparently the reasoning behind these celebrations is that the soul/ghost still is in contact either continuously or occasionally with the living. A placated ghost will disappear gradually, and his soul will be free to reside in the world of the ancestors. After the final one-year celebration, no further remembrance feast is held, and the name of the dead one is avoided for a while lest the ghost be reactivated. The soul becomes one of the nameless ancestors, all of whom are honored in a yearly ceremony (Maximoff 1947b: 42; Mitchell 1945: 47; Parry 1941: 40).

Mourning may last as long as one year, but the period can be cut short, sometimes at the request of the dying man himself. Full mourning—in terms of no shaving, no haircutting, no change of clothes, no cooking by members of the bereaved family—never continues for longer than one month. Partial mourning interdicts the playing of music, dancing, drinking hard liquor (beer is allowable), attending other people's celebrations, etc. The Big Man decides the length of the mourning period (unless the dead person wished differently), depending upon the exigencies of the local Gypsy situation, the degree of closeness of the relationship to the deceased, the number of people involved, the degree of possible danger to the band's leadership while mourning is in progress, etc. (Brown 1929: 168-70; Lee 1972; Myers 1945: 92; Yoors 1967: 77-80; Yoors 1971: 86-87).

The Gypsies are aware that death is inevitable for man. A person who has lived to see children grow up and have children of their own, who has achieved some modicum of success within Gypsy society and has earned the respect of the Rom as an individual has lived a full life. He has sampled life's offerings, both good and bad, and he has survived; his line is assured continuation through his offspring; his own reputation will endure as long as those who remember recount his "tales of reputation," as Gypsies sit in the quiet of the evening, relaxing from the experiences of the day and savoring the companionship of friends and relatives. When such a man dies, the Gypsies say "He has eaten his bread," and this simple statement aptly summarizes their estimate of a properly accomplished life cycle. Good fortune or adversity, happiness or sorrow, wealth or poverty, comfort or pain—in the ultimate analysis none of these are worthy of mention. What really is significant is that a Rom was born and, having been brought into this world, somehow managed to stay alive until old age. That is the final triumph of Gypsyhood.

10

RESERVOIRS OF GYPSY CULTURE

For the last hundred years outsiders have predicted the disappearance of the Gypsies. Nevertheless, these aliens in metropolis are still among us. How Gypsy culture has managed to survive is the subject of this chapter.

Temporary Contact: Nomadism as an Isolating Mechanism

For people to incorporate into another group, they must be in continuous, intimate contact with their neighbors, so that each side may get to know the other. A nomadic way of life, however, effectively reduces the amount of time during which a group may remain in association with others. Throughout their history, the Rom have kept their culture away from inquisitive eyes. In former times, they camped away from settlements; the longer the anticipated stay in one place, the more secluded the campsite selected. The Gypsies, on their part, were never much interested in the gajo way of life.

Now that the Rom are based in cities, one might anticipate a closer relationship with outsiders. However, this is not the case. A people can be nomadic even in a metropolis. New York City is large and crowded; it is inhabited by many different ethnic groups. Since the Gypsies maintain their nomadic patterns within the city, contact with any given group is usually brief. A band may move from Manhattan's East Harlem (mostly Puerto Rican) to Brooklyn's Crown Heights (with its concentration of Jews) to Queens' Jackson Heights (an area characterized by its

West Indian population). Therefore, the old situation of sporadic and superficial interaction with any one group of non-Gypsies continues unabated. So does the Romany distaste for what little they do see of gaǰo life.

Gypsy nomadism is not obvious to non-Gypsies. For example, a Gypsy ofisa may remain at the same address for months at a time. The store may remain the same in terms of location and decoration, but, behind the brightly colored curtains, the proprietors may change rapidly. The change of tenants is not usually apparent to the gaǰe, for one Gypsy woman looks pretty much like another. Untutored eyes see only the similarity in costume and not the facial differences. Neighbors or customers who become aware of the presence of different fortunetellers may be told a plausible, reassuring story, e.g., that the new occupants are sisters who are helping out because of illness in the family.

I know of high-income-producing ofisas that have remained open at the same locations for five years or longer; the personnel, however, has changed about once every six months. The urban environment in which Gypsies live encourages anonymity, and it contributes to their isolation.

Incomplete Contact: Prejudice as an Isolating Mechanism

Most Gypsies have great contempt for non-Gypsies; these feelings are often reciprocated by non-Gypsies themselves. One of the characteristics of prejudice is that it is a self-reinforcing system; selective observation helps fulfill one's expectations. Evidence to the contrary is overlooked or explained away as an exception.

Even if the Gypsies were to decide they wanted a closer contact with outsiders, they would not obtain it readily, because the gaǰe, for their part tend to fear and dislike Gypsies. They also have a lot of misinformation about them. For instance, Gypsies frequently have been accused of ritual murder or cannibalism in Europe. But homicide is avoided by Gypsies because of their fear of ghosts, and no Rom would condemn himself to "ghost sickness" by ingesting parts of a corpse. Nevertheless, fifty years ago, Gypsies were being killed in Central Europe for alleged cannibalism.

Buffered Contact: The Sexes as Separate Spheres of Influence

Inherent in Gypsy culture is still another mechanism for discouraging contact with outsiders; I refer to the sexual division of
labor. We have seen that the only members of a Gypsy society to
have continuous contact with non-Gypsies are the fortunetellers.
However, the non-Gypsy world represented by ofisa customers
is atypical. Most of the people seen are women, so the Gypsy
reader views the non-Gypsy world for the most part through
feminine eyes. Furthermore, Gypsy palmists are most often
patronized by the unhappy or emotionally disturbed, creating a
negative impression on the Gypsies.

Still, those few Gypsies who would like the freedom of non-
Gypsy women (perhaps convinced that they would handle situations in a better way) are in no position to effect such changes.
Their young husbands see no advantage to themselves in grant-
ing the wives more freedom, and their mothers-in-law also are
aware that compliant young women are necessary to perform
household chores and to contribute financially to the upkeep of
households. Thus, the young women would be the most likely to
profit by any changes in Gypsy culture, but they occupy too low a
status within their society to effect any changes. By the time the
women are sufficiently powerful to influence their groups, their
own self-interest militates against any changes, for now they are
wives of Big Men, mothers of adult sons, and therefore
mothers-in-law commanding a corps of daughters-in-law, who
must be kept compliant.

As far as the men are concerned, their sphere of activities
emphasizes the world of the Rom much more than that of the
gajo. Thus, they are less apt to come into close contact with
non-Gypsies. Today, when they do interact, their associations
(aside from secret visits to prostitutes) are with other men almost
exclusively. A young Gypsy husband has few responsibilities
imposed on him, and his life contrasts favorably with that of
young American husbands. Small wonder that young Gypsy
men see little reason to change their lifestyles. The relatively
infrequent complaint of twenty years ago that they were not
allowed to choose their own brides is not often heard nowadays,
not only because the Old Ones are more inclined to arrange
matches in accordance with the inclinations of the younger peo-

ple, but also because increasing Gypsy acceptance of love between husbands and wives has resulted in more personally satisfying unions.

Among the men, only the older ones have extensive contacts
with outsiders. But like the older women, the Big Men have a
vested interest in the status quo, and they are unwilling to effect
change.[1]

Flexibility: Delayed Enculturation and Readiness to Bend

The history of the Rom proves that a people and a culture can
endure great stress and environmental change and still survive;
they themselves seem to lack much historical perspective, for
their memory, as measured by the tales of olden times and by
their ability to recall their ancestors, encompasses no more than
five generations at most. However, each generation reaffirms
for itself anew that rigid, stubborn inflexibility makes survival
difficult. For example, the young girls experience a delay in
learning the details of their basic roles until after marriage. This
postponed enculturation acts as a mechanism to insure an easy
adjustment to the new band into which they marry, for they have
not acquired behavioral habits that would have to be changed.
Part of the early training also teaches them to expect that some
customs will be different after their marriage—perhaps even the
dialect of Romany will vary.[2]

Even the males are aware that great cultural and linguistic
diversity exists in the non-Gypsy world. The men are taught to
remain true to their Gypsy values, but they are warned that they,
too, must make readjustments as they travel among the gaje.
They are trained to look for different legal systems and regulations, to expect varying ways of doing business, to anticipate
variations in dress, food, etc. They learn of specific differences
through the factual accounts in "tales of truth." They are

[1]Sexual dichotomy as a deterrent to culture change has been argued in detail
in Cotten 1951.

[2]The attitude toward dialect differences among the Gypsies deserves special
comment. Even after long years of residence among speakers of other dialects,
Gypsy women preserve their natal dialect as a means of asserting their prove-
nance. There is no social pressure exerted by the husband's people for them to
change their speech habits; but their children are corrected sternly if they fail
to speak the dialect of the father's band.

cautioned to place themselves under the patronage and guidance of the resident Rom, should they have to relocate to unfamiliar areas, and they are warned that they will have to accept a lower status in the new situation until they can readjust. All of these attitudes nurture a psychological flexibility leading to a reduction of stress in the face of external changes and a strong belief that accommodation is not necessarily a renunciation of one's own ways.

Reinforcement: Gypsy Arts and the Kris

Gypsy values have another cultural avenue for their continuous, positive expression; this is by means of the arts. The Nomads' major art forms are song, dance, and story-telling. Of these, dance is the least important. Dancing is a frequent pastime; every Gypsy girl wants to be a good dancer, and young women consider it worthwhile to practice dance-steps whenever they can. However, individual solo steps are unique to each dancer (and jealously guarded); some emphasize graceful coordination of the body; some concentrate on the intricacies of the footwork; and some on the rapidity of executing the steps. There seems to be no particular meaning assigned to the various choreographies.

Similarly, the different types of dances—circle dance involving both sexes; men's dances in which several men occupy the dance-floor simultaneously; the solo wedding dance of young men; the dance involving an older man and a corps of young women; solo female dances; couple dances borrowed from the gaje—are performed only on certain social occasions; the dances themselves, however, are meaningless. On the other hand, dances carry latent psychological messages that can be analyzed by the anthropologist. For example, the reader will recall the interpretative discussion of the circle wedding dances. The highly gymnastic men's dance serves as a vehicle to emphasize male physical prowess. I have watched middle-aged men strain to surpass (or at least to keep up with) younger men, and I have seen their relief and self-satisfaction when they succeeded. The old men do not place themselves in this competitive position; instead, they dance with the young daughters and daughters-in-law in a proud assertion of their right to command the behavior of these young women (the older women never imitate this dance, but the dance-floor is yielded to them quickly during solo female performances).

The various kinds of Gypsy songs reflect the different social occasions during which they are sung. Some are dance-songs; but most songs are given the full attention of the audience without the competing distraction of dance. Instrumental accompaniment is not considered a necessity. Good singers may be called upon to perform for long stretches of time; other singers may join in and clap to mark the major beats of the rhythm. The Rom do not approve of the gratuitous introduction of syncopation by an onlooker, as I have discovered from experience.

The men sing the drinking songs and the dirges. Both sexes join in the long traditional epic songs; but the women, at least among the Mačvaja, tend to function as lead singers. The subject matter of drinking and dance songs is humorous. The dirges are full of defiance and pride. They may tell of the sadness of parting, but they also affirm the joys of having lived. Positive about the good points and negative about the bad ones, these songs reinforce Gypsy values and encourage the Rom to follow the dictates of their culture by leading exemplary lives like those of the people honored in the dirges.

Another set of songs deals with everyday occurrences. There are a limited number of basic melodies involved, but the words are new, improvised at the gatherings. The songs are about specific people, usually the important members of the group, and the singer-composers are free to criticize the Big Men without reproach. Some of these songs are used as a means of social protest: the texts may reflect the general sentiment of the Gypsy band toward one of the influential men (or women) and thereby act as a form of social control, praising or damning as the situation requires it. These songs are memorized immediately, then repeated far and wide, their contents being treated seriously by all. (The reputation of the Big Men depends in part both on the frequency with which their names are mentioned in the songs and on the nature of the comments.)

Daughters-in-law in the group find another important use for these songs. Ordinarily required to be self-effacing, when called upon to entertain as a singer, a bori occupies center stage. If her improvisations are clever and reflect a sharp mind, the young woman earns the recognition of the gathering.

Story-telling, like singing, is still very much a living art among the Rom. Fairytales are avowedly invented to entertain people. These stories are considered the exclusive property of the teller; only he can repeat them. The plots are action-oriented; frequently repetitive episodes are included in the full version of the story. Some of the tales relate the exploits of human beings: male or female, of noble or of humble birth, Gypsy or non-Gypsy. One particular category of fairytale is of the Foolish-Jack type; for example, a supposedly stupid youth gets the better of people who are apparently older, wiser, richer, more important than he, and in the process the entire social group is forced to acknowledge that it erred in its original judgment. These wish-fulfillment tales emphasize the importance of shrewdness, the need to rely upon one's intelligence for survival, the idea that appearances can be deceiving. They are not only entertaining but they are educational as well, serving to reinforce Gypsy cultural values.

"Tales of reputation" are stories about known individuals; they can be of two types. "True tales of reputation" deal with the virtues and achievements of an individual. "Lying tales of reputation," on the other hand, deal with the faults and foibles of a man, and are based on gossip. Tales of reputation spread quickly throughout Gypsydom. Who knows when one may meet its hero? It is helpful to know in advance the type of person whom one will be dealing with; therefore, many people are known by hearsay before they are ever met. I have found that many Rom "know" me, although we have never met before. It is not unusual for them to ask me to repeat certain incidents of my life in order to verify their stories!

"Tales of truth" are mostly didactic; they include narratives of survival: what business opportunities exist, how to tell fortunes in different languages, who to deal with among gajo authorities, etc. Others deal with religious beliefs and practices. In fact, these tales transmit essential knowledge of all kinds, except for that pertaining to the kris (Gypsy justice).

The kris tales, like the other stories, are important reservoirs of Gypsy lore, inculcating attitudes toward the Rom's place in the universe and behavior in the face of the uncertainties of life.

Pragmatism: Gypsy World View

Gypsy behavior in everyday circumstances seems to be governed by sheer practicality. In the protective circle of trusted relatives and friends, however, the Gypsy will discuss philosophical principles and ideals with passion, sincerity, and determination—an abstract topic, the subject of an intellectual exercise. Any problems an outsider may have in trying to understand the apparent inconsistencies of Gypsy attitudes and behavior are probably the result of a lack of familiarity with their underlying world view. To a Gypsy, we Americans must seem a simple-minded people because we think in terms of contrasting pairs: good or evil and all-or-none. The Gypsies see us as an un-individualistic, highly conforming people.

The Gypsies emphasize complexity: the keystone of existence is the harmony of the universe; such harmony requires the complicated orchestration of a multiplicity of entities and forces. The overall balance is a subtle, shifting counterpoise like the succession of seasons and years; spring inevitably follows winter, but one knows in advance that next year's spring will not be the same as this year's. Thus I may know the characteristics of springtime in general but I must also be prepared to find that this particular spring is unique. The logical extension of this attitude is that a man should be guided by general principles of behavior (corresponding to the general characteristics of springtime), but he cannot survive if he always applied concrete details of behavior successful in one particular circumstance (equivalent to "last year's spring") to another circumstance (equivalent to "this year's spring").

So the hidebound traditionalist is as foolish as the man who abandons completely the tried-and-true. On the other hand, an unknown road may sometimes be the only route available. There comes a time when life becomes so difficult that the best course of action is to take a chance for no better reason than that life could not possibly get worse. The idea, then, is to do something, anything; but to do it quickly and get it over with. The contradiction is more apparent than real, for one must first decide judiciously which course of action is the better one at any particular time and for a given set of circumstances, that of the usual or that of the anything-goes type. Furthermore, the very existence of such diametrically opposed choices discourages too mechanical an application of rules—*any* rules.

Romany attitudes toward time contrast strongly with ours, and the difference is even reflected in our languages. English verbs recognize a past, present, and future tense: "I rode the horse yesterday" or "I ride the horse today" or "I will ride the horse tomorrow." For us, there is a definite separation among all three states of existence, and our language structure makes this quite clear. In Romany, on the other hand, the present and the future are a single tense, different in form from the past tense: "I rode the horse yesterday" or "I ride the horse today or tomorrow." The Romany linguistic structure fits in well with Gypsy thought. What is significant about the past is what has continued to the present, and the rest can be allowed to fade away as inconsequential. As far as the future is concerned, it can only come into being if the present is given our careful attention. If we do not survive the present, there will be no future; therefore, the intelligent man concentrates on the present.

Gypsy beliefs affirming individuality and the need for flexibility lead to practical long-run benefits that may not be consciously recognized by the Gypsies but do strike the social scientist as obvious and important—perhaps the best phrase for it is one borrowed from gamblers: the technique of "hedging your bets."

Long-time gamblers learn from experience that betting all the money on one outcome results either in a large return for a successful bet or a complete loss for an unsuccessful one. In the long run, one loses a great deal more than one gets. But, if the betting money is spread over several possible outcomes, one stands a better chance of winning some money even if one loses some as well. The risks of failure are less even though the possible returns also are less; and in the long run, the gambler stands a better chance to keep some of his investment or to make a profit. In a way, cultures also gamble on possible outcomes; but in their case, the gamble involved is the preservation of the culture or the society itself. If all the units of a society react to an extreme emergency by adopting the same course of action, there is a failure to hedge the bet; either all of the society's units will survive or all will perish.

Gypsy culture characteristically hedges its bets by allowing each of the bands to adopt a different reaction to an emergency. Some bands are unlucky and perish; others are luckier and manage to survive; one or two may even "strike it rich" and thrive under the new conditions. What happens to any specific band is a matter of luck; but it is highly unlikely that all the bands will perish, and it is highly probable that the Gypsy culture as a whole will survive albeit with reduced numbers of Gypsies.

Gypsy variability baffles the nosy American anthropologist who likes his case histories in neat categories. I vaguely recall that I thought this variability was an important research problem during my first years of working with the Rom. However, after twenty-eight years, I find it is difficult not to think like a Gypsy, and I can no longer see variability as an important puzzle to be solved. I simply accept its existence and feel that the important issue is the reinforcement of two broad themes: keeping Gypsies in tune with the universe and preventing them from violating the kris.

Miniaturization: Safety in Replication

A mechanism that has helped to preserve the Gypsy way of life for well over half a millenium is what I call "miniaturization." The fundamental unit of Gypsy society is the extended family, a group of semi-independent nuclear families under the authority of the Big Man (ideally the sire of the sires of the nuclear families). The nuclear families may temporarily move away from the main corpus, either to return or to be followed by the others. But they separate permanently only when the total mass becomes too large for proper functioning. This happens when the member-nuclear families begin to marry off their sons and produce a generation of grandchildren.

The next larger unit, after the extended family, is the vitsa or band, a group of cooperating extended families that unite under the authority of a chief. A band is apt to affiliate with only a limited number of other bands within the same geographic area; this group of allied bands occupying the same territory is thought of as a "tribe" by the Gypsies. It lacks a political leader, and it has no real practical significance in Gypsy eyes.

An interesting feature of this type of social structure is that in its ideal form each larger unit is a logical outgrowth of the next smaller one. Normal increase in size of each unit comes through biological reproduction. The resultant larger size sets in motion pressures to reduce the unit back to its original size. The semi-independent nuclear family consisting initially of parents and children now becomes a unit of parents, children, and grand-children, with a corresponding increase in numbers of people. At this point it resembles the extended family, and indeed it splits off from the parent-extended family and becomes an extended family in its own right.

In similar fashion, the extended families that make up the band also undergo biological increase within their nuclear families and then bud off these larger nuclear families as new extended families. Total band size now includes many more individual Gypsies and a larger number of extended families. The band becomes too large for efficient functioning and di-vides into two or more daughter bands, which in course of time may grow and replicate several more times, extending their geographic spread and preserving the remembrance of a com-mon ancestry. In this manner tribes are formed.

This process of replication whereby new bands and lineages are formed is not unique to the Gypsies. It is characteristic of some East African and Central Asian groups as well. But the Romany version is different from these others insofar as it lacks a distinction between senior and junior lines—the new vitsas have the same status as the vitsa from which they budded off. All vitsas have potential equal rank in the societal hierarchy, and all compete as social peers for social recognition. This principle, of course, parallels the situation within the extended family, in which each son starts off with equal rank and then earns his own relative status through his individual efforts.

The pattern of authority and leadership remains the same, regardless of the level of unit examined. Headmanship is always provisional; absolute authority reposes only in the kris, never in a human agent. Leadership is always contingent upon the role-encumbent's ability to produce for his followers. Failure, even after years of successful service, dooms the leader to a loss of his power; a new leader is selected to carry on. These state-ments apply equally to the heads of families, the Big Men, and the chiefs of bands. The nature of the leadership role also is the same for families and bands; a man can perfect his leadership skills in a smaller unit (the family) and then progress to the leadership of a larger unit (the band).

The concept of miniaturization as found in Rom society is similar but not identical to a concept recently developed by British social anthropologists (e.g., Goody 1958 and, for the United States, Keesing 1970); these anthropologists speak of a "developmental cycle" of the family, emphasizing the similarity of the growth and development of an entire family to the growth and development within the human individual's life cycle. A particular family grows from establishment (equivalent to birth) through expansion (equivalent to childhood/adolescence) to reduction (equivalent to senescence), and final extinction (equivalent to death). But "miniaturization" concentrates rather on the proliferation and expansion of a nuclear family into extended family and then band.

Miniaturization also shares common features with the ideas set forth by Émile Durkheim in *De La Division du Travail Social* (1903). Durkheim would call Gypsy society a "segmented society," by which he means a form of social structure in which all parts replicate one another in form and functions. Such units emphasize kinship as the social bond holding them together. He contrasts segmented societies with organic societies; the latter emphasize a complex division of labor such that all of the subunits of the society can function only in the presence of the others. They are interdependent upon one another, just as one organ in the human body depends upon all the other organs for maintenance of life functions. Durkheim contrasts this organic solidarity to the "mechanical solidarity" of the segmented society, in which parts are held together merely through ties of similarity. Therefore, segmented societies, Durkheim claims, are subject to an easy severation of parts.

An example of organic society is our own industrialized society, with its emphasis on complexity and cohesion. I want to point out that, given a favorable environment, it is capable of great ultimate growth in size; however, when faced with adverse circumstances, the entire society is vulnerable to extinction if any of the necessary component parts cease to function. A segmented society, like the Rom, on the contrary, can survive adversity, for it can continue to function even if one of its parts is lost, as Durkheim indicated. With miniaturization the continued existence of just one unit guarantees the survival of the entire society, albeit perhaps in an abbreviated form. Furthermore, in a society with miniaturization, abbreviation is a temporary condition, remediable when circumstances improve, since each small unit carries the germinative seeds of the next larger unit within its own dynamic organization, and thus society can afford to lose a number of units without permanent injury being done to the whole.

Consequently, we see that the existence of even so small a Gypsy group as one adult man and one adult woman, both highly fecund and both committed to Gypsy culture, virtually guarantees the preservation of the Rom, especially in view of the high probability that, sooner or later as a result of their wanderings, they will find other similar survival units with whom to affiliate.[3]

Culling: The Elimination of Flaws

Survival of a society and its culture is not quite the same as the physical survival of a people. An entire people can be killed off by genocide; but by ethnocide a whole culture can be forced into extinction. What has not been universally acknowledged is that a viable culture can afford to lose a certain percentage of its members and still flourish. The amount of safe attrition is contingent on a number of factors, of course: the total population base currently extant; the minimum population base necessary to fulfill societal requirements; the rate of natural increase; etc. Thus, with a high rate of natural increase and a minimum societal base requirement—an accurate description of the Rom—prevalent death rates are well within the safe attrition range allowable for the preservation of Gypsy culture. Indeed,

[3]As I write, partial confirmation of this position has come in the form of a *New York Times* account (July 14, 1973: 27) of some Kalderaš Gypsies seeking asylum in this country from the attempts of Polish authorities to force assimilation. The scouting party consists of a 24-year-old man, his wife, their 4-year-old daughter, and the wife's unmarried 19-year-old brother. The little girl is proof of the couple's fertility, and the unattached youth is of proper age to effect marital affiliation with a vitsa already well established here.

considerably higher loss rates would be tolerable, and such losses have occurred throughout Gypsy history.

But from where do nonphysical losses stem? They result from sociocultural mobility, as it were. Individuals or families abandon Gypsy culture to be accepted and absorbed into surrounding societies each generation. A few leave of their own free will because they do not find the Gypsy way personally satisfying. Some leave-taking is involuntary, the result of a concatenation of peculiar circumstances: an individual male may make a solitary trip for purposes of seeking new business contacts or as an advance scout into unknown areas and somehow never manage to return or to find another Gypsy group.

Involuntary withdrawal from the Rom may be gradual and unnoticeable: a small family may leave temporarily to avoid economic competition (e.g., the usual summer break-up into small parties) and continue to exist over years without rejoining other Gypsies, all the while raising their children without contacts with their own kind. Should the parents suddenly die, the youngsters are left stranded, inexperienced in the ways of the Gypsy. I know of two such cases of potential loss where the young parents have failed to teach children Romany (most unusual, and probably indicative of a basic flaw in the parents' enculturation). Complete lack of contact has not occurred in these two cases, however, and the other Rom are making an effort to encourage the children to learn the language. But, if the youngsters fail to learn rapidly or they are again separated from the main body of Gypsies for an extended period, they may well be lost to Gypsy society permanently.

Forced removal from Gypsy life also may occur as punishment. An individual may be banished for breaking the kris, and the sentence may be permanent. An entire group also may be excommunicated. In such cases, commensality is interdicted, and no Gypsy group will be willing to furnish them with brides, forcing them to seek marriage outside the group.

Where the individual's separation from his society results from external causes, we may consider it an instance of accidental cultural death, a random happening of no significance to our discussion. However, the issue of arbitrary exile, whether self-imposed or coerced, is central to our present theme. It is a way to rid a society of those individuals who will not or cannot conform to its laws; we call such people "deviants" in social science terminology.

A deviant is much more than an embarrassment to other members of the society; his presence tends to upset normal societal interactions, and others must make constant readjustments in their thinking and behavior to compensate for his disconforming behavior. Worse yet, unless the deviant can be isolated in some fashion, his behavior is bound to spread to other members of the group. But if he remains at least partially functional, he may actually be accepted as a "normal" member of the group. The Gypsies handle mental retardation in this fashion. I know of two cases. The less severely handicapped youth is treated lovingly by his immediate kin and even attends some of the group gatherings; the family is trying unsuccessfully to find a wife for him. The other youth is too afflicted to function at all within the group.

The emotionally disturbed are handled in similar fashion. One young man I knew quite well suffered a sudden psychotic episode after the death of his father-in-law. He was hyperactive and suffered from auditory hallucinations; he also suffered from insomnia and fits of weeping. The Rom were aggrieved for him and his family and went to great lengths to ensure that the young man was always in the company of visitors. They also asked me to find a psychiatrist to treat him, specifying that they did not want him "locked up." ("Institutionalization" and "jail incarceration" are the same terms in Romany.) The patient recovered within several months under a regimen of intensive psychotherapy (at great financial cost to the group, I might add) and home care, much to everyone's relief and without any damage to his status within the group.

Gypsies will not tolerate homosexuality. If the individual is not successful in masking his private behavior by a public life of heterosexuality (Lee 1972 has an example), he is banished. Any man suspected of being a homosexual is ostracized. According to Gypsy thinking, mental retardation and some forms of psychosis only affect the patient himself; thus, those deviants are not regarded as socially contagious. A homosexual, however, requires a partner; they believe he is potentially "contagious" to other Gypsies. Furthermore, if he does not father children, he is in disharmony with the universe. I know of no instances of female homosexuality, and the Gypsies never mention it even as a possibility. I cannot explain it; I merely document it.

Another possible way of dealing with a deviant is to kill him. Murder is hardly a felicitous solution for Gypsies because of their fear of the malevolent ghosts of the dead; it is resorted to only in extreme cases.

The individual who deliberately denies the validity of Gypsy ways is socially dangerous. If by his actual behavior he is furnishing a flawed model for others to emulate or if he tries to persuade others to abandon aspects of Gypsy culture, he is a threat to Gypsydom. The cultural traitor is banished.

Gypsy culture perpetually is bombarded by outside influences and periodically besieged by strong coercive attempts to assimilate. Only those individuals who are unshakable in their convictions of the superiority of Rom-ness and only those units that can safeguard Gypsyhood by a judicious strategy of fission-and-fusion, bend-and-resist, cooperate-and-disband are capable of passing the Romany way on to the next generation. Only the fit need apply.

11

CHOICE-TAKING: A NEW THEORY

Conducting research is a way of life to scientists; it forms the basis both for data-collection on the input side of scientific endeavor and for theory-generation on the output side. As a group, scientists are thoroughly committed to researching, and, although they may think and write about such matters as "good research design," "replicable results," "reliability-versus-validity," etc., they rarely question their most basic assumptions about the research process itself. This is particularly true of anthropological research. The constraints of our work situations are significant variables to which we pay surprisingly scant attention. For example, fieldwork may require a time span of twelve to twenty-four months (the period devoted to living with and as a member of the group being studied). At this phase, the anthropologist is required to collect as much concrete data as possible about the people with whom he is living. This pressure to obtain as complete an outline of the total way of life as possible necessarily results in an overemphasis on the cultural ground rules and a neglect of such nuances as alternate patterning, variations in actual behavioral practices, and most importantly the dynamic nature of lives actually being lived. Whereas the anthropologist must devote his psychosomatic energies to learning the culture he is studying, the carriers of that culture are so much at home in it that they can thread their way through the maze of cultural possibilities without much effort. Not every person the anthropologist interviews is equally adept at maximizing potential advantages and minimizing potential risks, of course; relative expertise involves extent of knowledge of acceptable alternatives, ability to predict the consequences of these alternatives (in relation both to cultural ramifications and to individual reactions of particular personalities constituting the social group involved), unique individual intelligence, etc. Nevertheless, virtually every member of the society being studied takes for granted that which the anthropologist seeks to learn.

Moreover, the anthropologist wishes to know about everything all at once. If the people he is working with are accomplished metalworkers, he wishes to be taught the basics of metalwork *and* all of its refinements, all within a period of a few weeks. The fact that an accomplished smith may have devoted a dozen years or more to learning his art is unimportant. Similarly, the researcher hopes to live, at least vicariously, several lifetimes in his short sojourn; he expects to follow the full life cycles of many dissimilar people.

Thus, the field of anthropology would seem to be an enterprise devoted to the self-serving interests of egocentric fools. As an anthropologist, I am reluctant to accept this conclusion, and so I add quickly that anthropology has been in business for more than a century and has produced some very respectable results. Like man himself, the creation of anthropology as a meaningful field of research may be a statistical improbability, but it is here and it does function, however imperfectly.

Some particularly gifted fieldworkers in the past tried to point the way toward improved conceptualizations and more insightful analyses, but the trails they blazed were not followed by their successors to any great extent and have been overgrown through neglect. Ralph Linton (1936: 271-87) emphasized that the ways of a culture were not monotonously the same. He categorized cultural rules into three analytic groups: rules of proscription dictated what behaviors were absolutely forbidden to members of a society; rules of prescription listed those behaviors enjoined upon members of a society as absolute "musts"; and a large middle ground of alternatives, a series of possible, optional behaviors among which members of the society were free to choose.

Alfred Louis Kroeber (1944) also concentrated on alternatives, but his concern initially focussed on the totality available to different civilizations (i.e., cultures with urbanization, writing, etc.), and he concluded that the elaboration of the cultural inventory of any civilization was in part a function of the diversity of available alternatives, that rapidity of change depended partially on new alternatives being fed into the sociocultural system from other such systems (by borrowing and/or diffusion), and that the continued viability of a civilization required the encouragement of high levels of alternatives.

Ruth Fulton Benedict, who was a keen student of deviant behavior in various societies, was struck by the way those individuals who could not or would not conform nevertheless deviated in similar ways in each culture (1946: 232-57). She stressed that some of the infractions were not only quite common but also unofficially condoned. As a result, she talked about the apparent existence of "rules to break the rules" (classnotes, Columbia University, 1948).

Meanwhile, American anthropologists began to move away from the attempt to document cultures that were undergoing rapid extinction; instead, they began to study contemporary, flourishing cultures. They were disturbed by the discrepancy that existed between what the members of a culture said they did and what they actually did in their everyday lives. They emphasized a difference between what they called "ideal culture" and what they called "real culture." The large gap between the two was bridged by means of such explanations as the conflict existing between different social values and/or competition for resources (time, space, personnel, valuables, etc.). But the explanations tended to be *post hoc*, lacking predictive power. Others followed anthropologists like Leslie White (1947) who expounded in his theory of culturology the idea that it is possible to explain the various aspects of a culture exclusively within the context of its other aspects without the need to consider human beings as individual entities. He contended that variations in cultural phenomena can be accounted for sufficiently by such factors as "techno-environmental base" (Harris 1971) and "population density" among others. The idea of cultural determinism, an almost total denial of the ability of individuals to guide their life-courses to any important magnitude, is implicit in culturology.

Kenneth Pike, a noted linguist, was impressed by the ability of the science of linguistics to analyze any language of the world regardless of its differences. For example, a linguist can describe the sounds he hears from his informants in two basic ways. (1) In the phon*etic* approach, speech sounds are analyzed abstractly in terms of features that linguists can always recognize and that are potentially present in any given speech sound system. (2) In the phon*emic* approach, speech sounds are studied in terms of the significant differences recognized by native speakers of a particular language. The difference between the phonetics and the phonemics of a language has led to what is known in anthropological linguistics as the "-etic/-emic differentiation."

This -etic/-emic difference was elaborated upon by Marvin Harris (1964), who argued that the -etic approach was replicable and more objective; furthermore, it made easy cross-cultural comparisons. An -emic study, on the other hand, makes cross-cultural comparisons very diffificult since it is necessary (at least ideally) to know the totality of a culture in order to understand the viewpoint of the members of that culture. The implication by Harris and his followers is that an -etic approach is more scientific and hence preferable. Another implication is that participants in a culture lack complete understanding of all aspects of their own society and culture, just as native speakers of a language may ignore some of the subtleties of their own language, leading to the ego-nourishing conclusion that only professional anthropologists can comprehend cultures and only professional linguists can comprehend languages *in toto*.

Without getting into a full discussion about the feasibility of objectivity in a scientific approach and whether Heisenberg's principle[1] does or does not obtain for all situations, let me indicate that the word "subjective" (as opposed to "objective," its purported antonym) often is considered pejorative in science and implies that the observer is reacting to and reporting his uniquely individual (and, worse yet, emotional) state.

Scientists must be trained in the methods of observation considered proper to their fields of study; by the time their educa-

[1]As Heisenberg originally stated in the Principle of Indeterminacy, or Uncertainty Principle, the observer cannot simultaneously measure precisely both the position and velocity of a moving electron. By extrapolation, the principle is used in social sciences to refer to the inability of an observer to ascertain whether his research procedures have a significant effect on the data he is studying.

tion is completed, they possess shared conventions of thinking, talking, and acting. Consensus of opinion is both the symptom and the result. However, an anthropological field study also deals with a people's "consensus of opinion," just because it is indicative of shared conventions of thinking, talking, and acting—which is another way of defining a culture. The fieldworker may well be describing his informants' emotional reactions and thought patterns *but not necessarily his own*—for him, these are non-subjective data, replicable by all properly trained fieldworkers. Of course, fieldworkers have been trained to gather and classify their data in standard anthropological terms, but their informants may not recognize these terms. Their lives will be discussed in different terms. Thus, the -etic/-emic differentiation can be reduced to a matter of "language." Whose concepts are they, the informants' or the researchers'? Concepts recognizable by the informants are -emic, whereas concepts recognizable by the researchers are -etic.

In short, none of the current anthropological theories seems to be adequate for a meaningful organization of the data on the Gypsies I have collected or for an explanation of what I have observed. Doubtlessly, I would be more amenable to one or another of the extant theories if I had studied a number of different cultures over a short period of time—as so many of my colleagues do. But my interest in practicing and teaching applied anthropology aggravates my disenchantment, for I require a theory that not only explains what I have already observed but also predicts reasonably successfully what will happen in the future if a change is deliberately introduced. I would hope also that a theory would be able to reduce the chasm between concrete data and abstract generalizations.

Let us take a thought-journey through the data we have shared together to see if such a theory can be formulated. We shall weave together some of the threads already spun by others, but the resultant fabric will be different. In the first place, let us return to the raw material of any fieldwork, that which a person says or does. But already the true initial datum has been ignored, for the individual must have made several choices before saying or doing anything. That individual faces the option of *not* saying or doing something and has chosen to react behaviorally and observably in a given way. Or, in other words, any act of the will is the end-product in a complicated sequence predicated on making choices.

Human behavior involves the selection among possible options from the most trivial to the most crucial. The number of choices available at any one moment in time range from two ("yes"-or-"no") to any number of possibilities. Some of the options preexist in the whole area of *alternatives*: the culture provides a number of possibilities of which each is equally acceptable.

Life is not the discrete series of events that most anthropological theory implies. "Decision-making" is a term frequently used these days to encompass studies of how people in power—political leaders, business executives, elites of various kinds—decide how to act. But contrary to the opinion of social science, decision-making is not a special process limited to any select few; nearly all human beings make decisions innumerable times a day. I say "nearly all" because I am unsure how early after birth choosing starts.

At least in the beginning of fieldwork, the anthropologist becomes aware that a choice has been made when he observes a behavioral event; later on, he may come to realize that a choice had been made when an informant failed to perform in a preexistent situation where other informants subsequently are discovered to act characteristically.

The choice of whether or not to act (the yes-or-no option) applies to prescriptive, proscriptive, and alternative rules. At its most extreme, any individual may choose death in preference to obeying a requirement or suppressing a desire to do something forbidden. Among the Rom, the frustration of having to obey the dictates of older people may push a young person to commit suicide. A young man whose marital hopes are dashed may kill himself if he fails to persuade his family to arrange the desired marriage or if the girl's family marries her to someone else. Similarly, a young Gypsy girl who objects to accepting the traditional role of becoming a bori may run away to marry a non-Gypsy if she is willing to accept excommunication. Or, a desperately unhappy married woman who sees no other alternative to years of future misery may prefer death by suicide.

Insofar as situations with multiple potential alternatives are concerned, an individual might elect to do nothing at all instead of choosing among the available options. It would be possible for a Gypsy man to be carried along by allowing events to happen to him, remaining within his extended family and vitsa, and drifting along with the decisions made by the Old One and by his chief.

The synthesis of the basic premises of choice-making theory is indicated in the accompanying diagram (Diagram 11.1). The central focus is the choice-making itself, a process initiated by the examination of the preexistent situation (including both the actors and the circumstances). The preexistent situation itself is dynamic; it changes constantly because it is an open system not only subject to fluctuations within its own component parts (e.g., the actors are undergoing the normal life cycle of progression and change), but also sensitive to elements impinging from outside its own constituent parts (e.g., exposure to an incoming group of Gypsies, changes in the municipal code of the city of residence, etc.). Therefore, stasis requires compensatory changes within the system: maintenance of stability occurs only through continuous corrections of the preexistent situation.

Choice-taking being processual, it cannot function as the analytic unit; the individual or group of individuals must do the monitoring and choosing. The motivating directives for making choices are the immediate and future goals; these are shaped by both cultural ideals which have been internalized by the individual and by personal desires arising from the uniqueness of every human being (this being a basic assumption of anthropology and the behavioral sciences in general). Given the goal directives, the plan formulation involves: (1) an inspection of the options available from the cultural reservoir of alternatives; (2) a determination of possible new options; (3) a weighing of the results of steps 1 and 2 (are these options implementable in this specific context for these particular actors?); and finally (4) an examination of the possibility of success for each of the accessible options of step 3—a form of probability forecasting predicated on likely repercussions resulting from similar circumstances. Once a plan is formulated, it is put into action; and the outcome can be measured in terms of behavior. These, in turn, effect changes (desired or undesired, predicted and/or unforeseen) in the original preexistent situation, P_n, which now becomes the new preexistent situation, P_{n+1}.

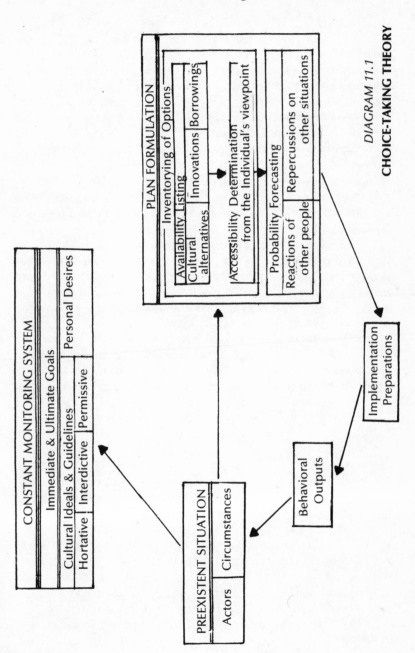

DIAGRAM 11.1
CHOICE-TAKING THEORY

Choice-taking theory has several advantages for the anthropologists of today. It affords a balanced treatment of "ideal" versus "real" culture, incorporating on an equal basis as it does both the ideal cultural constructs in the minds of the informants and also the actual behavioral events observable by the investigator. It takes biological variables into consideration both with respect to ecological factors in the preexistent situation and in relation to the physical attributes of the actors. (Some options are contingent upon the right age or sex; some are contingent upon physical fitness, etc.) An individual's options in a pluralistic society such as, for example, that of modern New York City might be limited by his being non-white or being unable to understand or speak adequately Standard American English in both its spoken and written variants.

Choice-taking recognizes and utilizes the dynamic nature of human variability. But despite its multi-variable, ever-fluctuating nature, the theoretical model is quantifiable, thanks to modern computer technology. Unlike many models in fashion today, this theory neither ignores the unique past history of the group nor the likely course of future events.

Perhaps one of the most exciting aspects of the theory to a professional anthropologist is that with it he can solve the problem of lack of cross-cultural correspondence to such traditional professional categories as economic structuring, social organization, and political classification. The neat little cubby-holes created by the social scientists simply do not fit the data of many cultures. What is political behavior (defined as the maintenance or restoration of normal functioning in the face of dissension) in one society may operate through the legitimate exercise of force by a policing group whereas in another restoration or supervision of the status quo may be the function of the priesthood. For the Nomad Gypsies, we cannot consider political behavior without considering kinship (in the determination of vitsa membership); this is not unusual in other cultures throughout the world as well. However, its relationship to the kumpanja, the economic unit, is less ordinary. Continuous membership in a kumpanja may in turn lead to new marriages and the formation of new bands and tribes, thereby affecting the political structure.

Furthermore, in studying a culture exposed to influences from other cultures (and today how many cultures are truly isolated from such exposure?), the choice-taking analysis not only indicates what options are available and accessible from outside of the society under consideration but also affords a method for quantifying the number of times such extra-societal options are exercised and whether this exercise is increasing along a time dimension.

A logical sequitur to the above point is that such a theoretical approach is just as feasible for a multi-ethnic, complicated, modern urban research situation as it is for a relatively isolated tribal or rural one.

When we study culture change, our predictive power is generated through the choice-taking approach, and this in turn makes the formulation of specific courses of action for directing such change less uncertain, since we may both think in terms of making more options available and accessible to the "target population" and also because we can design probability forecasting equations to determine the likelihood of succeeding with any number of possible strategies. (Note that this technique is identical to the one postulated by the theory itself.)

Admittedly, one can become overly impressed with one's own brain child, and I must concede that there still is much "softness" in the theory; however, additional applications to various cultures will help to smooth out the inequalities, as such testing always does. More disadvantageous, because they are firmly built into the theory itself, are: (1) the requirement that the anthropologist who begins work with a new group must commit himself to a long association with his informants (naturally twenty-five years is not *de rigueur*, but a three- to five-year study does seem to be a minimum); and (2) the data must necessarily remain incomplete because the approach presupposes an open system situation—with permeable boundaries, external influences affecting the internal structuring, inherent feedback and self-correction, structural elements only temporarily and delicately equipoised, etc.—and because of the probability of the introduction of new variables in the future, such as innovations. Indeed, the only ultimate limit for any group being studied is the death of the actor (or actor-group), either in terms of actual physical death or in terms of complete cessation of social role functioning (the sociocultural equivalent of biological mortality).

The theory's rejection of the social structure or the cultural system as its basic unit in favor of the set of actors and the behavioral events may also be regarded as a disadvantage or perhaps even a threat to the field of anthropology as we now know it. If the human actor is accepted as the major unit of study, social scientists might well derive a corollary position that anthropology as a separate and independent field of study is not necessary. I may find myself in the unenviable position of having talked myself out of a field of study for which I have devoted a lifetime. One possible consequence of this theory, then, is that anthropology will become superannuated. On the other hand, another possible consequence of this theory might be the formulation of a new kind of anthropology, incorporating data and approaches from many other fields, such as psychology, medicine, and systems analysis, and reaffirming the central importance of the "human" in what is, after all, the science of man. In the hope that the second choice will be taken, I propose that we refer to a sub-field called "humanistic anthropology," and I append a list of basic premises to start it on its way.

APPENDIX TO CHAPTER 11

BASIC PREMISES OF CHOICE-TAKING THEORY

Premise 1.0—Human beings continuously make choices.

Premise 2.0—In any behavioral situation, there always exists choice potential.

Premise 2.1—Minimally, there is always a yes/no potential choice, regardless of cultural rules.

Premise 2.2—A possible option is to take no action at all, even if many possible alternatives exist.

Premise 3.0—Every culture establishes behavioral guidelines for the members of its society.

Premise 3.1—Some of these guidelines are *hortative*; every culture establishes that certain behavior patterns must be followed (prescribed behaviors), given specific circumstances.

Premise 3.2—Some of these guidelines are *interdictive*; every culture establishes that certain behavioral patterns must not occur (forbidden behaviors), given specific circumstances.

Premise 3.3—Some of these guidelines are *permissive*; every culture establishes that certain behavioral patterns are possible (alternative behaviors), given specific circumstances.

Premise 4.0—Cultural rules do not and cannot program for all contingencies because they are predicated on specific circumstances triggering their initiation.

Premise 4.1—Cultural rules covering one set of circumstances may have little or nothing to do with the cultural rules pertaining to a different set of circumstances.

Premise 4.1.1—When sets of circumstances overlap, the pertinent cultural rules called into play are juxtaposed and may be partially conflicting or totally contradictory.

Premise 4.2—Circumstances may sort into a novel combination not readily covered by any set of cultural rules.

Premise 4.2.1—Lack of existent cultural rules creates a void.

Premise 4.2.1.1—This void may be met by confusion on the part of carriers of that culture and/or by disorganization within the societal structure.

Premise 4.2.1.2—This void may be filled by a new cultural invention which may then become part of the cultural inventory of options.

Premise 4.2.1.3—This void may be filled by a custom borrowed from another culture were there to be contact between members of different societies.

Premise 5.0—Cultural rules, as blueprints for action, are implementable only if all the necessary resources and conditions are present and accessible to the actors in a situation.

Premise 5.1—Necessary resources include usable manpower (with the appropriate skills, physical and intellectual abilities, etc.), available time, available space, and available natural resources.

Premise 5.2—Necessary conditions include the individual's knowledge of the existence of the rule and of the ways to implement it, the judgment that he has or will have the necessary resources, the premise that his plan is feasible and will not be conflictive.

Premise 6.0—In a given series of related choice-taking events, the choices made in the earlier part of the sequence may themselves have a limiting effect upon the alternatives available in the later part of the same sequence.

Premise 6.1—Some alternative options are incompatible with or preclude other alternatives in the same pool of potential choices ("choice dissonance").

Premise 6.2—Some alternative options tend to encourage the selection of others, either conjointly or sequentially ("choice coupling") within the same pool of potential choices.

Premise 7.0—Culture change can be analyzed through the choice-taking approach.

Premise 7.1—For any given point in time, T_x, alternatives can be enumerated and listed with their positive or negative values.

Premise 7.1.1—Valencing of each option (assignment of numerical values) can be determined by frequency studies (number of times of occurrence or avoidance).

Premise 7.2—For any later point in time, T_{x+y}, a new count and valencing may be computed.

Premise 7.2.1—Qualitative and quantitative changes can be determined thereby.

Premise 7.2.2—Some of the T_x options may have decreased or disappeared from the cultural repertoire.

Premise 7.2.3—Some of the new options at T_{x+y} may be invented by carriers of the same culture.

Premise 7.2.4—Some of the new options at T_{x+y} may have been borrowed from the repertoires of other cultures.

Premise 8.0—Given a valenced list of options at any given time, T_x, predictions of behavior in the immediate future may be made by performing the necessary computations.

Premise 8.1—In a directed culture change project, predictions of probable success also may be based on the valenced-list technique.

Premise 8.2—A directed culture change project must take into account both choice dissonance (Premise 6.1) and choice coupling (Premise 6.2).

GLOSSARY

AMARE ROMA. Literally, "our men." Used to indicate Ego's own group of Rom Gypsies.

ARXENTINA. A term used to designate a group of Kalderaš originally from Argentina and Brazil.

BAJUR. A Mačvaja term to refer to confidence game rackets. Sometimes called *xoxano baro*.

BARO. Literally, the "Big Man." A term used to refer to the heads of extended families.

BAXT. The Romany expression for luck.

BORI. "Daughter-in-law." A term used by all of the members of the husband's group.

ČURARA. A tribal designation for one group of Rom Gypsies. Supposed to be derived from *čuri*, "knife"; hence, "people of the knife." Probably equivalent to the English expression, "Killer Gypsies."

DEL. Romany for "God."

DIKLO. The headscarf that must be worn in public by all married women.

DIVANO. A term used to refer to the deliberations of the Council of Elders, the aggregation of the Big Men of a vitsa.

GAJO (MALE), GAJI (FEMALE), GAJE (PLURAL). A generic term for non-Gypsies.

GALBE. Gold coin necklaces.

HIRA. A term used to refer to anecdotal stories about actual people.

KALDERAŠ, KALDERAŠA. A tribal designation for one group of Rom Gypsies whose traditional occupation was coppersmithing.

KRIS. "Justice" or "court trial." This concept is central to Gypsy culture and refers to a whole complex of ideas and behavior patterns, including the whole body of customary law, the procedures of holding a court trial, and the underlying world view and value system.

KUMPANJA. The economic unit of Gypsy society.

LOVARA. A term used for one tribal division of Rom, supposed to be derived from *love*, "money," according to the Lovara themselves.

MAČVAJA, MAČVANA. A tribal designation for one group of Rom Gypsies.

MARIME, MAXRIME. A term used to cover the concept of ritual dangerousness and/or pollution. The opposite is *užo*.

MEKSIKAJA. A term used to designate a band from Mexico, sometimes identified as Mačvaja and sometimes as Kalderaš.

MULO MAS. Literally, "dead meat." A term used to cover the acceptable cooking and eating of dead animals who have died from natural causes.

MULO, MULE (PLURAL). Literally, the "dead one." A term used to refer to the much-feared ghosts of the dead.

OFISA, OFISO. The term used for a fortunetelling location.

PERINA. The traditional goosedown and feather quilts used as matresses and blankets.

ROM. Literally, "husband." The extended meaning is "adult male Gypsy." Also used to indicate the Nomad Gypsies as a whole.

ROMA. A plural formation for Rom in some dialects of Romany.

ROMANY. The language of the Gypsies. An offshoot of the tenth century A.D. Prakrits vernaculars, and therefore an Indo-Aryan language.

RUSS. A designation for a New York City group of Rom Gypsies who have intermarried with the Kalderaš and Russian Sedentaries.

SINTI, SINTE. A term applied to Sedentary Gypsies in order to differentiate them from the Rom Gypsies.

ŠEJ. Literally, "daughter." This term is expanded to mean any unmarried girl born into Ego's own group.

URSITORI. The spirits representing the Fates who establish the general direction of a newborn baby's life.

VARDO. The traditional living wagon of some of the Rom Gypsies.

VITSA, VITSI (PLURAL). A term used to designate a band but usually translated into English by the Gypsies as "family."

Xᴀ sᴀsᴛɪᴍᴀsᴀ. Literally, "Eat in good health." A mandatory verbal formula to be uttered by an individual who is not joining Gypsies who are eating.

Xᴀɴᴀᴍɪᴋ. Literally, "parents of my child's spouse." This relationship is culturally important to the Rom, for a marriage is regarded as a union between two extended families.

Xoxᴀɴo ʙᴀʀo. Literally, the "Big Lie." A Kalderaš term used to designate confidence game rackets. Sometimes also called *bajur*, especially by the Mačvaja.

NOTE:

Most vowels are pronounced as in Italian.
aj and ej are dipthongs.
č is pronounced like the "ch" in "church."
ǰ is pronounced like the "j" in "judge."
š is pronounced like the "sh" in "should."
x is a guttural fricative like the "ch" in Scottish "loch."
Aspiration of the plosives has been omitted because of typographic difficulties.

REFERENCES CITED

Bataillard, Paul. 1889-1890. "Beginning of the Immigration of the Gypsies into Western Europe in the Fifteenth Century; First Period, 1417-1435." *Journal of the Gypsy Lore Society*. 1(4): 185-212; 1(5): 260-286; 1(6): 324-345; 2(1): 27-53.

Benedict, Ruth Fulton. 1946 reissue of 1934 ed. *Patterns of Culture*. New York: Pelican Books, Penguin Books.

Bercovici, Konrad. 1928. *Story of the Gypsies*. New York: Farrar.

Bhargava, Bhavani Shanker. n.d. [1949]. *The Criminal Tribes: A Social and Economic Study of the Principal Criminal Tribes and Castes in in Northern India*. Lucknow: Universal Publishers.

Biswas, P. C. 1960. *The Ex-Criminal Tribes of Delhi State*. Delhi: University of Delhi.

Block, Martin. 1939. Transl. by Barbara Kuczynski and Duncan Taylor. *Gypsies, Their Life and Their Customs*. New York: Appleton-Century.

Bonos, Arlene Helen. 1942 (Apr.). "Roumany Rye of Philadelphia." *American Anthropologist*. 44(2): 257-74.

Borrow, George Henry. 1907 ed. *The Zincali; an Account of the Gypsies of Spain*. London: J. Murray.

Brown, Irving Henry. 1929. "The Gypsies in America." *Journal of the Gypsy Lore Society*. 3rd ser. 8(4): 145-76.

———. 1924. *Gypsy Fires in America; a Narrative of Life among the Romanis of the United States and Canada*. New York: Harpers Brothers.

Buettner-Janusch, John. 1973. *Physical Anthropology: A Perspective*. New York: John Wiley.

Cannon, Walter B. 1942 (Apr.). " 'Voodoo' Death." *American Anthropologist*. n.s. 44(2): 169-81.

Clébert, Jean Paul. 1963 [1961]. Transl. by Charles Duff. *The Gypsies*. New York: E. P. Dutton.

Cohn, Werner. 1973. *The Gypsies*. Reading, Mass.: Addison-Wesley.

———. 1969 (June). "Some Comparisons between Gypsy (North American *rom*) and American English Kinship Terms." *American Anthropologist*. n.s. 71(3): 476-82.

Çoker, Gülbün. 1966. "Romany Rye in Philadelphia: A Sequel." *Southwestern Journal of Anthropology*. 22: 85-100.

Cotten, Rena M. 1955 (Jan.-Apr.). "An Anthropologist Looks at Gypsiology." *Journal of the Gypsy Lore Society*. 3rd ser. 34(1-2): 20-37.

————. 1954a (July-Sept.). "Gypsy Folktales." *Journal of American Folklore*. 67(265): 261-66.

————. 1954b (July-Oct.). "An Anthropologist Looks at Gypsiology." *Journal of the Gypsy Lore Society*. 3rd ser. 33(3-4): 107-20.

————. 1951. "Sex Dichotomy among the American *Kalderaš* Gypsies." *Journal of the Gypsy Lore Society*. 3rd ser. 30: 16-25.

————. 1950. *The Fork in the Road: A Study of Acculturation among the American Kalderaš Gypsies*. Ph.D. Dissertation, Columbia University. Ann Arbor: University Microfilms.

Cowles, Frederic. 1948. *Gypsy Caravan*. London: Robert Hale.

Crooke, William. 1910. "Notes on the Criminal Classes in the Bombay Presidency." *Journal of the Gypsy Lore Society*. n.s. 4: 35-40.

————. 1888. "Notes on the Gypsy Tribes of the North-Western Provinces and Oudh." *Indian Antiquary*. 17: 68-75.

de Goeje, M. J. 1886. "A Contribution to the History of the Gypsies." In David MacRitchie: *Accounts of the Gypsies of India*. London: Kegan Paul, French. Pp. 1-61.

Ekvall, Robert B. 1968. *Fields on the Hoof: Nexus of Tibetan Nomadic Pastoralism*. Case Studies in Cultural Anthropology. New York: Holt, Rinehart and Winston.

Esty, Katherine. 1969. *The Gypsies, Wanderers in Time*. New York: Hawthorn Books.

Goody, Jack (ed.). 1971 reissue of 1958 ed. *The Developmental Cycle in Domestic Groups*. Cambridge Papers in Social Anthropology, 1. Cambridge: Cambridge University Press.

Grellman, H. M. G. 1807 Eng. ed. of 1783 ed. *Historischer Versuch über die Zigeuner*. Göttingen.

Grierson, G. A. 188 (Oct.). "Doms, Jâts, and the Origin of the Gypsies." *Journal of the Gypsy Lore Society*. 1(2): 71-76.

Groome, Francis Hindes. 1899. *Gipsy Folk-Tales*. London.

Gropper, Rena C. 1967. "Urban Nomads—The Gypsies of New York City." *Transactions of the New York Academy of Sciences*. ser. II. 29: 1050-56.

Harris, Marvin. 1971. *Culture, Man, and Nature: An Introduction to Cultural Anthropology*. New York: Thomas Y. Crowell.

————. 1964. *The Nature of Cultural Things*. New York: Random House.

Helm, June (ed.). 1968. *Essays on the Problem of Tribe: Proceedings of the 1967 Annual Spring Meeting of the American Ethnological Society*. Seattle and London: University of Washington Press.

Hopf, Carl. 1870. *Die Einwanderung der Zigeuner in Europa*. Gotha.

Huth, Ferdinand Gerard. 1945 (Jan.-Apr.) "The English Gypsy Tent." *Journal of the Gypsy Lore Society*. 3rd ser. 24(1-2): 30-43.

Kessing, Robert M. 1970. "Kwaio Fosterage." *American Anthropologist*. n.s. 72(5): 991-1020.

Kenrick, Donald, and Grattan Puxon. 1972. *The Destiny of Europe's Gypsies*. New York: Basic Books.

Krader, Lawrence. 1963. *Peoples of Central Asia*. Uralic and Altaic Series, vol. 26. Bloomington: Indiana University Press.

Kroeber, Alfred Louis. 1948. *Anthropology: Race, Language, Culture, Psychology, Prehistory*. new ed., rev. New York: Harcourt, Brace and Company.

————. 1944. *Configurations of Culture Growth*. Berkeley: University of California Press.

Lee, Ronald. 1972 [1971]. *Goddam Gypsy: An Autobiographical Novel*. Indianapolis, New York: Bobbs-Merrill.

Leland, Charles Godfrey. 1891. *Gypsy Sorcery and Fortune Telling*. New York: Charles Scribner's.

Linton, Ralph. 1936. *The Study of Man: An Introduction*. New York: Appleton-Century, Crofts.

MacRitchie, David. 1866. *Accounts of the Gypsies of India*. London: Kegan Paul, French.

Mandelbaum, David G. 1970. *Society in India: Continuity and Change, Change and Continuity*. 2 vols. Berkeley: University of California Press.

Maximoff, Matéo. 1949. *The Ursitory*. London: Chapman & Hall.

————. 1947a (July-Oct.). "Three Feast-Days among the 'Turco-American' Gypsies." *Journal of the Gypsy Lore Society*. 3rd ser. 26(3-4): 127-32.

————. 1947b (Jan.-Apr.). "The Gypsies of Montreuil-Sous-Bois: Some Observations on His Own Tribe." *Journal of the Gypsy Lore Society*. 3rd ser. 26(1-2): 37-42.

————. 1946a. *Les Ursitory: Roman*. Paris: Ernest Flammarion.

————. 1946b (July-Oct.). "Some Peculiarities in the Speech of the Kalderaš." *Journal of the Gypsy Lore Society*. 3rd ser. 25(3-4): 108-12.

Merton, Robert K. 1957. *Social Theory and Social Structure*. rev. & enl. ed. New York: The Free Press.

Miklosisch, Franz. 1972-80. *Über die Mundarten und die Wanderung der Zigeuner Europas*. Wien.

Mitchell, Joseph. 1945. "King of the Gypsies." In his *McSorley's Wonderful Saloon*. New York: Penguin Books. Pp. 39-59.

Moriarty, J. R. 1929. "A Gypsy Coppersmith Family." *Journal of the Gypsy Lore Society*. 3rd ser. 8(4): 176-81.

Myers, John. 1945 (July-Oct.). "Supplementary Jottings on the Customs of the 'Greek' Nomad Gypsies." *Journal of the Gypsy Lore Society*. 3rd ser. 24(3-4): 88-94.

Parry, Albert. 1941 (Feb.). "Children of Romany in New York." *Travel*. 77(4): 18-22.

Paspati, A. G. 1870. *Études sur les Tschinghianés ou Bohémiens de l'Empire Ottoman*. Constantinople.

Petrovič, A. 1939 (Feb. 11). "Diet of Serbian Gypsies." *Nature*. 143:248.

Pittard, E. 1902 (Jan.-Apr.). "Anthropologie de la Roumanie— Contribution à l'étude anthropologique des Tziganes Dit Roumains." *Bulletin de la Société des Sciences de Bucharest*. 11(1-2): 128-44.

Pott, A. F. 1844. *Die Zigeuner in Europa und Asien*. 2 vols. Halle: Ed. Heynemann.

Quintana, Bertha B., and Lois Gray Floyd. 1972. *¡Qué Gitano! Gypsies of Southern Spain*. Case Studies in Cultural Anthropology. New York: Holt, Rinehart and Winston.

Sher Singh 'Sher'. 1967. *The Sikligars of Punjab*. Jullumdur: University Press.

———. 1965. *The Sansis of Punjab: A Gypsy and Denotified Tribe of Rajput Origin*. Delhi: Munshiram Mansharlal.

Starkie, Walter Fitzwilliam. 1953. *In Sara's Tents*. London: John Murray.

———. 1937. *Don Gypsy: Adventures with a Fiddle in Southern Spain and Barbary*. New York: E. P. Dutton.

———. 1933 [1935]. *Raggle-taggle: Adventures with a Fiddle in Hungary and Roumania*. New York: E. P. Dutton.

Thompson, Thomas William. 1929. "Additional Notes on English Gypsy Uncleanness Taboos." *Journal of the Gypsy Lore Society*. 3rd ser. 8(1): 33-39.

———. 1922. "The Uncleanness of Women among English Gypsies." *Journal of the Gypsy Lore Society*. 3rd ser. 1(1): 15-43.

Tillhagen, Carl-Herman. 1947 (July-Oct.). "A Swedish Gypsy Investigation." Transl. by G. A. Urquhart. *Journal of the Gypsy Lore Society*. 3rd ser. 26(3-4): 89-115.

Turner, R. L. 1927. " 'The Position of Romani in Indo-Aryan': A Reply to Dr. J. Sampson." *Journal of the Gypsy Lore Society*. 3rd ser. 6(3): 110-35.

———. 1926. "The Position of Romani in Indo-Aryan." *Journal of the Gypsy Lore Society*. 3rd ser. 4(4): 145-89.

Vesey-Fitzgerald, Brian. 1944, *Gypsies of Britain: An Introduction to Their History*. London: Chapman & Hall.

Weybright, Victor. 1945 (Jan.-Apr.). "A Nomad Gypsy Coppersmith in New York." *Journal of the Gypsy Lore Society*. 3rd ser. 24(1-2): 2-8.

———. 1938 (Mar.). "Who Can Tell the Gypsies' Fortune? The Nomad Coppersmiths, Now at the End of the Gypsy Trail." *Survey Graphic*. 27: 142-45.

White, Leslie A. 1947. "Culturological vs. Psychological Interpretations of Human Behavior." *American Sociological Review*. Pp. 686-98.

Williams, H. L. 1912-1913. "The Criminal and Wandering Tribes of India." *Journal of the Gypsy Lore Society*. n.s. 6(1): 34-58; 6(2): 110-35.

Wlislocki, Heinrich von. 1891. *Volksglaube und Religiöser Brauch der Zigeuner*. Münster.

————. 1890. *Vom Wandernden Zigeunervolke; Bilder aus dem Leben der Siebenbürgen Zigeuner. Geschichtliches, Ethnologisches, Sprache und Poesie*. Hamburg.

Woolner, A. C. 1928 (July-Dec.). "Asoka and the Gypsies." *Journal of the Gypsy Lore Society*. 3rd ser. 7(3-4): 108-11.

Wright, Richardson. 1947 (July-Oct.). "Easter Celebrations of the Gypsy Coppersmiths in New York." *Journal of the Gypsy Lore Society*. 3rd ser. 24(3-4):132-33.

————. 1946 (July-Oct.). "The Gypsy Coppersmiths in New York: A Pictorial Supplement to Victor Weybright's Article." *Journal of the Gypsy Lore Society*. 3rd ser. 25(3-4): 116-20.

Yoors, Jan. 1971. *Crossing*. New York: Simon and Schuster.

————. 1967. *The Gypsies*. New York: Simon and Schuster.

————. 1947 (Jan.-Apr.). "Lowari Law & Jurisdiction." *Journal of the Gypsy Lore Society*. 3rd ser. 26(1-2): 1-18.

ANNOTATED BIBLIOGRAPHY
A Guide for Research

PART ONE
GENERAL REFERENCES ON GYPSIES

1. Bataillard, Paul. 1889-91. "Beginning of the Immigration of the Gypsies into Western Europe in the Fifteenth Century." *Journal of the Gypsy Lore Society*. 1: 185-212, 260-86, 324-45; 2: 27-53. An excellent summary presentation of early documents bearing on the subject.

2. Bercovici, Konrad. 1928. *The Story of the Gypsies*. New York: Farrar. Bercovici wrote extensively on the Gypsies in the 1920s. Unfortunately, much of his work was not only anecdotal but also sensationalistic, and it is difficult to determine how much is factual.

3. Boeckh, Sherry. 1974 (Oct.). "In Search of Gypsies." *Impetus* [magazine supplement to the Oct. 19, 1974, issue of *The Financial Post*.]. Pp. 40-44. Journalistic account of the Spanish Gitanos and an interview with a man claiming to be King of the Polish Gypsies. Author asserts there are 25,000 Gypsies in Canada and 12 million elsewhere. One color photograph.

4. Bhattacharya, Deben. 1965. *The Gypsies: Pictures and Music from East and West*. London: Record Books. Superficial textual treatment without reference to tribal provenience. Photographs and two small records of Gypsy music.

5. Black, George F. 1914. *A Gypsy Bibliography*. Gypsy Lore Society Monographs No. 1. Lists 4,577 works on Gypsies, often with table of contents and reviews available. Includes all European languages. Recommended as a shortcut into bibliography search of data published prior to 1913.

6. Block, Martin (transl. by Barbara Kuczynski and Duncan Taylor). 1959. *Gypsies: Their Life and Their Customs*. New York: Appleton-Century. This general reference work deals mainly with European Gypsies and frequently fails to indicate clearly the type of Gypsy being described. Apparently most of the data refer to southeastern Europe and non-Rom Gypsies. However, it does furnish a handy one-volume digest of what most Gypsy scholars thought as of the 1930s. Includes good photographs.

7. "Caravan of Mystery." 1950 (Aug.). *Coronet*. Pp. 111-26. A superficial, journalistic account of little value aside from the photographs.

8. Clébert, Jean-Paul (transl. by Charles Duff). 1963 (French ed., 1961). *The Gypsies*. New York: E. P. Dutton. This general reference work relies primarily on the writings of others for raw data; it reports the conclusions without much critical analysis. This book, like that of Martin Block (6. above) leaves the reader uncertain about geographical and tribal provenience much of the time. Surprisingly little new material is added by Clébert to the store of knowledge presented by Block. Includes photographs.

9. Cotten, Rena M. (now Rena C. Gropper). 1955 (Jan.-Apr.). "An Anthropologist Looks at Gypsiology—II." *Journal of the Gypsy Lore Society*. 3rd ser. 34(1-2): 20-37.

10. ———. 1954 (July-Oct.). "An Anthropologist Looks at Gypsiology." *Journal of the Gypsy Lore Society*. 3rd ser. 33(3-4): 107-20. An analytic secondary source. These articles attempt an overview of the state of knowledge on Gypsies and an appeal for more careful work in the future.

11. DP [Daphne Prior]. 1970 (Feb.). "The Exiles of Little Egypt." *The Sciences*. 10(2):30-34. Tertiary source. This is based on Clébert's book and on an extensive interview with Rena C. Gropper and Gropper's article (114. following).

12. Esty, Katherine. 1969. *The Gypsies, Wanderers in Time*. New York: Hawthorn Books. This book includes material on some of the Gypsy scholars of the past. Basically a secondary or tertiary source, it includes a chapter on a Kalderaš informant in Sweden ("Miloš: The Life and Death of a Swedish Gypsy"); a chapter on "Gypsies in America," dealing mainly with the Rom; and a chapter on "Magic and Fortune-Telling," with a major emphasis on the Rom, although it is not so indicated. Includes a few photographs.

13. Grellman, H(einrich) M(oritz) G(ottlieb). 1783. *Die Zigeuner. Ein historischer Versuch über die Lebensart und Verfassung, Sitten und Schicksahle dieses Volks in Europa, nebst ihren Ursprunge.* Dessau and Leipzig.

14. ———. 1807. *Dissertation on the Gipseys: Representing Their Manner of Life, Family, Economy, Occupations and Trades, Marriages and Education, Sickness, Death and Burial, Religion, Language, Sciences and Arts, etc. etc. etc. With an Historical Enquiry Concerning Their*

Origin and First Appearance in Europe. London: Effingham Gilson, William Ballintine. This is one of the earliest general references known and a classic to which all Gypsy scholars should refer.

15. Hopf, Carl. 1870. *Die Einwanderung der Zigeuner in Europa.* Gotha: Friedrich Andreas Perthes. A careful study of the chronicles relating to the early appearance of the Gypsies in Europe.

16. Kochanowski, Jan. 1963. *Gypsy Studies.* 2 vols. New Delhi: International Academy of Indian Culture. A linguistic study using modern anthropological techniques.

17. Lal, Chaman. 1962. *Gypsies: Forgotten Children of India.* Delhi: Publications Division, Ministry of Information and Broadcasting. A Hindu's presentation of research and reactions toward Gypsies of Europe. Tribal provenience is difficult for the reader to assign.

18. Miklosich, Franz Xavier. 1872-80. *Über die Mundarten und die Wanderungen der Zigeuner Europas.* Wien. Primary and secondary source, and a classic. The major emphasis is on early records, folktales, and language—all non-Rom.

19. Paspati (Paspates), Alexander G. 1870. *Études sur les Tschinghianés ou Bohémiens de l'Empire Ottoman.* A. Koroméla. This important source is available in English as *Memoir on the Language of the Gypsies as Used in the Turkish Empire* (1932: New Haven). It embraces far more than the language and includes materials on Rom Gypsies.

20. Pott, August Friedrich. 1844-45. *Die Zigeuner in Europa und Asien: Ethnographisch-linguistische Untersuchung, vornehmlich Ihrer Herkunft und Sprache, nach Gedruckten und Ungedruckten Quellen.* 2 vols. Halle: Ed. Heynemann. An important classic.

21. McDowell, Bart. *Gypsies: Wanderers of the World.* Washington, D.C.: The National Geographic Society. A journalistic account of a trip taken by the author and an English couple through Europe and Asia. The text is superficial and fails to differentiate among the different types of Gypsies. Includes many full-color photographs.

22. Tipler, Derek A. 1968 (Aug./Sept.). "From Nomads to Nation." *Midstream.* Pp. 61-70. A general survey article on Gypsies of Europe and North America with a journalistic account of the International Gypsy Committee. Mr. Tipler says he is a British Gypsy.

23. Wedek, H. E., with the assistance of Wade Baskin. 1973. *Dictionary of Gypsy Life and Lore*. New York: Philosophical Library. A tertiary source, with entries listed alphabetically according to no particular logical system. Since there is no crediting of the original source and no evaluation of the probable reliability of the information, this book would be difficult to use. A few photographs are taken from other sources.

PART TWO

REFERENCES TO NOMAD GYPSIES OF EUROPE

24. Ackerley, Frederick George. 1912-1913. "The Dialect of the Nomad Gypsy Coppersmiths." *Journal of the Gypsy Lore Society*. n.s. 6(4): 303-26; 7(3): 161-214. An old-fashioned initial treatment of the subject.

25. Andreas (Mui Shuko). *Gypsy Coppersmiths in Liverpool and Birkenhead*. Liverpool: Henry Young and Sons. I have not been able to locate this.

26. Anonymous. 1913. "The Coppersmiths (with Pedigrees)." *Journal of the Gypsy Lore Society*. n.s. 6(4): 241-43. Primary source.

24. Anonymous. 1908 (Oct.). "Poverty and a Song." *Journal of the Gypsy Lore Society*. n.s. 2(2): 118-19. Anecdotal primary source report of a day spent with the "German" Gypsies (Lovara), July 31, 1906. Includes a song with melody and text.

28. Bercovici, Konrad. 1928. *Story of the Gypsies*. New York: Farrar. Pp. 219-24 include an anecdotal primary account of an encounter with some Russian Kalderaš.

29. Ehrenborg, Harald. 1910 (July). "A Far-travelled Band in Sweden." *Journal of the Gypsy Lore Society*. n.s. 4(1): 72-73. An anecdotal primary source account of a one-day meeting with a small group of what are obviously Rom Gypsies.

30. Gjerdman, Olof, and Erik Ljungberg. 1963. *The Language of the Swedish Coppersmith Gypsy Johan Dimitro Taikon*. Uppsala: A-B Lundequisteka. Primary source data. A detailed linguistic analysis.

31. Labbati, Alfredo. 1908. "Gli Zingar a Roma." *Ars et Labor*. Milano. 63: 930-34. Photographs of Kalderaš according to Block's bibliography (no. 2440).

32. Macfie, Robert Andrew Scott. 1912 (Aug. 30). "The Gipsy Coppersmiths." *Manchester Guardian*. Primary source account. This describes the Liverpool "invasion" of 1911-12.

33. MacRitchie, David. 1886. "The Greek Gypsies at Liverpool." *Chamber's Journal*. 63: 577-80. Primary anecdotal account.

34. Maximoff, Matéo. 1950 (July 2). "Kamipe Romano, Amour Tzigane." *V*. No. 300: 8-9. Primary source story by a Kalderaš Gypsy, illustrated with posed photographs.

35. ———. 1950 (Sept.). "La Naissance chez les Tziganes." *L'Étoile du Forain*. Pp. 156-57. Primary source description of birth customs about and by a Kalderaš Gypsy.

36. ———. 1950 (Feb., Mar.). "Proverbes Tziganes." *L'Étoile du Forain*. 5(1): 18-19; 5(2): 43. Primary source. A discussion of some Kalderaš proverbs by a Kalderaš.

37. ———. 1947 (July-Oct.). "Three Feast-Days Among the 'Turco-American' Gypsies." *Journal of the Gypsy Lore Society*. 3rd ser. 26(3-4): 127-32. Primary source discussion of Rom who returned to Europe after having sojourned extensively in the United States, written by a European Kalderaš.

38. ———. 1947 (Jan.-Apr.). "The Gypsies of Montreuil-Sous-Bois: Some Observations on His Own Tribe." *Journal of the Gypsy Lore Society*. 3rd ser. 26(1-2): 37-42. Primary source data. Mainly demographic details.

39. ———. 1946. *Les Ursitory: Roman*. Paris: Ernest Flammarion. Primary source retelling of epic stories about a Kalderaš.

40. ———. 1946 (July-Oct.). "Some Peculiarities in the Speech of the Kalderaš." *Journal of the Gypsy Lore Society*. 3rd ser. 25(3-4): 108-12. Primary source data. A discussion of some proverbs and common linguistic mannerisms of the Kalderaš, written by a Kalderaš.

41. Starkie, Walter Fitzwilliam. 1937. *Don Gypsy: Adventures with a Fiddle in Southern Spain and Barbary*. New York: E. P. Dutton. Primary anecdotal source. Pp. 101-29 describes meetings with some Greek Kalderaš.

42. ———. 1935 (Eng. ed., 1933). *Raggle-Taggle: Adventures with a Fiddle in Hungary and Roumania*. New York: E. P. Dutton. Primary anecdotal source. Contains incidental references to meetings with Kalderaš.

43. Tillhagen, Carl-Herman. 1955 (Jan.-Apr.). "Married Life and Family Life among the Swedish Kalderaša Gypsies." *Journal of the Gypsy Lore Society*. 3rd ser. 34(1-2): 2-19.

44. ———. 1954 (July-Oct.). "Married Life and Family Life among the Swedish Kalderaša Gypsies." *Journal of the Gypsy Lore Society*. 3rd ser. 33(3-4): 129-50.

45. ———. (transl. by Frederick George Ackerley). 1950 (Jan.-Apr.). "Gypsy Clans in Sweden." *Journal of the Gypsy Lore Society*. 3rd ser. 29(1-2): 23-39.

46. ———. 1949 (July-Oct.). "Gypsy Clans in Sweden." *Journal of the Gypsy Lore Society.* 3rd ser. 28(3-4): 119-34.

47. ———. 1949 (Jan.-Apr.). "Gypsy Clans in Sweden." *Journal of the Gypsy Lore Society.* 3rd ser. 28(1-2): 1-17.

48. ———. (transl. by G. A. Urquhart). 1947 (July-Oct.). "A Swedish Gypsy Investigation." *Journal of the Gypsy Lore Society.* 3rd ser. 26(3-4): 89-115. Primary source data. Presentation of the results of an anthropological investigation.

49. Winstedt, Eric Otto. 1912-1913. "The Gypsy Coppersmiths' Invasion of 1911-1913." *Journal of the Gypsy Lore Society.* n.s. 6(4): 244-303. Primary source data recapitulating most of the contacts made by members of the Gypsy Lore Society and including anecdotal and analytic material.

50. Yates, Dora E. 1953. *My Gypsy Days: Recollections of a Romany Rawnie.* London: Phoenix House. An autobiographical account of a student of the Gypsies. Several chapters deal with anecdotal experiences with Rom Gypsies: "German Gypsies at Blackpool, 1906," on a Lovara invasion (according to Yoors); "Rumanian Gypsy Coppersmiths at Birkenhead and Liverpool, 1911-12," on Kalderaš; "Greek Gypsies from Corfu, 1934," probably on a Kalderaš group; "The Gypsy Story-teller of Montreuil, 1946-52" deals with Matéo Maximoff (see items no. 34-40). Some photographs are included.

51. Yoors, Jan. 1971. *Crossing.* New York: Simon and Schuster.

52. ———. 1967. *The Gypsies.* New York: Simon and Schuster.

53. ———. 1947. (Jan.-Apr.). "Lowari Law & Jurisdiction." *Journal of the Gypsy Lore Society.* 3rd ser. 26(1-2): 1-18.

54. ———. 1946. (Jan.-Apr.). "A Lowari Tale." *Journal of the Gypsy Lore Society.* 3rd ser. 25(1-2): 3-21.

55. ———. 1945 (July-Oct.). "Reminiscences of the Lowara. No. 2: A Lowara Camp." *Journal of the Gypsy Lore Society.* 3rd ser. 24(3-4): 81-88.

55. ———. 1945 (Jan.-Apr.). "Reminiscences of the Lowara. No. 1: Lowari Children." *Journal of the Gypsy Lore Society.* 3rd ser. 24(1-2): 8-17. Primary source data. Mr. Yoors was adopted by the Lovara Gypsies and spent about a decade with them. His material is eminently useful, sometimes as an analytic, descriptive account and sometimes in lieu of having a real, live informant with the reader.

57. Zielinski, Vladislaw Kornel, Ritter von. 1892. "Notes on the Nomadic Gypsies of Poland." *Journal of the Gypsy Lore Society.* 3: 108-09. No. 4470 of Black's bibliography.

PART THREE

REFERENCES ON GYPSIES OF
THE UNITED STATES AND CANADA

N.B. Most works refer to Nomad Gypsies, whether the author indicates such to be the case or not. Therefore, the bulk of the literature cited will be indexed under Part Four. It is also recommended that the scholar consult the *New York Times Index*.

58. Anonymous. 1835. "American Gypsies." *The Family Magazine*. 2: 86-87. No. 76 of Black's bibliography. I have not seen it.

59. Bercovici, Konrad. 1922 (Feb.). "American Gypsy." *Century Magazine*. 103: 507-19. Anecdotal primary source.

60. Berry, Riley Maria Fletcher. 1910. "The American Gypsy." *Century Magazine*. 80: 614-23. Anecdotal primary source on non-Rom Gypsies. Illustrated.

61. ———. 1902. "The American Gypsy: An Accurate and Picturesque Account, Embodying the Results of Long Personal Investigation." *Frank Leslie's Popular Monthly*. 53: 560-72. Anecdotal primary source on non-Rom Gypsies. Illustrated.

62. Bishop, William Henry. 1882. "Southern California." *Harper's Magazine*. 65: 863-82. This is No. 385 of Black's bibliography. Black indicates that p. 877 has an allusion to "English Gypsies" from Australia, and p. 875 has an illustration of a camp.

63. Brown, Irving Henry. 1929. "The Gypsies in America." *Journal of the Gypsy Lore Society*. 3rd ser. 8(4): 145-76. Primary source. This article is absolutely necessary to pursue studies on the Gypsies of the United States.

64. ———. 1927 (Oct. 1). "Children of the Earth." *Survey Graphic*. 59(1): 6-12. Primary source, mainly anecdotal, with photographs, and primarily on the Rom.

65. Burton, Sir Richard Francis. 1898. *The Jew, the Gypsy, and El Islam*. London: Hutchinson. Secondary source. Pp. 282-85 deal with "The Gypsy in America," and refer to non-Rom.

66. Clark, Marie W. 1967 (Summer). "Vanishing Vagabonds: The American Gypsies." *Texas Quarterly*. 10:204-10. I have not seen this article.

67. Dodd-Poince, Adah. 1908. "The Gypsies under the Stanley Government." *Ohio Magazine*. 4: 413-18. Primary source; journalistic interviewing. Deals with English Gypsies. Illustrated.

68. Goodwin, Joseph O. 1871. "Children of the Summer." *Harper's Magazine*. 43: 321-29. This is no. 1694 of Black's bibliography, and he says pp. 326-38 deal with Gypsies in America.

69. Jones, Alexander. 1834. "American Gypsies." *American Journal of Science and Arts*. 26: 189-90. Secondary source on French, non-Rom Gypsies in Louisiana.

70. Kegan, Arthur. 1889 (May 26). [No title] *Globe-Democrat, St. Louis*. No. 2276 of Black's bibliography. With illustrations.

71. Leland, Charles Godfrey. 1883. "Visiting the Gypsies." *Century Magazine*. n.s. 3: 905-12. Primary anecdotal source. Describes his visit to a Philadelphia encampment of non-Rom Gypsies.

72. ———. 1882. *The Gypsies of Russia, Austria, England and America*. London. I have not been able to locate this work.

73. ———. 1882. *The Gypsies*. Boston: Houghton, Mifflin. Anecdotal primary source. A whole section on "American Gypsies" will be found on pp. 227-271; actually these chapters deal with non-Rom Gypsies in Philadelphia and New Jersey.

74. MacLeod, William. 1909 (Oct.). "A New World Gypsy Camp." *Journal of the Gypsy Lore Society*. n.s. 3(2): 81-88. Anecdotal primary source report on some 300 Rom Gypsies in Boston, August 15, 1908. Not very informative aside from details of begging and chicanery.

75. Pennell, Elizabeth Robins. 1882. "A Ramble in Old Philadelphia." *Century Magazine*. n.s. 1: 655-67. Primary anecdotal source on English Gypsies. Reprinted in Leland's *The Gypsies* (71. above).

76. Shoemaker, Henry W. 1929. "Origins of the Pennsylvania German Gypsies." *Journal of the Gypsy Lore Society*. 3rd ser. 8(4): 181-83.

77. ———. 1925. "Gipsy Life and Gipsy Lore in the Pennsylvania Mountains; Address Delivered by . . . Civic Club, 1924." Altoona, Pa.: Altoona Times Tribune. Secondary source summation of what was known about this particular group of non-Rom Gypsies.

78. Tyree, Jessie Partlon. 1907. "The Nomads of Romany: A Visit to a Gypsy Camp." *Recreation*. 25: 221-24. Anecdotal primary source. These apparently were English Gypsies somewhere in the United States. Illustrated.

79. Wakeman, Edgar L. 1889 (Sept. 17). "American Gypsies." *Manchester Guardian*.

80. ———. 1889 (Aug. 19). "American Gypsies." *Manchester Guardian*.

81. ———. 1887 (Apr. 22). "American Gypsies." *Boston Daily Globe*. Primary anecdotal sources.

PART FOUR

NOMAD GYPSIES OF THE UNITED STATES AND CANADA
(Those references dealing specifically with New York City will be found in Part Five.)

82. Anderson, Gwen, and Bridget Tighe. 1973 (Feb.). "Gypsy Culture and Health Care." *American Journal of Nursing*. 73(2): 282-85. Primary source on Rom Gypsies in the Boston area, with a focus on the delivery of health care.

83. Bonos, Arlene Helen. 1942 (Apr.-June). "Roumany Rye of Philadelphia." *American Anthropologist*. n:s. 44(2): 257-74. Primary source. A rapid overview by a graduate student of anthropology who apparently did not complete extended fieldwork.

84. Brown, Irving Henry. 1924. *Gypsy Fires in America: A Narrative of Life among the Romanies of the United States and Canada*. New York: Harper & Brothers. Primary source, anecdotal account with some illustrations. The scholar should, of course, also consult 63. above.

85. Cohn, Werner. 1973. *The Gypsies*. Reading, Mass.: Addison-Wesley. Primary source analytic data by a sociologist. Professor Cohn worked with some of the Rom of western Canada and northwestern United States and then compared them with Gypsies in Europe. Photographs.

86. ———. 1970 (Sept.). "La Persistance d'un Groupe Paria Relativement Stable. Quelques Réflexions sur les Tsiganes Nord-américains." *Études Tziganes*. 16(2&3): 3-19. Primary analytic source. The focus is on the interaction with the outside world.

87. ———. 1969 (June). "Some Comparisons between Gypsy (North American *rom*) and American English Kinship Terms." *American Anthropologist*. 71(3): 476-82. Primary source analytic data.

88. Çoker, Gülbrün. 1966. "Romany Rye in Philadelphia: A Sequel." *Southwestern Journal of Anthropology*. 22: 85-100.

89. ———. 1965 (Mar.). "Aspects of Gypsy Social Organization: A Preliminary Report." *Bulletin of the Philadelphia Anthropological Society*. 17(1): 1-21. mimeo. Primary source. This is the work of a graduate student in anthropology and details primarily material on household structure.

90. Cotten, Rena M. 1954 (July-Sept.). "Gypsy Folktales." *Journal of American Folklore*. 67(265): 261-66. Primary source. Analytic approach to types of tales with important theoretical ramifications for folklore studies.

91. ———. 1950 (Jan.). "Gypsy Child Care." *Childhood Education*. 26(5): 228. Primary source. This is a brief description of Rom expectations pertinent to normal growth and development and methods of childcare.

92. ———. 1951 (Jan.-Apr.). "Sex Dichotomy among the American Kalderaš Gypsies." *Journal of the Gypsy Lore Society*. 3rd ser. 30(1-2): 16-25. Primary source. This is an analytic presentation of the natural division of labor and the delegation of different spheres of influence to males and females among the Kalderaš and the consequences in terms of culture change.

93. Demitro, Steve. 1927 (Oct. 1). "Folk Tales." *Survey Graphic*. 49(1): 17-19. Primary source. A young Kalderaš boy tells stories. Photograph.

94. Gatlin, G. 1925 (June). "Nomads of Our American Highways." *Travel*. 45: 12-14. I have not seen this article.

95. Godwin, R. K. 1920 (June 26). "Truant Tribe in School." *Survey Graphic*. 44: 447-48. I have been unable to locate this.

96. Kenny, Michael. 1969. "Educating Gypsy Children in Baltimore —A Proposal." Baltimore: Health and Welfare Council of the Baltimore Area. Primary source on the Rom of Baltimore. This is an analytic position paper with recommendations.

97. Kornblum, William, and Paul Lichter, 1972 (Oct.). "Urban Gypsies and the Culture of Poverty." *Urban Life and Culture*. 1: 239-53. Primary source contrasting Boyaš Gypsies of Paris with Kalderaš of Seattle, Washington, by two sociologists.

98. Lee, Ronald. 1972[1971]. *Goddam Gypsy: An Autobiographical Novel*. Indianapolis, New York: Bobbs-Merrill. Primary source, mainly anecdotal in approach. Mr. Lee is a Gypsy and details his interactions with the Rom of Canada.

99. LoBello, Nino. 1954 (Apr.). "Life Among the Gypsies." *Science Digest*. 35(4): 27-31. Primary source, mainly a journalistic approach, but based on fieldwork and interviewing during a summer period.

100. Maupin, Armistead. 1974 (July). "California Is the Best Place in the World for Gypsies." *Coast*. 15(6): 32-35. Journalistic primary source account of Kalderaš Gypsies.

101. McLure, Clare Edgar. 1927 (Oct. 1). "Gypsies in Halsted Street." *Survey Graphic*. 59(1): 13-16. Primary source account of Kalderaš Gypsies in Chicago. Illustrated with photographs.

102. Miller, Carol J. 1968. "Mačvaja Gypsy Marimé." Master's thesis, University of Washington. Primary source. This is a study by a graduate student in anthropology.

103. Moriarty, J. R. 1929. "A Gypsy Coppersmith Family." *Journal of the Gypsy Lore Society*. 3rd ser. 8(4): 176-81. Primary anecdotal source. This deals with a Kalderaš family in Canada.

104. Myers, John. 1945 (July-Oct.). "Supplementary Jottings on the Customs of the 'Greek' Nomad Gypsies." *Journal of the Gypsy Lore Society*. 3rd ser. 24(3-4): 88-94. Primary anecdotal source on Kalderaš.

105. Rice, Louise. 1927 (Oct. 1). "Puri Romani Dyes." *Survey Graphic*. 59(1): 25-26. Primary anecdotal source. Illustrated.

106. Schreiber, Ernest. 1973 (Aug. 5). "The Gypsies' Secret World." "Today": *The Philadelphia Inquirer*. Pp. 14-23. Primary source, journalistic account of Philadelphia Rom. Photographs, lexicon, and recipes.

107. Traverso, Georgina Jill. 1955 (July-Oct.). "Some Gypsies in Providence, Rhode Island, 1951-3." *Journal of the Gypsy Lore Society*. 3rd ser. 34(3-4): 115-29. Primary anecdotal source on Rom Gypsies.

108. Weybright, Victor. 1938 (July 31). "Reality Overtakes the Gypsy." *New York Times Magazine*. P. 10ff. Primary source, journalistic account of problems, cf. no. 109.

109. ———. 1938 (Mar.). "Who Can Tell the Gypsies' Fortune? The Nomad Coppersmiths, Now at the End of the Gypsy Trail." *Survey Graphic*. 27: 142-45. Primary source, journalistic account of problems. Photographs.

110. ———. 1927 (Oct. 1). "Why Live Like a Gypsy?" *Survey Graphic*. 59(1): 32-35. Primary source, journalistic account of Rom, especially Kalderaš. Photographs.

PART FIVE

NOMAD GYPSIES OF NEW YORK CITY

111. Baïracli-Levy, Juliette de. 1963. *A Gypsy in New York*. An anecdotal primary source detailing a winter season during which she met some Gypsies, not all Rom.

112. Bercovici, Konrad. 1924 (June). "Around the World in New York; The Gypsy Quarter." *Century Magazine*. 108: 231-40. Primary source, journalistic account, including a general survey of all types of Gypsies.

113. Cotten, Rena M. 1950. *The Fork in the Road: A Study of Acculturation among the American* Kalderaš *Gypsies*. Ph.D. dissertation, Columbia University. Primary analytic source, with numerous case histories by a graduate student in anthropology. Illustrated with diagrams.

114. Gropper, Rena C. 1967 (June). "Urban Nomads—The Gypsies of New York City." *Transactions of the New York Academy of Sciences*. ser. II. 29(8): 1050-56. Primary analytic source tracing thirty years of history of the Rom in New York City. Gropper is the former Rena M. Cotten.

115. Lynden, Patricia. 1967 (Aug.). "Last Holdouts." *Atlantic Monthly*. 220(2): 42-46. Primary source, journalistic account of the Rom of New York City. She did not like them very much. One small photograph.

116. Mass, Peter. 1974 (Sept. 23). "The Deadly Battle to Become King of the Gypsies." *New York*. 7(38): 26-40.

117. ———. 1974 (Sept. 30). "The Deadly Battle to Become King of the Gypsies: Part II." *New York*. 7(39): 31-41. Journalistic primary source account of Bimbo Kalderaš. Illustrated with photographs and drawings.

118. Mitchell, Joseph. 1955 (June 4). "Profiles—The Beautiful Flower." *The New Yorker*. 31(16): 39-89. Primary source, journalistic account of some of the Rom of New York City with additional interviewing of police.

119. ———. 1945. "King of the Gypsies." In his *McSorley's Wonderful Saloon*. New York: Penguin Books. Pp. 39-59. Reprinted from item no. 120.

120. ———. 1942 (Aug. 15). "King of the Gypsies." *The New Yorker*. 18: 21-26ff. Primary source, journalistic account of Johnny Nikanov.

121. Oujevolk, George B. 1935. "The Gypsies of Brooklyn in 1934." *Journal of the Gypsy Lore Society*. 3rd ser. 14(3): 121-27. Primary source data, best read after the researcher has had some experience. One photograph.

122. Parry, Albert. 1941 (Feb.). "Children of Romany in New York." *Travel*. 76(4): 18-22ff. Primary source, journalistic account of Rom Gypsies. Photographs.

123. Wallace, Ed. 1949 (Aug. 17). "Roll Jordan—on Gypsy Wheels." *New York World-Telegram*. P. 21.

124. ———. 1949 (Aug. 16). "Gypsies Turning from Old Trails." *New York World-Telegram*. P. 17.

125. ———. 1949 (Aug. 15). "Gypsy's Mystic Gyp." *New York World-Telegram*. P. 13. A three-article series on New York City's Nomad Gypsies and their problems; primary source, journalistic treatment. Photographs.

126. Weybright, Victor. 1945. "A Nomad Coppersmith in New York." *Journal of the Gypsy Lore Society*. 3rd ser. 24(1-2): 2-8. Primary source, journalistic account of some Kalderaš. Photographs.

127. Wright, Richardson. 1947 (July-Oct.). "Easter Celebrations of the Gypsy Coppersmiths in New York." *Journal of the Gypsy Lore Society*. 3rd ser. 26(3-4): 132-33. Primary source, journalistic account; predominantly photographic.

128. ———. 1946 (July-Oct.). "The Gypsy Coppersmiths in New York: A Pictorial Supplement to Victor Weybright's Article." *Journal of the Gypsy Lore Society*. 3rd ser. 25(3-4): 116-20. Primary source. Numerous photographs.

INDEX